The Irish Question

The Irish Question

Two Centuries of Conflict

Second Edition

Lawrence J. McCaffrey

THE UNIVERSITY PRESS OF KENTUCKY

Scholarly publisher for the Commonwealth,
serving Bellarmine College, Berea College, Centre
College of Kentucky, Eastern Kentucky University,
The Filson Club, Georgetown College, Kentucky
Historical Society, Kentucky State University,
Morehead State University, Murray State University,
Northern Kentucky University, Transylvania University,
University of Kentucky, University of Louisville,
and Western Kentucky University

Editorial and Sales Offices: The University Press of Kentucky
663 South Limestone Street, Lexington, Kentucky 40508-4008

Library of Congress Cataloging-in-Publication Data

McCaffrey, Lawrence John, 1925–
    The Irish question : two centuries of conflict / Lawrence J.
McCaffrey.
        p.   cm.
    Includes bibliographical references (p.) and index.
    ISBN 0-8131-1928-6 (acid-free paper). —ISBN 0-8131-0855-1 (acid
-free paper).
    1. Ireland—Politics and government—19th century. 2. Ireland—
Politics and government—20th century. 3. Great Britain—Foreign
relations—Ireland. 4. Ireland—Foreign relations—Great Britain.
5. Nationalism—Ireland—History. 6. Home rule—Ireland. 7. Irish
question. I. Title.
DA950.M327   1996
941.508—dc20
                                                                    95-6860

To
Joan

Contents

Preface

In the mid-1960s when I was teaching modern British history at Marquette University in Milwaukee, I noticed that although the Irish Question was one of the most important, and certainly the most divisive and defining, issue in nineteenth-century British politics, few textbooks gave it sufficient attention. To assist my own and other students in American colleges and universities in their understanding of the Irish dimension of modern British history I wrote *The Irish Question, 1800-1922*. Since the University Press of Kentucky published it in 1968, the crisis in Northern Ireland has revived the Irish Question as a major factor in Anglo-Irish relations and as a disturbing element in British life and politics. The massive expansion of Irish historiography since the original publication of *The Irish Question* is another good reason for taking a further look at the relationship between Ireland and Britain. Therefore, I was most happy to accept the invitation of the University Press of Kentucky to revise my original manuscript and to extend its narrative beyond the beginning of the Irish Free State.

In this new version of *The Irish Question* I do not use footnotes, but pay tribute to the research of the many scholars who contributed to my knowledge of Irish history in the Recommended Reading section of the book. In addition, I would like to thank the graduate students I have worked with over the years: Eileen Brewer, Michael Funcheon, Brian Griffin, Terrence La Rocca, Eileen McMahon, Michael Murphy, Kevin O'Neill, Timothy Sarbaugh, Maryann

Gialanella Valiulis, and Andrew Wilson, Loyola University of Chicago; Elizabeth S. Meloy, Northwestern University; Frank Biletz, University of Chicago; and Troy Davis, Marquette University. Their research and writing have affected my interpretation of Irish history in positive ways.

I also learned a great deal from associations and conversations with such close friends as Thomas N. Brown, Patrick Casey, Vincent Comerford, Thomas Cunningham, Joseph M. Curran, Thomas Flanagan, Thomas E. Hachey, Joseph M. Hernon Jr., T.W. Heyck, John Kelleher, Emmet Larkin, Sean Lucy, Ailfrid MacLochlainn, John A. Murphy, Maureen Murphy, Janet Nolan, Harold Orel, Ellen Skerrett, Mary Helen Thuente, and Alan Ward.

I owe a special debt of gratitude to my wife, Joan; children, Kevin, Sheila, and Patricia; their spouses, Jean Luft, Fernando Trigosa, and Bob Jacques; my grandchildren, Sean, Emily, Brian, Kathleen, and Alex; and my West Highland White Terrier friends, Andy and the late Fergus, for frequent morale boosts.

Much of this book is the result of my own research and writings on Irish nationalism, as indicated in the 1968 publication. In my discussion of the recent troubles in Northern Ireland, I borrowed from my *Chicago Tribune* essay of May 10, 1981, "Crisis in Northern Ireland."

Introduction

In many ways a study of the experience of the British in Ireland and Irish reactions to their unwanted presence provides insights into our world of disappearing empires, emerging nations, cultural conflicts between affluent and underdeveloped countries, and ethnic and religious feuds within and between nations.

Traditional and popular versions of Irish history have traced the origins and attributed the success of Irish nationalism to the failure of Britain to react adequately or in a timely manner to the basic religious, political, economic, and social needs that created and encouraged opposition to the Union. They have described most British concessions to Irish demands as expedient measures designed to frustrate agitations before they became insurrections. According to this thesis, these hastily designed sops to Irish Catholic complaints were palliatives rather than remedies; their deficiencies created new and deepened old grievances, and, in the long run, antagonized rather than conciliated majority Irish opinion.

There can be little quarrel with the thesis that Irish nationalism owed much to British ignorance of and insensitivity toward conditions in Ireland and Irish points of view. Still, it is too easy to blame sectarian strife, economic exploitation, and the denial of political and cultural sovereignty in Ireland entirely on the inadequacies of British politicians. Even when viewed from a contemporary perspective the complexity of the Irish Question defies simple solutions, and in their attempt to respond to Irish discontent British

jmh

leaders have been confronted with the limitations placed on political action by the party system; economic and political dogmas; cultural, religious, and class conflict in Ireland; and the pressures and prejudices of British public opinion.

At first glance the Irish Question appears to have been essentially religious in nature. Protestants controlling the Irish Parliament in 1800 accepted the Act of Union as a compact with coreligionists on the other side of the Irish Sea to maintain their privileged position. Although the Crown and the Tory party endorsed Protestant Ascendancy, the Catholic majority in Ireland refused to accept an apartheid policy that would condemn it to a permanent inferiority. But sectarianism in Ireland involves much more than theology.

For the most part, Protestants were the educated, propertied, prosperous, and politically and socially dominant class. Ulster Presbyterians were businessmen, shopkeepers, professionals, members of the gentry, and tenant farmers. As Noncomformists dissenting from the Protestant Church of Ireland, they suffered discrimination for a considerable period of time, but not nearly to the same extent as Catholics. In the late eighteenth and early nineteenth centuries, New Light Presbyterians, influenced by the liberal spirit of the Enlightenment, displayed tolerance toward Catholics. But the Evangelical triumphed over the New Light strain, and Anglicans and Presbyterians found common ground in fervent no-popery. At the beginning of the nineteenth century there was a substantial Catholic middle class, a small aristocracy and gentry, and a few successful professionals, but in general Catholics represented the landless, rack-rented, illiterate, and politically underprivileged portion of the Irish population. While most of the emotional content of the Irish Question centered on the sectarian issue, its essence was the attempt of a besieged minority, aided by an alien legislature, to maintain religious, political, economic, and social dominance over a deprived and resentful majority increasingly aware of the power of organized and disciplined numbers.

Irish nationalism emerged in the nineteenth century as a badge of dignity and a promise of hope for a people who in the century before had lost these qualities. As a mass enterprise, nationalism was born in the struggle for Catholic Emancipation and revitalized in the agitations for Repeal, Home Rule, and tenant right. Because the demoralized Irish masses at the beginning of the nineteenth century had little sense of ethnicity, the United Kingdom

Parliament might have forestalled Irish nationalism by immediately including Catholic representatives and by quickly addressing problems in Ireland. When it failed to do so, Daniel O'Connell mobilized Catholics for religious and political purposes, creating a political nationalism; later Young Ireland defined and propagandized a cultural dimension of Irish nationality. Together they made Irish Catholics conscious of their strength, provided them with an identity, and convinced them of a spiritual superiority over the "materialistic" and "bloodthirsty" Sassenachs holding them in bondage. The obstinancy of the Protestant Ascendancy in resisting logical and just concessions to the religious, economic, and political needs of the Catholic majority, coupled with the repeated failures of Westminster to cope with these problems, strengthened the political and cultural aspects of the national movement and made a solution of the Irish Question short of self-government unlikely.

Generally Whig, Radical, and Liberal politicians found it easier to deal with Irish discontent than their Tory and Conservative counterparts. On the British left there was considerable support for such reforms as Catholic Emancipation, an expanded Irish suffrage, a state system of Irish elementary education, and restrictions on the wealth and influence of the established church. Nevertheless, in the first half of the nineteenth century, even those with a liberal disposition exhibited mental and emotional blocks when confronting Catholic demands. Laissez-faire doctrines, an important element of the liberal creed, served the interests of industrial England, but were inapplicable to such Irish problems as landlord-tenant relations, unemployment, overpopulation, and the consequence of these difficulties—famine. Radical advocates of the separation of church and state obstructed the development of adequate systems of secondary and university education in Ireland because the Irish, Catholic and Protestant, were reluctant to accept any plan that separated religious and secular schooling. All leftist factions, though friendly to various forms of Continental and Latin American nationalism, were cool to Irish claims of sovereignty. They insisted that the Union was essential to Britain's defenses and to the maintenance of the empire, and they accepted the common Protestant position that the purpose of Irish nationalism was Catholic supremacy.

After 1868 the Liberal party made it increasingly clear that it was willing to go to previously rejected lengths to pacify Ireland. This remarkable change of position resulted from William Ewart Gladstone's sincere desire to solve the Irish Question, Liberal abandonment of doctrinaire laissez faire for a more flexible approach to economic problems, and Charles Stewart Parnell's success in organizing a disciplined, talented, and determined Irish parliamentary party. More importantly, late nineteenth-century Liberals could not ignore the appeal of chauvinistic and imperialistic conservatism to the impulses of a substantial section of the newly enfranchised working class. To balance the growing appeal of the Conservative party, Liberals needed a working arrangement with Irish nationalists in the Commons. This fit the needs of Parnell, who realized that the success of Home Rule necessitated an accord with one of the British parties. Since the Liberals needed the Irish, even at the cost of limiting the property rights of landlords and establishing a legislature in Dublin, and the Irish needed the Liberals, though it meant cooperation with British secularists, Parnell and Gladstone concluded an alliance that weathered many storms and persisted into World War I.

Conservative politicians could not bid as high as Liberals for Irish party backing because they were bound by religious convictions, class privileges, and property concerns to the Protestant Ascendancy in Ireland. Irish Protestants depended on British Conservatives to champion their cause in Parliament against the ambitions of the Catholic democracy. In doing so, Conservatives at Westminster were protecting their own interests. They knew that concessions to Irish-Catholic agitations would establish precedents encouraging radical assaults on the property and power of the British upper classes.

Since Conservatives controlled the House of Lords, they could veto legislation tending to curb their class privileges or to weaken the connection between Britain and Ireland. When the House of Lords made it clear in 1893 that it would never consent to Home Rule, Irish nationalists finally realized that constitutional methods of agitation would not succeed as long as the peers enjoyed the power to prevent Irish independence. Therefore, elimination of the veto power of the Lords became a major plank in the Irish party platform. This helped narrow the gap between Irish nationalists, British radicals who viewed the Lords as an obstacle preventing the final victory of democracy, and Labour MPs who considered the peers a barrier to socialism.

Conservative resistance to Irish reform and self-government rested on a strong foundation, the anti-Catholic essence of British nativism. Since the religious conflicts of the sixteenth century, the

English considered Catholicism a menace to British traditions, values, and institutions. "Bloody" Mary's persecution of Protestants; Spain's employment of Catholic subversives to dethrone Elizabeth I; the Armada threat; the Catholic issue in the struggle between the Stuarts and Parliament; and the contests of the seventeenth, eighteenth, and early nineteenth centuries with Catholic France all gave Catholicism an alien and subversive image in Britain. As late as the early twentieth century, respectable British newspapers and periodicals frightened and excited their readers with "revelations" of popish plots and Jesuit conspiracies to undermine the Protestant foundations of the British constitution. Since the British Catholic population was timid, quiet, and relatively small, Ireland with her millions of discontented Catholics served as a convenient whipping boy for no-popery zealots.

After the Act of Union Britons were reluctantly forced to acknowledge the existence of the Irish Question. Irish debates occupied a disproportionate amount of parliamentary attention, to the detriment of vital British and imperial legislation. Irish agitations—Catholic Emancipation, the tithe war, Father Mathew's temperance movement, the anti–Poor Law campaign, tenant right, and Repeal—were reported, distorted, and exaggerated in the British press. Curiosity about a geographically close but culturally remote partner in the Union guaranteed interest in Irish writers and journalists who described Ireland and the Irish for British readers. Nineteenth-century economic developments also encouraged Irish-British contacts. Every year substantial numbers of Irish peasants supplemented meager incomes by working the British harvest, and factory employment possibilities attracted permanent Irish settlement in British industrial cities.

Newspaper stories about Ireland and personal associations with the Irish did not encourage British respect. Many Britons decided that contempt for law and order was part of the Irish national character. Their Protestant, nativist sensibilities were offended by the militant Catholic and anti-British views of popular Irish leaders. Britain's industrial and agrarian working classes resented the competition of Irish labor. All levels of British society rejected Irish immigrants, who spoke English in a strange if melodious manner, demonstrated prodigality in financial matters, drank to excess and engaged in drunken brawls, worshipped God in a "superstitious" and "idolatrous" manner, and were overly submissive to their clergy, agents of the dreaded and hated pope in Rome.

In reality, Irish working-class conduct was not much different from that of the English, Scots, and Welsh of the same social strata. But, aware of British hostility and lonely and uncomfortable in an urban environment, transplanted peasants from Ireland clung together in tenement neighborhoods. In doing so they accentuated their ethnic vices and peculiarities. British critics of the Irish seldom tried to understand the psychological or sociological reasons for Irish delinquency and clannishness. Instead, they preferred to bolster their egos by attributing Irish behavior patterns to a basic weakness of character and the malignant nature of popery. From 1800 to 1922 the Irish played a role in the British mindset similar to blacks in the American. They had a useful economic function doing the menial work other people were too weak or too proud to do; they entertained (the happy, shiftless stage Irishman with the rich and comic brogue); they frightened (they were brutal, wild, lawless, uncivilized); and they were convenient targets for the release of inferiority complexes and sadistic tendencies. In response to social and economic conditions, their own weaknesses, and British attitudes, many Irish cultivated the stereotype that the British had designed for them.

British anti-Irish Catholic opinion, made more formidable by each expansion of the electorate, was a significant emotional factor in British politics, making it difficult for Parliament to approach Irish issues objectively. In the 1840s Sir Robert Peel, as part of his Irish policy, attempted to detach the Catholic hierarchy and clergy from the ranks of Irish nationalism by easing the financial burdens of their church. His efforts antagonized British opinion and the ultra-Tory wing of the Conservative party, which had never forgiven him for conceding Catholic Emancipation in 1829. In revenge for Peel's endowment of the Roman Catholic seminary at Maynooth and his work in repealing the Corn Laws, ultra-Tories, combined with Whigs and Irish Repealers, turned Peel out of office. The cost of vengeance was a seriously weakened Conservative Party and the political confusion and instability of the 1850s and 1860s.

British nativism continued to influence the course of British politics in the last half of the nineteenth and the early decades of the twentieth centuries. Gladstone also discovered that British opinion could respond unfavorably to government efforts to satisfy Irish-Catholic needs and demands. Like Peel, he split his party in an attempt to solve the Irish Question. With the completion of the Irish-Liberal alliance, followed by a Liberal schism over Home Rule, the anti-Catho-

lic, anti-Irish orientation of British opinion became the most powerful weapon in the Conservative, renamed Unionist, party arsenal and
the Irish alliance the most vulnerable chink in Liberal armor.

Peel's and Gladstone's attempts to reconcile Irish aspirations
with British domestic and imperial interests in the face of hostile
British opinion and dissent within their own parties produced some
of the most dramatic episodes in nineteenth-century British history.
However, the most illuminating example of the influence of the Irish
Question on British politics, and the difficulty of solving this question in an atmosphere dominated by no-popery sentiment, occurred
between 1910 and 1914, when the third Home Rule bill brought
Britain to the precipice of civil war.

By 1910 reforming Liberal and Unionist governments had laid
to rest almost all Irish grievances concerning land, religion, voting,
and education. But Irish nationalism had survived and taken on an
existence independent of the issues that had created and nourished
it. In 1910 and 1911 Irish nationalists played the leading role in the
dramatic defeat of their old enemy, the House of Lords. When the
third Home Rule bill came before Parliament in 1912, it brought
about a direct confrontation between Irish nationalist-British Liberal
and Irish Protestant-British Tory alliances. British politicians had no
bribes left to offer as an alternative to Home Rule, and without the
absolute veto of the Lords there was no legal barrier to its ultimate
victory. Since Unionists had lost the constitutional game, they decided to encourage and support Ulster Protestant threats of civil war.
In August 1914 Britain was rescued from the grim dilemmas of the
Irish Question by the onset of World War I.

When Sir Edward Grey, the foreign secretary, told Parliament
on August 3, 1914, that Germany's invasion of Belgium would lead
to a British declaration of war, John Redmond, chair of the Irish
parliamentary party, rose in the Commons and said that Irish nationalists were prepared to join with Irish unionists in a war against
German authoritarianism and militarism and in defense of the integrity of small nations such as Belgium. Parliament passed the Home
Rule bill, and the government suspended its operation until after the
war so that the problem of Ulster Protestant opposition to Catholic
majority rule could be dealt with in a calmer atmosphere.

British Conservative and anti–Irish Catholic antagonism to
Home Rule and the limp response of the Liberal government to
Ulster Protestant intimidation began to damage the reputation and

standing of the Irish party. When the slaughter on the Western Front ended, a weary Britain encountered a new generation of Irish nationalists disillusioned with British politics and British constitutionalism. They placed their confidence in the bullet and the grenade.

During Easter Week 1916, members of the Irish Republican Brotherhood and socialist James Connolly's Irish Citizen Army engineered a revolt against British rule. Armed might crushed the Dublin rising, but the decision of the Westminster government to execute its leaders achieved the "blood sacrifice" goal of Patrick Pearse, poet-leader of the rebellion. People who had opposed the rebels now honored them as martyred heroes.

In the December 1918 general election, the heirs of Easter Week running as Sinn Féin republicans destroyed the Irish party. Victorious candidates refused to go to Westminster, established an Irish parliament, the Dáil, and tried to govern the country in the name of the Irish Republic. In January 1919 passive resistance to British rule evolved into a guerrilla war of liberation. But Ireland's most valuable weapon in the struggle was British and world opinion, which insisted that Britain heed its World War I claim to respect national self-determination. After failing to appease Irish nationalism in 1920 by the creation of two Home Rule parliaments, one for six of the nine Ulster counties, the other for the rest of the country, in 1921 Prime Minister David Lloyd George finally offered Sinn Féin rebels dominion status in the form of an Irish Free State.

Because it involved an oath of allegiance to the British monarch, a considerable minority fought a brutal and costly civil war against dominion status. The Free State prevailed and then demonstrated that the treaty with Britain was a steppingstone to complete independence. Its delegates to Commonwealth conferences expanded the definition of dominion self-government, culminating in the 1931 Statute of Westminster that declared the freedom and equality of all Commonwealth members. Employing opportunities provided by the Statute, Eamon de Valera, the leading political opponent of the Free State, as leader of the Irish government was able by 1939 to make his country a republic in fact if not in name. Resisting tremendous pressures from Britain and the United States, Ireland demonstrated her sovereignty by maintaining neutrality in World War II. In 1948 a coalition government, deciding to steal a march on de Valera's Fianna Fáil party, left the Commonwealth and declared Ireland a republic.

One of de Valera's stated reasons for neutrality was British occupation of Northern Ireland. From the early days of the Free State until quite recently, partition has perpetuated bitterness in Anglo-Irish relations. The situation has been exacerbated by the discrimination that the majority Protestant population has inflicted on the Catholic minority, and the indifference of British governments to injustices in the six counties. Although Ulster Protestants insist on a cultural and religious uniqueness and a Britishness that separates their community from Catholic Ireland, politicians in the south have reenforced the psychological border that divides the two Irelands by fostering a Gaelic Irish identity and a confessional state that reflects the values, ethos, rules, and regulations of the Catholic church.

After 1922 most Northern Ireland Catholics retreated into ghettos of despair; a few joined the Irish Republican Army in its futile efforts to end partition through violence. In the late 1960s well-educated Catholic moderates whose social mobility had been blocked by institutional and Protestant discrimination, joined with socialists, liberal Protestants, and radical university students in a civil rights movement to establish equality in housing, employment, voting, and social services. When Protestant mobs, encouraged by the Royal Ulster Constabulary and prominent Northern Ireland politicians, began to assault civil rights demonstrators, violence erupted. To protect Catholic ghettos from Protestant rage, Britain sent soldiers into the six counties in August 1969. Until they functioned as agents of the Northern Ireland government, Catholics welcomed them, but since early 1971 the IRA has been at war with British troops. For over twenty years Northern Ireland has experienced bombings and terrorist attacks by the IRA on the army, and a pattern of sectarian murders. At present the death toll exceeds 3,100.

At first, conflict in Northern Ireland intensified old animosities between Ireland and Britain. But when television cameras focused on Northern Ireland and publicized the discrimination that existed there and Britain's neglect of civil rights violations and social inequities, Westminster finally accepted responsibility for the situation. In March 1972 it suspended the Northern Ireland Parliament and ruled the six counties from Westminster. Since then Britain has tried to establish power-sharing assemblies in Northern Ireland, and has speeded up the effort started by the deposed Northern Ireland government to end sectarian discrimination in housing, voting, government employment, and social services. At present Catholics control local government in areas where they are a majority.

Meanwhile, in the Irish Republic politicians recognized that Ulster violence was spreading from north to south. They also realized that the Republic's emphasis on the Gaelic tradition and its catering to Catholic interests and pressure groups made it impossible to achieve a pluralistic society necessary for a united Ireland. Consequently, since the 1970s the Republic has become more secular in spirit and institutions. These changes have made little impression on Ulster Protestants, but they have made life more pleasant and promising for citizens in the twenty-six counties.

Since the beginnings of the Northern Ireland crisis cooperation and mutual understanding have replaced animosity and suspicion in Anglo-Irish relations. From the Sunningdale meeting in December 1973 through the Downing Street conference in December 1993, leaders of Britain and Ireland have worked out a common approach to Northern Ireland. Britain has extended to the Republic an advisory role in the administration of the six counties, has agreed not to stand in the way of a united Ireland, and promised to implement such unity if it ever has the consent of a majority of Northern Ireland citizens. Ireland has said that it will not try to end partition by force, has accepted the principle that the fate of Northern Ireland depends on the will of its majority, and has promised to investigate and probably change those elements in its constitution offensive to Northern Ireland Protestants, specifically territorial claims on the six counties.

Although the British and Irish governments have reached a consensus on the present and future of Northern Ireland, one that has the approval of most people in the two countries, the future of the six counties remains unclear. At the end of August 1994, Sinn Féin, the political arm of the Republican movement, persuaded the IRA to agree to a ceasefire as a prelude to negotiations on the future of Northern Ireland. In October unionist gunmen also agreed to stop shooting. Shortly after, Britain's prime minister, John Major, agreed to negotiations involving Britain, the Irish Republic, and all interested parties in Northern Ireland. But it will be difficult to maintain peace and to achieve a consensus between unionists and nationalists. Most Protestants and Nonconformists continue to consider themselves British and culturally distinct from Catholics. Some Catholics, less fanatic in their Irishness than Protestants are in their Britishness, are prepared to accept equality in the United Kingdom as a more realistic and practical priority than an undivided Ireland. But there is a militant Catholic minority, some fed on the mythology of "blood sacrifice" Irish republicanism, who insist that Britain must withdraw from Northern Ireland, and that the six counties must join the other twenty-six in an undivided Irish nation. Finding a lasting compromise between these extremes will tax the ingenuity of British and Irish governments, and test the goodwill that has recently developed between them.

1

Catholic Emancipation 1800–1829

Although the English were in Ireland as early as the twelfth century, they never gained effective control until Hugh O'Neill, the Earl of Tyrone and the leader of Ulster resistance, surrendered to Lord Mountjoy, Queen Elizabeth's deputy, on March 30, 1603, six days after her death. Elizabeth introduced the most important factor, religion, into the complexity of the Irish Question. Since his church retained traditional theology, the Mass, and the sacraments, Henry VIII's defiance of papal authority did not greatly disturb Irish Catholics. Elizabeth's church, however, was Protestant in doctrine and worship, and she planted Protestants on lands seized from Catholic rebels. Catholics, heretofore lukewarm papists, began to defend their religion against Protestantism as a dimension of English conquest and colonization. Since early in the seventeenth century, religion in Ireland has symbolized culture and nationality.

Despite a small number of English and Scottish intruders, before 1607, when O'Neill, Hugh O'Donnell, and other northern clan chiefs fled Ireland in fear of their lives (the "Flight of the Earls"), Ulster was the most Gaelic, and therefore the most potentially rebellious Irish province. To remedy this situation, James I, the first Stuart king, planted colonies of English Protestants and Scottish Presbyterians on lands confiscated from departed clan chiefs.

With woeful consequences, Old English Catholics, descendants of Henry II's Norman vassals, and Gaelic coreligionists tried to reverse their misfortunes by siding with Charles I during his war with

Parliament in the 1640s. Oliver Cromwell crushed them, confiscating their property, "driving them to Hell or Connacht." Not discouraged and still trying to recoup losses, Irish Catholics joined James II when he fought for his throne in Ireland. In 1691 William III, the victor, signed a benevolent peace treaty with Old English and Gaelic Catholics, but the exclusively Protestant Irish Parliament, demanding revenge, refused to honor the king's agreement. Instead, it enacted legislation restricting the Catholic Church and depriving Catholics of property and political rights. Officials lightly enforced the religious aspects of the Penal Laws, but rigidly imposed their political and property clauses. Anti-Catholic legislation coerced most members of the Catholic aristocracy and gentry to either leave the country or to turn Protestant in order to protect their property and retain political and social status. Middle- and lower-class Catholics remained true to their faith.

The Penal Laws divided Ireland between a virtually propertyless and powerless 75 percent Catholic majority and a 25 percent Protestant Ascendancy and Dissenter minority. Like Catholics, Dissenters, largely Presbyterian, were less than first-class citizens, a fact that drove hundreds of thousands of them to North America. But the Protestant Ascendancy Irish Parliament passed toleration acts for Nonconformists and shared with them an intense hatred and suspicion of Catholics.

During the eighteenth century, English colonists in Ireland and America became Anglo-Irish and Anglo-American patriots, using Lockean political theory to demand an increase in self-rule. Exploiting Britain's preoccupation with the war in America, Anglo-Irish volunteers, mobilized to defend Ireland against a possible Bourbon invasion, intimidated the British into conceding free trade and Irish parliamentary sovereignty.

A Dublin parliamentary majority insisted on maintaining Catholic exclusion from the Irish nation. Britain, however, had a different agenda. Engaged in a life-and-death struggle with the armies of the French Revolution, England feared that France would attempt an invasion of the British Isles, and that Ireland, with its class and religious antagonisms, was a natural target for such a strategy. If France invaded and occupied Ireland, Britain would be trapped in a vise between an Ireland dominated by an old enemy and a Western Europe infused with the spirit of revolution. British politicians also wanted the best possible relations with their Austrian Hapsburg

Catholic ally in the struggle against France. Therefore, London pressured Dublin into modifying the Penal Laws. The Irish Parliament removed penalties involved in mixed marriages, permitted Catholics to have schools, to enter the legal profession, to vote on an equal footing with Protestants, to bear arms, and to be eligible for minor civil and military positions. In 1795 the Irish government endowed a Roman Catholic seminary at Maynooth in County Kildare to keep Irish candidates for the priesthood away from the Continent and French Revolution ideology. Despite these concessions, the Irish Parliament still denied Catholics access to political office.

Inspired by the liberal tenets of the Enlightenment and the French Revolution, a number of Protestants and Nonconformists in 1791 organized the Society of United Irishmen to promote parliamentary and political reform, including Catholic Emancipation. Frustrated by government oppression, the United Irishmen, in alliance with Catholic agrarian radicals, turned from reform to revolutionary republicanism.

The United Irishmen flourished in Ulster, providing subsequent republican movements with a once-upon-a-time myth of Catholic-Protestant unity against the English oppressor. But the Orange Order founded in 1795—the product of a bloody skirmish in County Armagh (the Battle of the Diamond) between two agrarian secret societies, the Catholic Defenders and the Protestant Peep O'Day Boys—was probably a more accurate barometer of Ulster Protestant sentiment than the United Irishmen. Orangemen then and now have been dedicated to a never-ending war against popery and Catholic nationalism.

In 1798 widespread rebellion broke out in Ireland. In Wexford, Orange yeomen from Ulster crushed a Catholic peasant revolt, and in Antrim the government used Catholic militiamen to smash a Protestant rising. In Mayo, French General Humbert arrived with a thousand soldiers. Pike-carrying Catholic peasants joined him not to fight for "liberty, equality, and fraternity," but for the "pope and the Blessed Virgin." After a string of stirring French victories, Lord Cornwallis defeated Humbert. British authorities executed Catholic rebels while returning French captives to their homeland.

The unsuccessful but destructive 1798 rebellion confirmed British anxieties, shared by many members of the Irish Protestant Ascendancy, that French-inspired political radicalism and an aggressive

Catholicism endangered the stability of Ireland and the security of Britain. William Pitt the Younger, the British prime minister, and his Cabinet decided that the Irish Parliament lacked the public confidence and the financial resources to insure the tranquility of Ireland or her immunity from French intrigue. Lord Cornwallis, the lord lieutenant, and Lord Castlereigh, the chief secretary, approached John Fitzgibbon, the earl of Clare, and other Irish Protestant leaders with an offer of union with Britain.

Although many members of the Protestant Ascendancy were attracted by the British offer, believing that a joining of the two islands would prove economically beneficial to Ireland while at the same time guarding their privileged position against the threats of French radicalism in the form of Jacobinism and Romanism, a majority of Protestant leaders were hostile to Pitt's plan. They felt that the British Parliament might make concessions to Catholic agitation, and that the transfer of power to Westminister would diminish the political influence of the Irish aristocracy and threaten Irish economic interests. British negotiators won substantial support from Catholic prelates, namely, Dublin's archbishop, John Thomas Troy, by suggesting to them, with the approval of Pitt, an advocate of Catholic Emancipation, that a Westminster Parliament would deal more objectively with their claims than the Protestant Ascendancy Parliament in Dublin. Disagreeing with their bishops, many patriotic Catholic lay leaders preferred to place their hopes for a better Irish future in an Irish Protestant Parliament than in an alien British legislature.

The Irish Parliament rejected the notion of a united kingdom in 1799, but a year later the British government acquired a few converts from among anti-unionists, and persuaded a large number of neutrals to endorse the British connection. That year a majority of the MPs in the Irish Parliament voted the extinction of their country's legislative independence. Traditional interpretations of the Act of Union have attacked Britain for using patronage positions and peerages to bribe members of the Irish Parliament. But the use of patronage to win votes was an accepted practice in eighteenth-century Ireland and Britain. And those who voted for the Union did so for a variety of reasons, as did those who voted against it. Motives on both sides were sometimes disinterested and thoughtful, sometimes selfish and mercenary.

In 1800, then, members of the Protestant Ascendancy traded

Ireland's sovereignty for a guarantee of their privileged position, one hundred seats in the British House of Commons and thirty-two places in the House of Lords (four bishops and twenty-eight lay peers), a merger of the Churches of England and Ireland, and the amalgamation of the Irish and British treasuries (completed in 1817). But associations between Britain and Ireland were not as complete as those between England and Scotland. Ireland retained an administration comprised of a lord lieutenant and a chief secretary and their staffs, and separate courts, police, prisons, and a number of agencies and departments of government.

Throughout the nineteenth century law-and-order mandates indicate that from a British perspective Ireland was more a colony than an integral part of the United Kingdom. To curb agrarian violence and to prevent insurrection the Westminster Parliament frequently passed coercion bills that temporarily shelved the British constitution in Ireland by suspending habeas corpus, imposing curfews, and permitting arms searches. As Irish chief secretary (1812-18), and later as British home secretary, Sir Robert Peel created police forces on both islands (which is why the Irish have called constables "Peelers" and the British have referred to them as "Bobbies"). Policemen in Britain functioned quite differently from those in Ireland. In England, Scotland, and Wales, constables served and protected their communities. In Ireland they not only prevented and punished crime and disorder, they also acted as a security force sustaining British rule. By 1867 Peel's Peace Preservation Force had evolved into the half-police, half-soldier Royal Irish Constabulary, a model for paramilitary security units throughout the empire.

The Dublin Parliament held its last session in College Green on August 2, 1800; on January 28, 1801, Irish representatives took their places at Westminster. Now that Ireland was a part of the United Kingdom, the Irish Question took center stage in British politics. It became the most perplexing, persistent, emotional, and perhaps the most difficult problem confronting Britain and Ireland during the two succeeding centuries.

While the Act of Union was not responsible for the social, religious, economic, or even all of the political dimensions of the Irish Question, it complicated an already difficult situation. Religion was the most obvious area of tension in Irish society. Due to the opposition of the king, the House of Lords, and the British public, Pitt could not keep his promise to emancipate Catholics. Therefore, the Irish majority entered the Union as second-class citizens. In addition, they were taxed to support the established church, which ministered to the spiritual needs of only about 13 percent of Ireland's people (Presbyterians, Methodists, Quakers, and other Nonconformists also paid tithes). The Protestant minority not only enjoyed a favored religious position but also owned most of the property in the country and occupied a monopoly of Irish seats in Parliament and positions in government.

When Ireland became part of the United Kingdom it had a small Catholic gentry and an expanding Catholic middle class, the product of the early Penal period when Catholics, denied property purchase, had to turn their energies and ambitions to commerce and the lower ranks of the professions. Although the position of the Catholic gentry and middle class had substantially improved in the course of the eighteenth century, they still were frustrated by remaining Penal Laws, which denied them a significant role in directing Irish affairs. They agitated for relief legislation that would permit them to sit in the House of Commons and the House of Lords, hold government office, advance in the professions, and win social prestige in the Irish community. In their agitation for political rights, they had little contact with or concern for the lower classes, comprising the overwhelming majority of the Catholic population.

Most Irish Catholics during the early nineteenth century were tenant farmers or agricultural laborers. As a group they were dehumanized, demoralized, and largely illiterate, possessing neither the hope of progress nor the desire for improvement. Few tenants had farms larger than fifteen acres; many had only about five. Agricultural laborers were fortunate to have the use of an acre to grow food for their large families. A typical rural dwelling was a mud cabin with a dirt floor that could turn into a muddy mire in heavy Irish rains, and a vermin-saturated thatch roof. Often there was not even one window to let in fresh air. Since a pig was often the only valuable family possession, it was kept in the cabin in bad weather. Naturally these living conditions resulted in disease and an extremely high mortality rate. If a person somehow managed to survive childhood, scurvy, cholera, tuberculosis, and malnutrition would probably cut him or her down before middle age. But despite the prevalence of disease and hunger and the lack of medical care, Ireland had a population explosion that began midway through the eighteenth century and lasted into the early nineteenth. In 1781 the estimated population of

Ireland was 4,048,000; in 1841 the census recorded it at 8,175,000, an increase of more than 100 percent in sixty years.

Irish men and women tended to marry young and their large families produced a population growth that triumphed over high infant mortality rates, sickness, subsistence sized agricultural plots, and famine. Poverty seems to encourage the sexual urge, and for Irish Catholics desire was satisfied in marriage. In their miserable existences, sex and the companionship of husbands, wives, and children, like good and even bad whiskey, were a comfort and an escape. But an important factor encouraging relatively early marriages, and the consequent fecundity of Irish women, was the potato, a vegetable that is easy to cultivate, flourishes in bad soil, and makes a nutritious meal. In the period before the Great Famine, most rural folk ate only potatoes and drank a little milk to wash them down. The average Irishman devoured ten pounds of potatoes a day, sometimes consuming them half cooked so that they would take longer to digest. Unhappily, reliance on the potato meant frequent famines. The Great Hunger (1845-49) was not the first time fungus and/or bad weather had ruined the potato crop.

A rapidly expanding population strained an already weak agrarian economy. Except for linen manufacturing and shipbuilding around Belfast, there was little industry in Ireland to provide an employment alternative to farming. Exploiting a land shortage, landlords were able to raise rents for holdings far beyond their value, and they could always find desperate people willing to pay. To accommodate a growing population and to earn a few shillings and pence to pay their landlords, tenant farmers subdivided their small plots. As Irish farms decreased in size, Irish agriculture increased in inefficiency. Land hunger fostered avarice, evictions, class war, and violence.

Since landlords had the support of the law and the authorities, a number of secret societies such as the Ribbonmen and the Whiteboys flourished in Ireland. They burned hayricks and maimed cattle to punish landlords and those who occupied farms of those evicted for nonpayment of rent; they also shot bailiffs who represented rack-renting landlords. But class conflict extended beyond landlords and tenants. Quite often tenant farmers exploited agricultural laborers who also organized secret terrorist groups to impose some sort of moral economy in rural Ireland. Occasionally, secret societies also targeted Catholic priests with reputations for charging excessive dues and fees for religious services such as baptisms, marriages, and funerals. Protestant tithe collectors were other victims of intimidation and violence.

Frequently, Irish landlords lived in Britain, and this absenteeism aggravated rural social and economic problems in Ireland. Resident landlords were more likely to be interested in the quality of agriculture practiced on their estates. They might work at improving the cultivation techniques of their tenants and show a humane interest in their welfare. Agents of absentee landlords, on the other hand, were often quick to evict and were likely to pay more attention to the collection of rents than to increasing the productivity of the estate. Of course, it is difficult to prove that absentees were not as kind or humane as resident landlords, but they did deny to Ireland the income derived from their property, thus frustrating the development of domestic trades and industries. Non-resident proprietors were more British than Irish in points of view, and the loss of such a large proportion of the aristocracy retarded the development of a vital, intelligent, and influential Irish political and economic opinion.

Relations between landlords and tenants were more cordial in Ulster than in Leinster, Munster, or Connacht. Ulster custom permitted a tenant to sell his interest in the farm when he left, protecting him somewhat against eviction and an unfair rent increase. But in the south and west, if a tenant improved his farm by draining, fencing, or fertilizing the land, or by repairing buildings, he increased its value and the landlord might raise the rent. If the tenant could not pay, the landlord could evict him without compensation for the changes he had made. As a result, tenant farmers in Leinster, Munster, or Connacht seldom improved their farms, and the quality of agriculture in Ulster was much higher than in the rest of the country. Perhaps landlord-tenant relations in Protestant Ulster were relatively harmonious because shared religious beliefs muted class conflict.

Intelligent observers recognized the unhealthy condition of the Irish economy, but politics, religious divisions, and classical liberal economic theories prevented remedies. All shades of British political opinion, refusing to consider limitations on property rights, argued that the agrarian situation in Ireland was a moral problem beyond political solution. Although Whigs and Radicals were willing to give the Irish a greater share in shaping their destiny through political reform, and were sympathetic to equality between Catholics and Protestants, laissez-faire dogmatism, so important in their circles, opposed suggested government public works or emigration projects. While some people on the left were prepared to consider alterations in Irish economic and social structures, Tories were adamant in opposing any concessions that might diminish Protestant Ascendancy. They considered criticisms of the privileged position of the Protestant Church and the Protestant aristocracy and gentry an assault on property rights. They were convinced that Catholic Emancipation would encourage Irish agitation and nationalism and open the door to further demands for reform. They thought that radical change in Ireland would endanger the Union and ultimately the empire, and inspire assaults on the British status quo.

In Ireland, the Catholic Committee, representing the upper social and economic levels of the Catholic community, conducted the campaign for Emancipation. Before it could prevail upon Whigs and Radicals to translate good intentions into a specific policy that would defeat Tory obstinacy, the Committee had to mobilize the peasant majority and clergy behind Emancipation. This was a difficult task because members of the Catholic upper and middle classes had little contact with or respect for the rural proletariat, and tenant farmers and agricultural laborers, oppressed by political and economic systems, were poor materials for a successful agitation. Catholic Ireland needed a leader possessing the genius to unite and lift the spirits of its demoralized and depressed people, and to give them the hope and confidence necessary for effective political action.

Daniel O'Connell, the architect of modern Irish political nationalism, answered this need. No other Irish leader has had as much local or international significance. In the early nineteenth century he was one of the most discussed personalities in Europe: to the embattled left he was a symbol of hope and a promise of the future; to the nervous aristocracy on the right he represented the enemy attempting to tear down the walls of entrenched privilege. O'Connell dedicated his talents and his energy to the interests of Ireland, but the principles he represented, the objectives of his ambitions, and the methods of his agitations had consequences for democratic and liberal causes in every country within the framework of or in contact with Western civilization. In the aristocratic and ultra-conservative age of Metternich, he was a successful tribune of the people. O'Connell translated democratic theory into successful practice by mobilizing millions of illiterate Irish peasants into a disciplined, organized national force. Using it as a weapon, he compelled a powerful, aristocratic British government to make concessions to Irish-Catholic demands.

Of course, members of the British establishment despised O'Connell. Their newspapers and periodicals described him as a mendacious, avaricious vulgarian stirring up the Irish masses in order to fill his pockets with donations from ignorant and impoverished peasants. Conservative journalists and politicians told the British public that the Irish demagogue was the leader of a vast conspiracy to subvert the constitution and empire by imposing popery on the British Isles and separating Ireland from Britain. Since hostility to Catholicism was the basic ingredient in British nativism, O'Connell was a natural target for British Tories manipulating Protestant passions to preserve and perpetuate existing economic, social, and religious structures throughout the United Kingdom.

With O'Connell's entry into politics, the Irish Question became the leading emotional issue dividing British parties and public opinion. O'Connell gave lessons to British politicians in the techniques of political organization and agitation. His successors in the leadership of Irish nationalism continued the instruction.

Born on August 6, 1775, O'Connell in British terms was a member of the Irish Catholic gentry, but to Irishmen he was a Kerry clan chieftain. His father was Morgan O'Connell, but his childless uncle Maurice, head of the family, adopted him. Maurice, through the friendship of Protestant neighbors, had managed to maintain his property during Penal times, and had substantially increased the family wealth in successful smuggling operations. Some of the O'Connells had earned military reputations in the service of the Bourbons and Hapsburgs. Because the Penal Laws prohibited open Catholic education in Ireland, Maurice sent his nephew first to St. Omer and then to Douai in northern France for secondary schooling. Because of the chaos caused by the French Revolution, O'Connell finished his studies in London and stayed there to train for the bar at Lincoln's Inn. Conservative clerical teachers and exposure to the French Revolution on the Continent influenced O'Connell to become a permanent opponent of the use of physical force for political change. Theobald Wolfe Tone, his Society of United Irishmen comrades, and Robert Emmet occupy prominent places in the pantheon of Irish nationalist heroes; O'Connell saw them differently, describing 1798 as a foolish waste of lives and property and the misdeed that led to the Act of Union. Robert Emmet's 1803 Dublin insurrection was a miserable failure, but his articulate and passionate speech from the dock inspired generations of Irish nationalists. O'Connell was not moved by Emmet's bravery or oratory, stating that a man who caused so much bloodshed and so many deaths had no right to compassion.

O'Connell's antipathy to revolutionary violence, however, did not erect a mental block against liberal reform. While at Lincoln's Inn he avidly read such exponents of liberal democracy as William Godwin, Thomas Paine, and Jeremy Bentham. Echoing the principles of Godwin and applying them to his own country, he argued that Ireland's freedom would be won through the pressures of mobilized public opinion rather than bullets or bayonets. O'Connell defined himself as a Utilitarian, and became a friend and loyal disciple of its founding father, Bentham. For a time he rejected the tenets of orthodox Christianity and embraced Deism. In time he regained his faith, but retained the liberal political attitudes of the Enlightenment.

Because he intended to practice law in Ireland, O'Connell finished his studies at Dublin's King's Inn, and in 1798 was admitted to the Irish bar. In 1802 he married his cousin Mary O'Connell of Tralee. Uncle Maurice at first disapproved of what he considered an unwise match, but Mary proved an asset to Daniel's political career. She provided him with a great deal of love, wise political advice, and the peace and security of a happy home. Seven children born of their marriage—four sons and three daughters—reached adulthood.

Since they were barred from government office and the honors of their calling, the law was a difficult profession for Catholics. They had to be content with unimportant cases and meager fees. O'Connell worked diligently and used his perceptive insights into the Irish character as well as his superior intelligence, quick wit, and oratorical skill to become the best cross-examiner and persuader of juries in Ireland. Fees for defending Irish Catholics were small, but his practice was large. By 1828 he had a yearly income of between £6,000 and £7,000.

O'Connell used courtroom settings to propagandize his political convictions. In addressing juries, he often criticized British rule in Ireland, and appealed for Catholic civil rights. When O'Connell entered politics, Catholic Emancipation was the big issue. Leadership of the Catholic Committee was in the hands of a small Catholic aristocracy and gentry with the support of a larger but just as moderate middle class. At Westminster, Henry Grattan, hero of 1780s

Anglo-Irish patriotism and a foe of the Act of Union, commanded the parliamentary advocates of Catholic civil rights. The cause attracted most Whigs and a few Tory MPs, and on occasion could mobilize a parliamentary majority. In defying Irish-Catholic and parliamentary opinion, Tory administrations could rely on George IV's Protestant conscience, the House of Lords, and anti-Catholic British opinion.

Catholic Emancipation did have a compromise chance of success: an arrangement limiting the independence of the Catholic Church in Britain and Ireland. Tory leaders indicated a willingness to repeal political restrictions on Catholics in exchange for government input into and veto rights over Rome's selection of bishops for the United Kingdom. Most prominent British Catholics, some of the Irish Catholic hierarchy, most notably Archbishop Troy, Grattan, the British Whigs, and even Pope Pius VII, anxious to have British support against Bonaparte, found the compromise acceptable.

O'Connell joined a number of other Catholic laymen in opposing the veto. As a proponent of separation of church and state, he argued that government intervention in the affairs of the Catholic Church would be detrimental to both religion and politics. His main motive in resisting a Britain-Rome compromise was his commitment to Irish nationalism. O'Connell realized that the Emancipation issue could arouse and recruit Catholics in Ireland for nationality. He understood that although the vast majority of Irish bishops and priests, to mollify British and Anglo- Irish Protestant and Ulster Presbyterian anti-Catholicism, had not participated in politics, most were the sons of farmers and shopkeepers, and enjoyed the confidence and respect of the laity. Therefore, they were natural leaders of the rural populace. If the government gained control over the nomination of bishops, it could use them as tools of British policy in Ireland. O'Connell knew that an indifferent or hostile hierarchy would stand in the way of an effective national movement. He reasoned that it would be better to postpone Catholic Emancipation if it meant the sacrifice of the most important institution in Ireland to British influence. He succeeded in rallying a considerable segment of hierarchical and clerical opinion against the veto. His efforts delayed Catholic Emancipation, but they enlisted bishops and priests for Irish nationalism.

The veto issue split Catholic ranks, and for years the Emancipation cause drifted. But in 1823, O'Connell, Thomas Wyse, and Richard Lalor Sheil, a Vetoist, met at the Wicklow mountain home of Christopher Fitz-Simon, O'Connell's son-in-law, and founded the Catholic Association. It took time for the new organization to catch on. During the first few months, meetings were poorly attended. Then in 1824 O'Connell formulated the strategy that made the Catholic Association the model for all popular agitations in Britain and Ireland during the nineteenth century. O'Connell borrowed organizing and fundraising techniques from eighteenth-century British Methodism and radicalism. Full members of the Association paid a guinea in yearly dues, but anyone could become an associate member for just a shilling paid in penny monthly installments.

Catholic chapels became recruiting centers for the Emancipation agitation. In sermons priests urged parishoners to join the Association. Encouraged by strong messages from the pulpit, Catholics paid their penny dues at tables set up outside chapel doors. The "Catholic rent" not only swelled the Association's treasury, it also enlisted mass support and enthusiasm. With little money to spare, tenant farmers were giving up the pleasures of liquor and tobacco to advance Catholic Emancipation. Their sacrifice committed them to a cause that provided a cohesive group identity, a purpose, and hope for the future.

From the beginning it was obvious that the Catholic Association was more than just a vehicle for Emancipation. O'Connell and his colleagues demanded a variety of reforms, including Repeal of the Union. British politicians recognized the danger to British rule in Ireland from a movement with such popular support and with such a vast income. In mass meetings O'Connell condemned violence and insisted that his followers employ constitutional methods to secure their civil liberties. He argued that mobilized public opinion was a more effective instrument of change than physical force. Nevertheless, behind O'Connell's explicit constitutional rhetoric there was an implicit threat of force. He warned British politicians that if they were not prepared to come to terms with a constitutional agitation, the Irish masses, now mobilized and full of expectations, might turn in frustration to leaders preaching violence as a solution to their problems.

When the government outlawed the Catholic Association, O'Connell used his legal dexterity to reorganize and expand its activities. In meetings at the Dublin Corn Exchange, Association members protested tithes and demanded mass education, rights for tenant farmers, an expanded suffrage, the secret ballot, parliamentary reform, and repeal of the Union. Irish newspapers paid more attention to Association proceedings than they did to Westminster debates. In fact, the Association had become an unofficial Irish-Catholic parliament. During the Catholic Emancipation agitation, O'Connell had expanded a Catholic into an Irish identity, and injected liberal-democratic principles into the bloodstream of Irish nationalism.

The 1826 general election was the Association's first test of strength. Thomas Wyse created a powerful Catholic organization in Waterford and nominated a pro-Emancipation Protestant, Villiers Stuart, to challenge Lord George Beresford, who had held the seat for twenty years. Priests steeled the courage of forty-shilling freeholders (lifetime leaseholders of a house or land with an annual rent of forty shillings) to vote against the wishes of their landlords. The Association's Waterford triumph encouraged a number of other constituencies (Louth, Monaghan, Westmeath, Cork City, Galway) to support other pro-Emancipation Protestant candidates, and priests again successfully competed with landlords for the votes of tenant farmers. Victories in 1826 elated the Catholic Association, strengthened the confidence of Catholics, alarmed the Anglo-Irish Protestant Ascendancy, and troubled the government.

Six months after the election, poor health necessitated the resignation of Lord Liverpool as prime minister. Since George Canning, his successor, was sympathetic to Catholic Emancipation, O'Connell slowed down the pace of agitation to give Canning time to author and present to Parliament a Catholic relief bill. Within a few months, Canning was dead, the Duke of Wellington was prime minister, and another anti-Catholic, Peel, was home secretary and government leader in the Commons. Wellington appointed C.E. Vesey Fitzgerald, MP for Clare, to the presidency of the Board of Trade, forcing him to contest his seat in a by-election.

Fitgerald was a popular landlord and a friend of Emancipation, but the Association decided to oppose him with a Catholic candidate. O'Connell reluctantly accepted the challenge. Engaged in a direct struggle with the enemy, the government threw massive resources and energy into the contest. But O'Connell had the priests and the tenant farmers behind him, and together they easily defeated the government, Fitzgerald, and Clare landlords.

Returns from Clare compelled Wellington and Peel to make a difficult decision. In conscience they opposed Emancipation but the alternative was bleaker. Irish Catholics could become dangerous if denied the fruits of victory. Government suppression of their hopes could encourage an increase in anti-Union sentiments. In addition there was the possibility that O'Connell's followers might reject his constitutional methods and attempt to gain their objectives through physical force. In any event, if the government did not concede Emancipation, the task of ruling Ireland would be difficult and costly. And if there was a rebellion in Ireland, many pro-Catholic MPs in the Commons would criticize the government more harshly than Irish rebels. Politicians also feared that turmoil in Ireland would encourage lawlessness in other parts of the United Kingdom. Industrialism had fostered economic and social discontent in Britain, manifested in riots, destruction of machinery, and demands for parliamentary reform.

In order to preserve the Union and peace and stability in Britain as well as Ireland, Wellington and Peel decided to ignore British anti-Catholicism and the right wing of their own party by conceding Emancipation in the 1829 Catholic Relief Bill. But playing the role of vindictive rather than good losers, they also strengthened Irish landlord political influence by abolishing the forty-shilling franchise, forced O'Connell to recontest Clare (he won at considerable expense), outlawed the Catholic Association, and made elected Catholic MPs take an insulting oath of allegiance.

Many of his followers criticized O'Connell's sacrifice of forty-shilling voters as a betrayal of nationalism and democracy. Indeed, it is difficult to understand his surrender on this issue. He protested publicly but without enthusiasm. In 1825, during failed negotiations, O'Connell had agreed to exchange government endowment of Catholic priests (a contradiction of a former position) and the end of the forty-shilling franchise for Catholic Emancipation. At the time, he expressed the opinion that the landlord-controlled tenant farmer vote was not a free expression of opinion. Catholic Emancipation's victory, however, had demonstrated the nationalistic and democratic potential of the peasant electorate. Perhaps O'Connell in 1829 did not energetically defend the interests of people who brought him election wins in 1826 and 1828 because he was unwilling to split Catholic leadership ranks; many upper- and middle-class Irish and British Catholics were not admirers of peasant democracy.

After the Catholic Relief Act Catholics could sit in both houses of Parliament and were eligible for all offices in the United Kingdom except those of regent, lord chancellor, and lord lieutenant and lord chancellor of Ireland. The elimination of the forty-shilling vote reduced the Irish electorate from over one hundred thousand to about sixteen thousand. Still, it was theoretically possible that Irish Catholics could return a substantial number of their coreligionists to the Commons. Wellington expected Catholic Emancipation to result in sixty Irish-Catholic MPs. He exaggerated Catholic possibilities. Since MPs were not salaried, and election campaigning and London residency during parliamentary sessions were costly, few Catholics could afford political careers. As late as 1874, after a considerable extension of the suffrage and the adoption of the secret ballot, a general election returned only forty-nine Irish Catholics. But there were Protestant nationalists and liberals prepared to serve Irish-Catholic constituents at Westminster.

While Catholic Emancipation elevated the significance of Irish opinion in Parliament, it also altered British politics. The Tory party, which Peel rechristened Conservative in 1834, was never the same after the Catholic Emancipation crisis. Its ultra-right wing fought and rallied British and Irish no-popery opinion against concessions to Catholics to the bitter end. Ultras never forgave Wellington and Peel, particularly the latter, for betraying the Protestant British constitution. Under Tory pressure, Peel had to surrender his seat for Oxford, though he won another for Westbury. A number of ultra-Tories embraced parliamentary reform because they said that the people were more reliably conservative and anti-Catholic than the aristocracy and gentry. Charging that Parliament had surrendered to popery in defiance of the constitution and British public opinion, in 1830 they joined Whigs in toppling the Wellington administration, clearing the way for a reform Parliament.

Realizing that British democracy, although it embraced no-popery, posed as much of a threat to their vested interests as Irish nationalism, Tories soon abandoned their brief flirtation with populism. Their distrust of Peel, however, was permanent, opening a fissure in Conservative unity that never completely closed, deepened under the stresses of the 1840s, and finally split the party into progressive and reactionary wings.

Events in Ireland during the 1820s offered valuable examples and precedents for British radicalism. O'Connell launched the first successful democratic mass movement in Europe. In efforts to reform Parliament, the British left followed O'Connell's formula for mobilizing public opinion, collecting funds and pressuring the government with the alternatives of reform or possible revolution. Radical political unions resembled the Catholic Association. Later, free-traders would also borrow O'Connell's techniques in their victorious campaign against the Corn Laws.

Catholic Emancipation encouraged the spread of popular sovereignty beyond parliamentary reform. In 1829 George IV lost a major battle with Parliament, signalling the declining power of the monarchy. Emancipation also was a victory of the Commons over the Lords, an initial triumph in a long struggle for power that would finally conclude with the 1911 Parliament Act, another Irish nationalist contribution to the evolution of British democracy.

By conceding Catholic Emancipation, Peel and Wellington hoped to preserve law and order and the Union. They also intended to squelch Irish nationalism by lessening Irish-Catholic discontent. But Britain had delayed Catholic political rights too long, and only conceded them under duress with humiliating strings attached. Instead of gratitude, Irish Catholics felt confidence in their united strength. Emancipation encouraged them to use the power of mobilized and disciplined opinion to demand other changes, such as religious equality, security for tenant farmers, an expanded suffrage with a secret ballot, and, eventually, self-government. The agitation for Catholic Emancipation had fostered Irish nationalism, enhanced O'Connell's position as leader of the Irish Catholic nation-in-waiting, and launched a new era in Irish protest that would complicate British politics and alter British institutions.

Unfortunately, the rise of a Catholic peasant democracy with national aspirations heightened sectarianism in Ireland. Protestants worried about the permanence of their Ascendancy, and became more emotionally attached to the Union as their salvation. Even more than before, religion in Ireland symbolized cultural and political loyalties as well as faith and worship.

Catholic Emancipation reverberated beyond the United Kingdom. With its commitment to liberal democracy, O'Connell's nationalism politically civilized its ally, Catholicism. When Alexis de Tocqueville made his journey through Ireland in 1835 he was amazed at the enthusiasm for popular sovereignty among Catholic bishops and priests at a time when Rome championed aristocratic power and privilege. During the nineteenth century Irish immigrants became the religious, political, education, and labor leaders of an expanding

American Catholicism. Their adherence to liberal democratic values
hastened their adjustment to the American political consensus, and
enabled them to direct other European Catholics who followed them
to the United States into a similar accommodation. Irish emigrants
to various parts of the British Empire (which would evolve into
Commonwealth nations) have had a similar experience.

2

Repeal
1829–1845

When O'Connell entered the House of Commons in 1829, most political experts predicted that he would fail in his new role and disappear as a significant factor in British and Irish politics. They said that since it took years to acquire the skills and influence to become a leader in the Commons, he was too old at fifty-four to launch a parliamentary career. According to pundits, a man had to be a skilled debater to command the attention of other MPs. They predicted that while O'Connell's demagogic style, which combined earthiness, blarney, exaggeration, and invective, might impress Irish peasants, it would only antagonize British gentlemen.

The experts underrated O'Connell. He was an immediate force at Westminster, laboring hard for his country while adroitly playing the parliamentary game. To please the folks back home, O'Connell on occasion would scurrilously bait opponents, but most often he adapted his style to the Westminster setting. Even enemies had to concede that he was one of the leading debaters in the Commons. He had a melodious, powerful voice and effectively used it to present his country's grievances, pleading the case for Irish reform and self-government.

In the early 1830s O'Connell fought for repeal of the Act of Union, but Tory and Whig governments were equally determined to destroy nationalist agitation in Ireland. In fact, the Whig administration that took office in 1830 demonstrated more diligence in curtailing repeal efforts than had Wellington and Peel. Although Whig leaders courted O'Connell's support with offers of government office, Lord Anglesey, the lord lieutenant, and Lord Stanley, the chief secretary, quickly outlawed every political organization the Irish leader initiated.

O'Connell deserves much of the credit for the passage of the 1832 Reform Bill. His influence was both direct and indirect. Radical leaders who led the agitation in Britain for parliamentary reform modeled their tactics on O'Connell's Emancipation campaign. Their political unions were copies of the Catholic Association. Radical newspapers reported and exaggerated discontent in Britain, warning the government that there were only two alternatives: reform or revolution. Not all Whig leaders were convinced that revolution would follow a failure to reform, but like Peel and Wellington in 1829, they could not afford to take a chance.

O'Connell directly aided the cause of parliamentary reform by supporting it with public speeches and with Irish support in close votes. Liberal values and Irish nationalism motivated his conduct in the Commons. In many ways his Benthamite Utilitarianism was more applicable to urban industrial Britain than it was to rural agrarian Ireland. But as a champion of popular sovereignty he wanted to make the Commons more representative of public opinion, and as an Irish nationalist he hoped that a liberalized British Parliament might concede reform and perhaps even Repeal to Ireland.

The Reform Bill did not satisfy O'Connell's expectations. It increased the Irish electorate to around 93,000 (less than the pre-1829 total), and raised Irish representation in the Commons from 100 to 105. But in comparison to other segments of the United Kingdom, the Bill shortchanged Ireland. The Catholic Relief Bill had established a £10 freehold county franchise in Ireland. The Reform Bill included a £10 borough franchise and added holders of land worth £10 with a twenty-year lease to the county franchise. None of these changes significantly increased the electorate or diminished the influence of the landlord class. As a result of the Reform Bill, 1 person in 115 voted in Irish county elections in contrast to 1 in 24 in England, 1 in 23 in Wales, and 1 in 45 in Scotland. In Irish cities the franchise was 1 in 22, in England and Wales it was 1 in 17, and in Scotland 1 in 27. O'Connell insisted that an increase of five MPs in the Commons did not adequately represent the quickly expanding Irish population, but British politicians replied that Parliament represented property, not people.

Despite his disappointment with the Irish Reform Bill, O'Connell refused to cut his ties with the Whigs and ignored the condescending manner in which Lords Grey and Melbourne and other members of the Whig aristocracy treated him. He believed that the Tories would always sustain Protestant Ascendancy in Ireland, and that the Whigs offered the only possible avenue to constructive change.

In the 1830s—as it had in the 1820s and would continue to do—the Irish Question helped to ideologically clarify and define British politics: Catholic Emancipation divided the Tories, and Whig responses to O'Connell's demands split their party. In 1834 important Whigs such as Sir James Graham, Edward Stanley, the earl of Ripon, and the duke of Richmond left the Cabinet protesting proposed legislation that would permit the government to interfere with property rights and violate the Protestant church by applying its surplus revenues in Ireland to general public services. Before the end of the 1830s, these defectors had moved to the Conservative benches.

Under the pressure of Irish nationalist opinion, but against his better judgment, O'Connell introduced a Repeal motion in the Commons in 1834. The humiliating results—only one British MP supported it—convinced him that the British Parliament would never seriously consider Irish self-government until it had the backing of an organized, disciplined, massive, and enthusiastic agitation.

During the first five years that O'Connell supported the Whigs his rewards were meager. Only Lord Stanley's 1831 Irish Education Bill, establishing a state-supported system of national elementary schools, made a significant positive change in Irish life. In order to minimize religious conflict, national schools offered nondenominational instruction in secular subjects but various sects could provide religious lessons for their own members.

Protestants objected to a "Godless" system outside their control. At first, most Catholic leaders welcomed the opportunity to raise the cultural level of their people, but later, when the church hierarchy developed a spirit of boldness and self-confidence, Archbishops Paul Cullen (Dublin), the ultramontane, and John MacHale (Tuam), the nationalist, condemned the national schools. The former said they were instruments of Protestant proselytism; the latter considered them agents of British rule. When Catholics began to attack the national schools, Protestants switched their position and began to defend them to avoid government financial aid in support of a denominational education system where most of the schools would be Catholic. However, by the mid-nineteenth century the national schools had already in fact if not in name become denominational. In Catholic districts priests headed school boards, and in Protestant areas parsons or vicars performed the same function.

The national system of education in Ireland had implications for Britain. In Ireland the government had experimented with a system of state-supported, theoretically secular education at a time when it was afraid to take such a risk in Britain. The Irish experiment was a victory for British radicalism, increasing pressure for nondenominational state-financed schooling in Britain.

For five years the Whigs enjoyed the benefits of Irish nationalist support without the inconveniences of an open alliance. Then, in 1835, the balance of political forces in the House of Commons forced them to come to terms with O'Connell. The Lichfield House Compact, an alliance between Whigs, Radicals, and Irish Repealers, promised O'Connell improvements in the administration of Irish affairs in exchange for his guarantee to keep the Whigs in office and aid them in their efforts to govern Ireland. In effect, this meant that O'Connell had agreed to abandon the agitation for Repeal in return for a promise of reform. Of course, the Tories denounced the Whig-Radical-Irish combination as a dishonorable and unholy alliance and some Irish nationalists agreed with that interpretation. Lords Russell and Melbourne replied that there was nothing in the Lichfield House Compact contrary to Whig principles, and O'Connell insisted that his arrangements with the Whigs did not violate his political convictions.

O'Connell advocated Repeal as the only plausible answer to the Irish Question. He said that only the Irish could solve the political, religious, social, and economic problems unique to their agrarian, almost feudal and manorial country. O'Connell knew that because they were the only people who could afford the luxury of politics—with its election expenses and service without compensation—upper-class Protestants would dominate an Irish parliament. But he was confident that Irish Catholic opinion and a large Catholic electorate would influence Protestant members of an Irish Lords and Commons. And he expected that time would bring changes increasing Catholic representation in a Dublin legislature.

Although O'Connell believed that under the Union Irish

needs were subordinate to British interests, and urged self-government for his people, he was willing to let British politicians prove him
wrong. The Irish leader often said that he would accept the Union
as a permanent arrangement on the following conditions: that Britain
treat Ireland as an equal partner and endeavor to promote her prosperity, and that Parliament discuss Irish issues in Irish and not British
terms, giving them a sympathetic hearing.

Except when making speeches to Irish audiences, O'Connell
was not a fanatic nationalist. He did not subscribe to the romantic
cultural nationalism that emerged in the early nineteenth century. As
a disciple of Bentham, he was more interested in the personal liberty,
happiness, and economic security of the Irish people than in such
abstract concepts as cultural sovereignty or the folk soul. Although
he doubted that the Protestant-dominated Parliament, representing
an increasingly British urban industrial society, could ever have the
patience, the sympathy, or the understanding to solve the problems
of Catholic, agrarian Ireland, O'Connell, in the Lichfield House
Compact, gave the Whigs another opportunity to prove to Ireland
the advantages of the Union.

Melbourne's administration did place three important Irish
bills on the statute books. In 1838 it commuted the tithe to a tax on
landed property, theoretically freeing Catholic tenant farmers from
the obligation of financing Protestantism. That same year, Parliament
applied the controversial principle of the British Poor Law—the
workhouse test for relief—to Ireland, but the Irish Poor Law did not
go into effect until 1842. The Irish Municipal Reform Bill, which
cleared Parliament in 1840, opened Irish city government to Catholic
participation. Of these three bills, the Poor Law is perhaps the best
example of the insensitivity of a British Parliament legislating for
Ireland.

In 1833 the British prime minister, Lord Grey, appointed the
Irish Poor Law Commission, including prominent Catholic, Protestant, and Presbyterian clerics, to investigate poverty in their country
and to recommend remedies. After two years spent collecting and
evaluating evidence, the Commission submitted a report in 1836
rejecting the British Poor Law as inappropriate for Ireland. It pointed
out that poverty was not a disgrace there and that the pauper had an
important role in society. Wandering beggars brought news and
entertainment into peasant cottages and provided people with an
opportunity to practice Christian charity. Commissioners said that

Irishmen would resent the government locking the poor in workhouses like criminals. And they insisted that Ireland could not afford the British system. Nearly two-and-a-half million people in Ireland were on the verge of starvation. To place all of them in workhouses would overburden the financial resources of an underdeveloped country, and paying poor rates would reduce many others to mendicancy. Instead of a poor law, the Commission recommended more voluntary relief agencies, public works projects to provide employment and improve the economic potential of the country, and state-financed emigration.

Lord John Russell, Whig leader in the Commons, ignored the report of the Irish Poor Law Commission. According to his Utilitarian logic, what suited Britain would fit Ireland. He sent George Nicholls, a British Poor Law official, across the Irish Sea to conduct another poverty survey. After only six weeks of research, he advised a British model poor law, and Russell and Parliament accepted his recommendation.

O'Connell was not satisfied with the fruits of the Whig alliance. The Tithe Act failed to meet his demand for the disestablishment of Protestantism, and it did not keep landlords from raising rents to compensate for the tax they paid to the established church. While O'Connell's arrangement with the Whigs prevented him from vigorously opposing the Poor Law, he voted against it. He also complained that the Whigs did not increase the Irish parliamentary franchise or Irish representation in the Commons, and that they did not do enough to curb Protestant Ascendancy.

Although Whig legislation disappointed O'Connell, Thomas Drummond, Irish undersecretary, did diminish Protestant influence. He appointed Catholics civil servants, magistrates, and other legal officials, and he told landlords that they had duties as well as rights. Drummond also outlawed and drove the Orange Order underground. Unfortunately, the liberal and tolerant spirit in Dublin Castle died with Drummond in 1840.

In 1838 O'Connell decided to warn Melbourne that he must earn continued support from Irish nationalist MPs. He organized the Precursor Society as a prelude to a revival of Repeal agitation and again demanded substantial Irish reforms. When it was clear that the Whigs would not introduce any more important Irish legislation, O'Connell decided to implement his threat. In April 1840 he chaired the first public meeting of the National Association of Ireland, rechristened in 1841 as the Loyal National Repeal Association. Like the Catholic Association, the new organization met at the Corn Exchange, Burgh Quay, Dublin, and later at a new nearby building, Conciliation Hall. Only a hundred people attended the first meeting, and just fifteen of them applied for membership. This apathetic response was an indication that many nationalists feared that O'Connell's alliance with the Whigs revealed his insincerity in regard to Repeal, and that he intended the new organization only as an instrument to intimidate Melbourne.

O'Connell modeled the Repeal organization on the Catholic Association. Members paid one pound in annual dues. Those who contributed ten pounds or more were called Volunteers, and could wear a uniform similar to the one worn by the Irish Volunteers when they forced a British government, fearful of a French invasion, to grant free trade and parliamentary sovereignty to Ireland in 1782. To obtain mass support for Repeal, O'Connell followed the Catholic Association formula, inviting tenant farmers and city and town workers to become associate members for a shilling a year, paid in installments of a penny a month or a farthing a week. In urban and rural parishes, Repeal wardens, men selected by local clergy and approved by the Association, collected dues and sent them, along with names of contributors, to Dublin. They also encouraged Repeal enthusiasm in their districts and established reading rooms where those involved and/or interested in the movement could read nationalist newspapers and pamphlets. Performing functions associated with later Irish-American precinct captains, wardens were the main cogs in the Repeal machinery.

For its first three years, the Loyal National Repeal Association made little progress in its goal to enlist the backing of Irish opinion. Most of the energetic and bright lawyers who had helped O'Connell construct an effective Catholic Association were now successes in their profession, reluctant to jeopardize their economic and social standing by supporting an anti-British movement with few prospects of success. Many, such as Richard Lalor Sheil, were loyal Whig MPs, and some held government office. Until 1843 even the Catholic hierarchy seemed indifferent to Repeal. But in late 1842 O'Connell did acquire lieutenants from a new generation of talented young men.

On October 15, 1842, the first issue of the *Nation* appeared. It combined the talents of Thomas Osborne Davis, John Blake Dillon, and Charles Gavan Duffy—three young men in their twenties, trained in the law and experienced in journalism. Davis was an Anglo-Irish Protestant; Dillon and Duffy were Catholics; Davis and Dillon had attended Trinity College; Davis was from Dublin, Dillon from Connacht, and Duffy from Ulster. Liberalism and romantic nationalism inspired all three.

Duffy, Dillon, and Davis founded the *Nation* "to create and foster public opinion and make it racy of the soil." They defined a nation as something beyond a political state; it was essentially a cultural and spiritual entity formed by history and tradition. They insisted that true Irish sovereignty depended on cultural independence and integrity as well as self-government.

Although Continental cultural nationalism inspired Young Ireland, as the *Nation* writers came to be called, they also drew from local sources. Influenced by the Scotsman James MacPherson's somewhat bogus translations of the Ossianic poems and tales, some Anglo-Irish Protestants in the late eighteenth century, intellectually fascinated with the Gaelic past, founded the Royal Irish Academy. In their poetry, patriotic ballads, and harp festivals, the Society of United Irishmen also furthered interest in Irish antiquities. Early in the nineteenth century, Thomas Moore's *Irish Melodies* and the historical novels of Lady Morgan (Sydney Owenson), the "Wild Irish Girl," both popular in Irish and British circles, romanticized Gaelic Ireland. In the 1830s Eugene O'Curry and John O'Donovan, two Catholics involved in the Ordnance Survey, 1831-1846, that remapped Ireland in a scientific manner, recovered and translated many old manuscripts, establishing a scholarly foundation for Gaelic studies.

Samuel Ferguson, a Trinity-educated Belfast Protestant, was another important early Gaelic scholar. In the 1830s he wrote for the *Dublin University Magazine*. The *DUM* was a Tory voice, but it promoted Irish cultural nationalism to save and strengthen the Union. Ferguson and his colleagues pleaded with Irish Protestants to form a common bond with the Catholic majority through interest in Ireland's history and culture, especially the Gaelic tradition. They believed that cultural nationalism could be a satisfying alternative to political nationalism, and that a distinct Irish identity could exist within the context of the United Kingdom.

If Young Ireland did not quite create Irish cultural nationalism, the young men at the *Nation* packaged and presented it better than those who had come before. O'Connell's political nationalism, forged in the struggle for Catholic Emancipation, provided the *Nation* with an eager audience. In their weekly paper, Davis, Dillon, Duffy and their colleagues favorably compared the spiritual qualities of peasant, agrarian Ireland with the materialism of urban, industrial Britain. An Irish Parliament, they said, would protect their country from the contamination of an alien, decadent culture. Young Irelanders blamed the British-planned, -organized, and -controlled national schools for sabotaging the Irish cultural heritage and imposing British values. (Actually, the national schools expanded the reading audience for the *Nation*.) They envisioned their role as assuming the responsibility of educating their countrymen to know and appreciate their own history, language, and culture.

Among others, the *Nation* attracted the talents of Thomas MacNevin, Daniel Owen Madden, John Mitchel, John O'Hagan, Thomas D'Arcy McGee, and Thomas Francis Meagher. In their essays they praised the high standards of early Christian Irish culture and the contribution made by Irish missionaries to the spread of civilization in Western Europe. They also wrote about the Irish patriots who resisted Dane, Norman, and English invaders. The *Nation* did more than exalt the past; it also tried to encourage a cultural revival, publishing the best in contemporary Irish writing. Poems by James Clarence Mangan and stories by William Carleton, probably the two most significant literary talents in Ireland during the first half of the nineteenth century, and the work of other creative writers and scholars appeared in the *Nation*. The paper invited readers to submit essays, poems, and ballads. Many of the nationalist songs still enjoying popularity among the Irish at home, in Britain, the United States, and throughout the Commonwealth first appeared in the *Nation*.

The Irish language was an important Young Ireland cause. The *Nation* urged its preservation where it survived and its revival where it had vanished. Young Irelanders said that Irish expressed the mind and soul of a unique, indigenous culture, and that English, a foreign tongue, represented cultural as well as political colonialism.

Dillon, Duffy, Davis, and associates attempted to separate the Irish and Catholic identities. They pleaded for harmony among all religious communities and stressed the common nationality of all those calling Ireland their home. The *Nation* gave equal attention to the patriotic contributions of people from all traditions. In discussing common grievances, it insisted that everyone in Ireland would profit from Repeal.

News coverage played a secondary role to the *Nation's* cultural and propaganda efforts. The paper usually borrowed news stories from other newspapers, and centered Young Ireland talent on editorials, poetry, historical essays, biographical sketches, patriotic ballads, and reviews. In addition to advocacy of the Irish language, editorials endorsed and preached cultural and political nationalism, sectarian harmony, tenant right, mass education (cultural and vocational), and political reforms consistent with liberalism and democracy. The *Nation* had such an immediate impact that it quickly attracted the attention of Parliament. British MPs lauded Young Ireland ability, but condemned its radical anti-British ideology.

Neither the appeals of the *Dublin University Magazine* nor the *Nation* enlisted much Anglo-Irish Protestant or Ulster Presbyterian enthusiasm. To them the Gaelic tradition represented Catholicism and nationalism, both dangerous to their security and standing. They continued to look to the British connection as their safeguard. But Young Ireland ideas found a home in the hearts and minds of those in an insecure Irish-Catholic middle class looking for a message that would lift their egos by telling them that they were products of and participants in a unique and significant historical and cultural tradition.

O'Connell welcomed Young Irelanders to the Loyal National Repeal Association, but he was always a little suspicious of his young allies. Since his Irish commitments were rooted in a Benthamite concern for the bread-and-butter issues of politics, he never really understood the uncompromising cultural nationalism of Young Ireland. On political platforms, O'Connell never hesitated to tell the Irish that they were the most virtuous, handsome, and intelligent people in the world, and that they lived in a country unmatched in physical beauty or in economic potential. This was not cultural nationalism; it was blarney used to lift spirits demoralized by over a century of ignorance, oppression, and poverty.

O'Connell sincerely loved his country and its people, Protestant, Nonconformist, and Catholic, and he was proud of his position as the Irish chieftain. He had little time, however, for excursions into the Gaelic past. His Utilitarian views are well illustrated by his attitude toward the Irish language. Unlike the Young Irelanders, he knew, spoke, and occasionally used Irish in political speeches, sometimes to confuse police reporters, but he was opposed to preservation efforts. To him, the Irish language was a symbol of inferiority and a barrier to progress. O'Connell was so occupied with the future of

Ireland that he had little time for its past. He wanted the Irish to have all of the cultural and technological advantages of nineteenth-century living. O'Connell, an enthusiastic reader of Dickens, did not hate England or English culture. He admired Britain's technological advances, its constitution, political institutions, and liberal tradition, and wanted them for his own people.

Since the cosmopolitan O'Connell could not understand or sympathize with the spirit of cultural nationalism that had spread through Europe and entered his own country in the form of Young Ireland, he distrusted the militant tone of the *Nation* and sometimes ridiculed its literary efforts. On the other hand, Young Irelanders were often impatient with O'Connell's pragmatism, flirtations with the Whigs, vulgarity, willingness to compromise Repeal for reform, affinity for the Catholic hierarchy and clergy, and despotic control over the Repeal Association. The *Nation* and O'Connell disagreed on British Chartism (a British working-class effort to achieve economic and social change by democratizing the political system), Corn Law repeal, and federalism. Young Ireland viewed the Chartists as representatives of the British democracy, and therefore natural allies of Irish nationalism against the common enemy, the British aristocracy. O'Connell condemned the Chartists, particularly his old enemy Fergus O'Connor, for employing methods of agitation that tended to encourage violence. True to his Utilitarian, free-trade convictions he opposed the Corn Laws. In rebuttal, the *Nation* held the position that protection was necessary for the welfare of the Irish agrarian economy, and that free trade would benefit industrial Britain at the expense of Ireland. Young Ireland was prepared to work with Irish federalists in a common attack on British domination in Ireland, but considered the limited Irish Parliament they proposed as inadequate for Irish needs. O'Connell was inclined to accept a federal arrangement as a settlement of Irish claims if he could get British politicians to make—and Irish opinion to accept—such an offer.

Despite differences in temperament, methods, and policy, Young Irelanders realized that O'Connell had the allegiance of the Irish masses and that without him the national movement would collapse. Therefore, they were gentle in their criticism of the old man. They submitted to his leadership in the Repeal Association, and their propaganda efforts contributed to the revival of national enthusiasm. About eight thousand people purchased the *Nation*, but its influence extended beyond that number. The paper was in

Repeal reading rooms, and all over the country illiterate peasants crowded into thatch-roofed cottages to listen to the local scholar read Young Ireland poems, essays, and editorials.

While O'Connell served as first Catholic lord mayor of Dublin, Repeal was moribund in 1842. When he completed his term, his old enemy, Sir Robert Peel, was prime minister of a Conservative government, and the Loyal National Repeal Association was meeting weekly at the Corn Exchange. Few English politicians or journalists took it seriously. Writers in British newspapers and periodicals described O'Connell as a washed-up old demagogue agitating Repeal to keep his name before the Irish masses so he could collect money from naive, duped peasants. If this was his motive, he was unsuccessful. The Irish people demonstrated their apathy toward Repeal by not contributing their farthings and pennies to the Association. Only the success of the *Nation* indicated that the goals of nationalism had a following.

British and Irish indifference to Repeal irritated O'Connell, who loved the limelight, needed the annual tribute he received from the Irish people (financial compensation for sacrificing his law practice in order to serve in their interest), still had work to do for Ireland, and could not achieve his goals without the support, financial and moral, of the Catholic populace. So in January 1843 he decided to wage one more campaign for an Irish parliament or Irish reform, knowing that he had at his disposal the necessary ingredients for a successful agitation.

Although Catholic Emancipation, reform of the municipal corporations, the national schools, and the conversion of the tithe to a rent charge paid by the landlord satisfied some Irish needs, these were halfway measures enacted in a surly, reluctant manner, and therefore did not extinguish Irish discontent. Poverty, Protestant Ascendancy, and the tenant-right issue remained to perpetuate tensions between Britain and Ireland. When the government put the Poor Law into operation in 1842, all segments of Irish society expressed displeasure. Catholic, Protestant, and Presbyterian leaders united to condemn the workhouse test and the refusal to give outdoor relief (charity provided directly to people outside of an institutional framework). Irish Nationalists, Tories, and Whigs all protested the despotic powers of the Central Board of Poor Law Commissioners and complained about the expenses of operating a system designed for an industrial rather than an agrarian country.

Members of the upper and middle classes expressed their disapproval of the Poor Law in petitions to Parliament, platform speeches, and letters to newspapers. Tenant farmers often resorted to more spectacular and sometimes violent tactics. In many sections of the country they refused to pay poor rates, even when the government sent the army to collect them. O'Connell, aware of how opposition to the Poor Law stimulated anti-British passions, encouraged the protest, and included an anti-Poor Law plank as a major part of his Repeal platform. His strategy produced quick results. In the spring of 1843, as the anti–Poor Law agitation tapered off, the Repeal Association grew in strength, numbers, and financial income.

At the beginning of 1843 the most popular and influential man in Ireland, next to O'Connell, was Theobald Mathew, a Capuchin friar. Mathew had enrolled between four and five million people in his Temperance Society with a branch, complete with reading room and colorfully uniformed musical bands, in almost every country town. Even Ascendancy-dominated newspapers praised Mathew's efforts to curb the tendency of the Irish poor to escape misery in the bottle and the jug. Because temperance had continued the mass-movement style that O'Connell had originated in the 1820s, the Repeal leader considered the self-control and the enthusiasm of Father Mathew's teetotalers a potential fountain of Repeal strength. He tried to lure them into the ranks of Repeal by endorsing their cause, describing temperance as the most powerful weapon in the arsenal of moral force. He said it would discipline nationalists and strengthen them for their struggle against British domination.

Hoping to avoid partisan politics, Mathew refused to alienate Irish and British non-Catholics by associating temperance with Irish nationalism. But since he could not control or dictate the political loyalties or opinions of his followers, O'Connell succeeded in capturing their attention and loyalty. At the height of Repeal enthusiasm, temperance bands played an important role at public meetings, and the *Nation* was prominent in Society reading rooms.

After O'Connell had snared anti–Poor Law protesters and teetotalers, he persuaded the Dublin Corporation, along with other municipal and public bodies, to petition Parliament for a Repeal of the Union. Government officials aided Repeal recruiting by a series of tactical blunders. They awarded the Irish mail-coach contract to a Scottish company in preference to an Irish concern already holding the concession, thus forcing thousands of Dublin workers to face the prospect of unemployment in an already job-starved city. Then they dismissed Dr. Phelan, the only Catholic Poor Law commissioner, without an explanation. When the government finally decided to amend the Poor Law, it made concessions to the gentry while ignoring tenant farmer complaints.

While the Repeal agitation was gaining momentum, Wellington and Peel pushed an Irish Arms Bill through Parliament curtailing civil liberties, and the Irish lord chancellor, Sir Edward Sugden, dismissed magistrates who attended Repeal meetings (though he admitted they were legal and constitutional). The Arms Bill and the dismissal of the magistrates rallied Catholic barristers and solicitors to the Repeal standard, giving O'Connell the support of an influential segment of the Catholic middle class that had largely deserted him after Catholic Emancipation.

In the spring of 1843 O'Connell began to hold Sunday public assemblies to petition Parliament for a Repeal of the Union, located in a different part of the country every week. Thousands crowded the roads on early Sunday mornings; many journeyed a long distance to attend the meetings. Priests said Mass for them on the hillsides, before they cooked potato breakfasts over turf fires. Priests, temperance bands, local dignitaries, and lines of marching Repealers met O'Connell as he approached the selected town. They detached the horses and pulled his carriage by hand through the streets as women and children threw flowers in the path of the "Liberator."

At these mass rallies, O'Connell told audiences of hundreds of thousands that they were the bravest, strongest, and most patient and virtuous people on the face of the earth. He predicted that before the year was out they would have a Dublin parliament, acomplished by the force of moral persuasion. He said that they would never fight unless attacked, but that would not happen. Peel and Wellington would surrender to Irish national opinion as they had in 1829. O'Connell assured Repealers that an Irish legislature would solve the country's problems. Tenants would be secure on their farms, trade and commerce would flourish, and culture would thrive. Catholics, Protestants, and Nonconformists would live in harmony. There would be liberty of conscience with no established church. A free Ireland faithful to the Crown would live in peace with Britain.

O'Connell always encouraged loyalty to Queen Victoria. He told his listeners that if her ministers, "Orange Peel" and Wellington, the "stunted corporal," denied Ireland its due, Victoria would use her royal prerogative to establish a Dublin parliament. In preparation for independence, O'Connell promised to summon a pre-parliament, the Council of Three Hundred, and to establish arbitration courts so the people could seek an Irish rather than a British version of justice. By autumn, arbitration courts existed and operated with surprising efficiency and effectiveness.

These Monster Meetings, as newspapers described them, were a tremendous success. Contributions poured into the Association treasury. Five times during the late spring and summer the weekly Repeal rent exceeded £2,000, a fortune for the time. Much of the money came from the Irish in Britain and the United States, despite considerable Irish-American resentment of O'Connell's condemnation of slavery and its supporters. He said that he could not take blood money from defenders of black slavery to free Irish helots. O'Connell was ahead of his time in demanding not only emancipation but also full political and civil rights for blacks, fellow sons and daughters of God and equal members of the human race.

Crowds at Monster Meetings and the size of the Repeal rent frayed Irish Protestant and Presbyterian nerves. They insisted that the government suppress the agitation and outlaw the Repeal Association. Earl DeGrey, the anti-Catholic lord lieutenant, supported their demand.

Not until May of 1843 did Peel realize that O'Connell had mobilized a formidable challenge to British authority. As soon as he recognized the danger, the prime minister told Parliament that he would preserve the Union at all costs, but found it difficult to deal directly with O'Connell's agitation. Peel feared that anti-Repeal legislation might unintentionally embrace the Anti-Corn Law League, modeled on O'Connell's recipe for agitation. An attack on Repeal might unite Radicals, democrats, free-traders, and Irish nationalists in a common crusade in defense of civil and political liberties. This would make O'Connell respectable in Britain and both the anti-Corn Law and Repeal agitations would become more difficult to handle.

Once Peel rejected an anti-Repeal strategy that could provide O'Connell with British allies, he was forced to treat revitalized Irish nationalism with a policy of calculated indifference. His refusal to respond with coercive legislation or military action to O'Connell's boastful and aggressive orations infuriated the reactionary, anti-Irish, no-popery Tory core of the Conservative party, but his indifference masked a carefully calculated plan to destroy O'Connell's influence in Ireland while at the same time eradicating the roots of Irish nationalism. By not acknowledging the significance of Repeal by either coercion or immediate conciliation, Peel hoped to demonstrate to Irish Catholics that the scarcely veiled threats of the agitation would not intimidate the government into conceding either Repeal or reform. He hoped that once they comprehended that O'Connell could not redeem any of his extravagant pledges, the Irish public would lose confidence in him and his tactics. Repeal would then dwindle into insignificance, and the British army could easily handle any nationalist hotheads who reacted with physical violence.

While Peel and Sir James Graham, the home secretary, waited for their policy of indifference to deflate the Repeal balloon, they planned a long-range Irish policy to satisfy some of the needs and ambitions of the various components of the anti-Union coalition, and thus destroy Irish nationalism by eliminating the grievances that had created and nourished it. The government, however, had no intention of initiating reforms while agitation flourished and O'Connell enjoyed the confidence of Irish Catholics. Peel thought that concessions to Irish demands in 1843 might encourage nationalists to believe that the government was susceptible to intimidation and inspire O'Connell to intensify agitation. He wanted an Irish policy that was more than a frightened, ill-considered response to Irish discontent. He intended to lay the Irish Question permanently to rest, and to make the Union between the two islands a true community of interests and loyalties.

Of course, there was a danger that O'Connell, to maintain his standing with his followers, would commit to revolutionary conspiracy. There also was the possibility that he might lose the reins of Irish nationalism to advocates of physical force. So Peel and Graham took out an insurance policy against the failure of their Irish strategy. They dispatched troops, weapons, ammunition, and supplies to Ireland, and stored arms there for possible use by Protestant and Presbyterian yeomen. The prime minister and home secretary also were determined that O'Connell and his chief lieutenants would suffer the consequences of their audacious challenge to British authority. Graham instructed the Irish law officers to collect evidence of sedition.

When Peel told Parliament in May of 1843 that he was ready if necessary to use military force to maintain the Union, and when Sugden acted on this declaration by dismissing Repeal magistrates,

O'Connell was convinced that the government would employ coercion to smash his movement. In an effort to make Peel reconsider, and to preserve the enthusiasm and confidence of his supporters, he adopted a militant tone in his public speeches. He went so far as to suggest that he was prepared to conduct a defensive war against British troops.

By late summer, however, O'Connell realized that Peel was out to destroy Repeal by undermining the confidence of Irish nationalists in his ability to deliver on his promises of freedom and reform. He feared that if the prime minister's strategy succeeded his followers might abandon constitutional nationalism. To protect them from those with dangerous messages and from the bullets and bayonets of British soldiers, O'Connell adopted a softer line in his speeches. He stopped promising Repeal in the near future, and said that it would be impossible to summon the Council of Three Hundred before the year was out. Instead of guaranteeing quick victories, O'Connell now asked Irish nationalists to support him in a long struggle for freedom. He warned against men who counseled violence and insisted that moral force would eventually triumph over the Tories and anti-Irish British opinion.

By early autumn it was apparent that Peel's patience had achieved its objectives. O'Connell was preparing his followers for disappointment, the Repeal rent had declined, and Irish tenant farmers were neglecting agitation to concentrate their energies on an abundant harvest. Now that the enemy was in retreat, Peel made preparations to assume the offensive. He decided to prosecute Repeal leaders for sedition, and sent Lord DeGrey and Sugden to Dublin to supervise the arrest and prosecution of O'Connell and his lieutenants. They also received instructions to prevent the Repeal meeting scheduled for Sunday, October 8, in Clontarf, which was to be the year's last Monster Meeting. A tremendous crowd was expected to gather in the Dublin suburb; Repealers from Irish communities in Britain were crossing the Irish Sea for the event.

Late Saturday afternoon, October 7, DeGrey issued a proclamation outlawing the Clontarf meeting because the original announcement—written and distributed when O'Connell was not in Dublin—indicated that it was designed as a military demonstration to intimidate the government. Rather than risk a massacre, O'Connell complied with the order. A week later, authorities arrested him and six others (including Charles Gavan Duffy) and charged them with sedition and attempting to subvert the loyalty of soldiers stationed in Ireland. In February 1844 a jury convicted, and a judge fined O'Connell and his associates £2,000 and sentenced them to a year in prison.

In September 1844 the British law lords, by a one-vote margin, reversed the decision of the Irish court on the grounds that the prosecution had drawn up an improper indictment and tried its case before a packed jury. After their release from Richmond prison, O'Connell and his friends were received as heroes by Dublin Repealers. Celebration bonfires burned throughout the country. But O'Connell seemed to have little zest left for agitation. His decision to abandon the Clontarf meeting and his failure to exploit his legal vindication by intensifying nationalist activity did much to crush the Repeal spirit and to undermine confidence in constitutional methods of agitation. But the defeat of O'Connell and Repeal in 1843 was not a product of cowardice or faulty tactics so much as it was a misreading of the times.

Like most political leaders, O'Connell became a captive of past successes. He expected Peel and Parliament to react to the popular outcry for Repeal in the same way they had to the Catholic agitation of the 1820s. In 1828-29 he had convinced Tory leaders that if they did not concede Catholic rights, the extremist element in Ireland might push him aside, take control of the movement, and then substitute physical for moral force. Fifteen years later, he seemed to assume that if Peel again faced the alternatives of concessions to Irish nationalism or the potential chaos of violence, he would follow precedent and select the former. If the prime minister refused to bow to expediency, O'Connell hoped that Whig leaders in the Commons would exploit the Irish crisis to embarrass and perhaps topple the Conservative government. He thought that once in power, Russell and his colleague, Lord Palmerston, would probably try to quiet troubled Irish waters with a policy of conciliation and a renewal of the alliance with Irish nationalism.

Apparently, O'Connell did not understand that while the Irish mood of 1843 resembled the one of 1829, the same was not true of the temper of the British Parliament. In the 1820s there were a considerable number of enlightened MPs favorable to Emancipation; Peel and Wellington knew in 1829 that any attempt to suppress the Catholic Association without conceding its goal would antagonize a considerable portion of the House of Commons. If an Irish revolutionary movement in resistance to government despotism enjoyed the sympathy of a respectable body of British opinion, the seeds of rebellion might spread to and take root in a Britain already saturated with social, political, and economic discontent. Catholic Emancipation was an Irish issue with British implications, and the government's responsibility to preserve the Union and peace and order throughout the United Kingdom necessitated a compromise of Protestant principles.

In 1843 Whigs and Radicals as well as Conservatives and Tories rejected Repeal as a satisfactory solution to the Irish Question. They all agreed that an independent Ireland would weaken Britain's defenses and prepare the way for a dissolution of the empire. Conservatives and Tories also insisted that Repeal would permit an Irish Catholic majority to oppress an Irish Protestant minority. Whigs and Radicals maintained that the Union, if properly managed, could bring peace and prosperity to Ireland. During the Repeal crisis of 1843 British no-popery joined pro-Union parliamentary opinion against Irish nationalism. Whigs and Radicals did not hesitate to exploit Irish discontent to embarrass the Conservative government, but Peel could count on their support in his determination to preserve the Union.

When Peel challenged O'Connell on the Clontarf meeting, the Irish leader had no realistic choice but to retreat. His nonviolent convictions, his commitment to constitutional methods of agitation, and his common sense would not permit him to lead his followers to slaughter in a futile insurrection against disciplined British troops. When he surrendered to the government ultimatum, O'Connell removed the most effective weapon from the arsenal of constitutional agitation—the implied threat of physical force if Britain refused to submit to the demands of majority Irish opinion.

Confident that Repeal no longer was a live issue, by the beginning of 1844 Peel and Sir James Grahamwere ready to convert their Irish policy into legislation. Before doing so, Peel instructed reluctant officials in Dublin Castle to appoint as many Catholics as possible to government office, indicating Britain's intention to prove that the United Kingdom embraced all of the Irish people, Catholic, Protestant, and Nonconformist as equal citizens, and demonstrating that the Union promised rich benefits for their country. When De-Grey, the lord lieutenant, protested that few Catholics had the qualifications for government positions, Peel replied that if some exceptions were not made, Catholics would never have the ambition or incentive to acquire the necessary credentials for occupational and social mobility.

Although it included concessions to each of the clerical, agrarian, and middle-class components of the nationalist coalition, the main purpose of Peel's new Irish policy was to detach priests from popular agitation. Peel accepted a thesis popular in British intellectual and political circles that members of the Irish Catholic clergy fermented populist protests because they were financially dependent on the ignorant anti-British masses. He decided that the best way to detach the clergy from mass movements was to guarantee them and their church economic security. Peel also knew that separating priests from nationalism presented many risks. If the task was not handled with tact and superb diplomacy, it would alienate British no-popery, reactionary Tories in the Conservative party, the Irish Catholic hierarchy and clergy, and even Rome.

The government began its operation by asking Pope Gregory XVI to condemn the nationalist activities of Irish bishops and priests. By pointing out to Prince Clemons Furst von Metternich the dangerous implications of clerical nationalism in Ireland for all of Europe, and particularly for the multi-ethnic Hapsburg empire, the British persuaded the Austrian premier to endorse their request to Rome. William Petre, the British emissary to the Vatican, told the pope that if his government could obtain the support of the Catholic Church in Ireland for efforts to maintain the Union and social order, Peel's Irish policy might culminate in the endowment of Catholicism in that country. Rome welcomed this possibility and the opportunity to establish friendly relations with Britain, so Cardinal Fransoni, prefect of propaganda, wrote to the Irish hierarchy advising them to cease political activities and to concentrate their energies on spiritual matters. Only a small minority of the bishops heeded his counsel.

In the autumn of 1844, Peel and Graham initiated the legislative phase of their Irish policy with the Charitable Bequests Act, which eliminated many remaining Penal Law restrictions on the Catholic Church's opportunities to inherit or bequeath property. Peel and Graham intended the Charitable Bequests Act as a demonstration of government intentions to render justice to Catholics. In addition, Peel also hoped to use Catholic bishops on the Charitable Bequests Board as agents in his effort to persuade Irish-Catholic clerical and middle-class opinion that cooperation with the British government promised more benefits than anti-Union agitation.

O'Connell condemned the Charitable Bequests Act as inadquate and as a lever for the British government to exert influence over the hierarchy and clergy. Archbishop MacHale and a number of other bishops also attacked the measure. Archbishop Daniel Murray and a few other prelates accepted the Act and agreed to sit on the Charitable Bequests Board. This schism in the ranks of the hierarchy enlarged a split that had begun with the debate over the national education system in the 1830s. Murray viewed the national schools as imperfect but still a progressive infuence in Irish life. MacHale and his friends wanted an open system of endowed Catholic education. The feud within the hierarchy was bitter, with both sides frequently appealing to Rome.

In the spring of 1845 Peel made another friendly gesture to Irish Catholicism by introducing a proposal to increase and convert into a permanent endowment the annual grant to the Roman Catholic seminary at Maynooth. In the 1790s the Irish Parliament had established the seminary in Kildare to keep Irish candidates for the priesthood out of French Revolution–influenced seminaries on the Continent. After the Act of Union, Britain believed it had an obligation to continue maintaining Maynooth. Yet, every year when the grant came up for renewal, it provoked a wave of anti-Catholic hysteria, embittering relations between Britain and Ireland. Peel hoped that the Maynooth Bill would remove the seminary as an annual issue and at the same time convince Catholic bishops of his government's friendly attitude, thereby smoothing the way for a more extensive endowment of their church. However, the hostility of British no-popery to the bill, in and out of Parliament, offended Irish Catholics and ensured that the government would approach further endowment with caution. Nevertheless, Peel courageously resisted Tory-engineered anti-Catholic prejudice, and with the support of the Whigs passed the Maynooth Bill.

Following the Maynooth controversy within his own party, the prime minister turned to the educational needs of the Irish middle class, providing them with something more than Protestant Trinity College as a higher education opportunity. The government's Irish Colleges Bill established three provincial Queen's colleges (at Cork, Galway, and Belfast) organized on the principle of mixed or nondenominational education. Peel assumed that the first two would have

Catholic majorities while the last would enroll mostly Presbyterians. Peel and Graham hoped that in a university setting, Protestants and Catholics would mingle in a secular environment, emancipating middle-class Catholics from nationalism and clericalism by making them realize that they had interests independent of religion and more important than Repeal. In Britain the Colleges Bill met minimum opposition, but in Ireland O'Connell attacked mixed education as anti-Catholic in spirit and forced the church hierarchy to condemn the bill's provisions.

In 1841 and 1848, on the urging of Archbishop MacHale, the pope condemned the Queen's Colleges. At the Synod of Thurles in 1850, with Archbishop Cullen of Armagh presiding, the Irish hierarchy forbade Catholics to attend or to accept teaching or administrative posts in the colleges. The following year Rome endorsed the decision of the Irish bishops.

Because O'Connell's position on the Colleges Bill was inconsistent with his freedom of conscience views and his appeals for Catholic-Protestant harmony, it is fair to assume that he was sacrificing principle for his perceived need to keep Catholic bishops in the nationalist fold. Believing that Catholic-Protestant interaction in colleges would result in a decline of sectarianism and an increase in a common Irish identity, thus strengthening nationalism, Young Irelanders endorsed mixed education. This disagreement over higher education initiated an open feud that ended with the secession of Young Ireland from the Repeal Association in 1846.

The Colleges Bill was the last portion of Peel's Irish policy to pass through Parliament. He attempted to conciliate Irish tenant farmers by appointing the Devon Commission to investigate their relations with landlords and then to recommend legislation. Lord Stanley introduced a bill in the House of Lords based on the findings of the Devon Report and designed to introduce a moderate tenant right. But the government withdrew from the legislative contest when many Whigs and Conservatives indicated that they would not tolerate even a minor limitation on property rights.

Peel's Irish policy achieved many of its desired goals. Rome had condemned active clerical nationalism, and several Catholic bishops were cooperating with government efforts to lighten the financial burdens on their church. The Charitable Bequests Board gave Peel the opportunity to continue negotiations with them in his effort to demonstrate the Union's potential benefits for Irish Catholicism. And despite the negative response in Britain to the Maynooth Bill, the Irish hierarchy and clergy appreciated Peel's generous intentions and his courage in the face of British anti-Catholicism. Finally, although O'Connell, the bishops, and the pope condemned the Queen's Colleges, the education issue did create a conflict within Irish nationalism, an ideological clash between Young and "Old" Ireland which eventually destroyed the unity of Repeal.

O'Connell denied Peel total victory by shrewdly playing on Irish-Catholic suspicions of British intentions. During the Charitable Bequests debate, he told the Irish people that the British government was attempting to conclude an arrangement with Rome at the expense of Irish liberty. O'Connell's tactics forced the bishops to publish the Fransoni letter, intensifying distrust of British motives and lessening respect for Rome among Irish Catholics. Publication of Fransoni's epistle also forced Archbishop Murray and British officials to deny any intention of a concordat between the British government and the Roman Catholic Church. By emphasizing the danger of an understanding between London and the Vatican, O'Connell repaired the breach in Catholic nationalist unity opened by Peel's Irish policy to a certain extent, and made the hierarchy cautious about considering endowment by the British government. When British anti-Catholicism reacted to the Maynooth Bill, it helped O'Connell persuade his constituency that Peel's generosity was not a reflection of British popular attitudes toward the Irish. Even the split in Repeal ranks over the Colleges Bill did not appear fatal in 1845. Old and Young Ireland were still in basic agreement on the aims and methods of agitation.

It is impossible to evaluate accurately the success of Peel's Irish policy by the only valid test—its influence on the course of Anglo-Irish affairs. In 1845 famine devastated Ireland, provoking social disorder, forcing Peel to temporarily abandon his efforts to fully integrate Ireland into the United Kingdom. In the spring of 1846, arguing that the potato blight in Ireland necessitated putting an end to agricultural protection, the prime minister introduced legislation repealing the Corn Laws. Confronted with agrarian crime, he also introduced an Irish coercion bill. The government's "protection of life" bill would have placed considerable police power in disturbed districts, imposed a curfew on the population, sentenced its violators to fifteen years transportation, and collected fines to compensate victims of violence. On the afternoon of June 25 the Lords passed the free trade measure. That evening in the Commons, protectionist Tories, in a vengeful mood, joined Whigs, Radicals, and Irish nationalists in defeating Peel on Irish coercion, destroying his Conservative government. The Corn Law dispute emphasized a split in the Conservative party that began with Catholic Emancipation and intensified during Peel's effort to solve the Irish Question through fairness to Ireland's Catholic majority.

Since Peel's aborted effort to destroy Irish nationalism through concessions to its various interests contributed to the fall of his administration, no British leader dared confront the Irish Question in all its complexity until Gladstone took office in 1868. By that time Irish nationalism had assumed an identity independent of the economic, political, and religious grievances that had created and nourished it, and Britain had forfeited an opportunity to destroy it with justice and kindness.

3
Famine, Revolution, Republicanism 1845–1870

At the beginning of 1845, O'Connell, now approaching seventy and no longer energetic or robust, still chaired Repeal Association meetings. While he had lost his zest for mass agitation, he had proved a clever tactician in responding to Peel's efforts to destabilize Irish nationalism. Beginning with the dispute between O'Connell and Davis over the Colleges Bill, factionalism disrupted the Repeal Association. Young Irelanders distrusted O'Connell's renewed flirtation with the Whig party as a cynical betrayal of Irish nationalism. They described his Benthamite Utilitarianism as a materialistic "pig" philosophy, inappropriate to Irish needs or traditions, and they decried the sectarian tone of his nationalism. Although most were Catholic, Young Irelanders wanted to remove religious colorations from Irish identity and unite Catholics, Protestants, and Nonconformists in a common nationality. O'Connell, a believer in private conscience and separation of church and state, did not intend to replace Protestant with Catholic Ascendancy, but he knew that it was Catholic issues and Catholic mobilization that had produced Irish nationalism, and he was not convinced that it was yet strong enough to survive without the cooperation of bishops and priests. O'Connell also distrusted what he considered intellectual pretensions and secularism among Young Irelanders. He also worried that many of the articles in the *Nation* praising the Society of United Irishmen and the revolutionary heroes of 1798 might inspire violence among people tormented by the Great Famine.

In July 1846, in an attempt to purge physical force elements in the Repeal movement, O'Connell introduced a resolution demanding that all members reject revolution or leave the Association. After Thomas Francis Meagher, with great fervor, insisted that the Irish, like the American founding fathers, had a right to defend liberty with their lives, Young Irelanders, led by William Smith O'Brien and Charles Gavan Duffy, walked out of Conciliation Hall and founded the Irish Confederation. O'Brien, a Protestant landlord and Whig MP from County Clare, had decided in 1843 that the British Parliament would never render justice to Ireland. The next year he joined the Repeal Association and served as its acting head when O'Connell was in prison. Young Ireland's idealism attracted O'Brien; O'Connell's pragmatism often revolted him. When the showdown came, he chose idealism.

Despite O'Connell's genuine fears, revolution was only a theoretical issue in 1846. Young Irelanders were still constitutional Repealers. Although scarlet fever had taken the life of Thomas Osborne Davis in 1845, the Irish Confederation had most of the talent, but O'Connell had the numbers. Most Irish nationalists followed their priests in remaining loyal to the Liberator and "Old Ireland." The split in Irish nationalism was certainly ill-timed, occurring when Ireland was going through a crisis that would alter its history.

In 1845 a potato fungus originating in North America arrived in Ireland via the Continent, causing a famine that persisted through 1849 with aftershocks that were felt until 1851. Since they had to sell their grain crops and livestock to pay excessive rents, millions of people depended on the potato as their sole means of sustenance. During the Famine at least a million and a half died of starvation or from diseases associated with hunger—cholera, fever, and scurvy; many millions came close to death; and at least another million crossed the Atlantic in fever-infected coffin ships or swarmed across the Irish Sea to Cardiff, Glasgow, and Liverpool.

Irish nationalists in the nineteenth century claimed—there are still people in Ireland and among the Irish of the diaspora who hold this view—that Ireland suffered so much and lost so many people during the Famine because the British government tried to solve the Irish Question by exterminating a large proportion of its population. This is too simple an explanation for a complex situation. Much Famine misery resulted from an inefficient and unproductive agricultural system that had existed before the Union. Death, disease, and emigration were also the products of a population explosion encouraged by a primitive agrarian economy and a potato diet. When the Famine began to decimate Ireland, British officials diligently labored to mitigate the disaster, often donating their own money to feed the Irish poor. Many British physicians fell victim to fever while treating the Irish sick. People in Britain, including the queen and members of the royal family, contributed to Famine relief. British religious groups, particularly the Quakers, raised funds, ministered to the sick, and distributed food to the hungry. On rare occasions, never involving Quakers, some Protestant groups insisted Catholics change religion in exchange for food, giving rise to the denigrating term "Souper" in Ireland for a person who sells his faith for a mess of pottage.

In the Famine's first year, Peel's administration spent £8,000,000 in relief efforts. In contrast, the Whig government's reaction to the crisis did give Irish nationalists an excuse to raise the genocide charge. In a period when the Irish masses were dying of hunger and disease or were going into exile, the United Kingdom was the most prosperous country in the world. Yet the government refused to use the full resources of Britain and the empire to save its Irish partners in the Union. From 1845 to 1851 Britain spent only £15 million on Famine relief (compared to the £70 million later expended during the Crimean War). Committed to laissez-faire dogmatism, government officials did not provide enough food to meet immediate needs or design public works projects to stimulate the economy. They argued that Famine relief should not interfere with normal commercial activity, compete with private business, discourage personal initiative, make the Irish psychologically dependent on government charity, or interfere with private property or individual responsibility. In the Famine's darkest hours, Nassau Senior, a distinguished economist prominent in Whig circles, lamented that in 1848 only a million Irish people would die, an insufficient number to solve the population problem.

Anti-Catholicism certainly figured in British responses to Irish hunger. Many English, Scots, and Welsh believed that poverty and ignorance were endemic to Catholicism, and that the Irish were paying for their religious choice. Sectarian prejudice influenced Charles Edward Trevelyan, undersecretary of the Treasury, the man most responsible for government relief measures, who proclaimed the Famine a divine punishment on a wicked, perverse people.

In many ways the Irish suffered an experience during the

Great Famine similar to Jews a century later. Both groups were victims of what Albert Camus defined as ideological murder, the sacrifice of the lives of men, women, and children to economic, social, or political theories. Certainly the Nazis were more ruthless, heartless, and consistent in the application of racist principles than Trevelyan and his colleagues were in enforcing the dogmas of political economy, or in designing a Famine relief policy that reflected their dislike of Catholicism. But Irish people dying of hunger or crowded into the bowels of an emigrant ship in the 1840s would have had scant consolation in knowing that their predicament was not the result of race hate but the price they must pay for their religion and for Britain to maintain a free-enterprise economy.

The Famine was the most significant event in nineteenth-century Irish history: it destroyed whatever chance Peel's Irish policy had of soothing Irish-Catholic opinion; left the Irish with bitter memories and an intense hatred of Britain, emotions they would pass on to their children and grandchildren on both sides of the Atlantic; pushed the agrarian issue into the forefront of the Irish Question; multiplied and institutionalized emigration; and altered the direction of Irish nationalism and the complexion of Irish politics.

O'Connell returned to the Whig alliance in 1845, helping to depose Peel in 1846, and then giving the Russell administration his loyal support. Still, the Whigs never adequately rewarded the Irish leader for his years of service. In the 1830s O'Connell had kept them in office and helped push their legislation through the Commons. Whigs repaid him by cheating Ireland in the 1832 Reform Bill and proposing solutions to Irish problems concerning tithes, municipal government, and poverty that were inadequate or unsuitable for the Irish situation. Through it all O'Connell retained confidence in them as the only realistic hope for Irish reform, and in the Famine crisis he again turned to them for help. In February 1847, as a fading old man with a voice not much louder than a whisper, he rose in the House of Commons and begged Britain to help his starving people. British MPs listened with attention, then ignored his plea. Broken-hearted and close to death, O'Connell set out for Rome in late March of 1847. In Paris he received the homage of French liberals for his contributions to the advance of liberalism and democracy. O'Connell never reached the Holy City. He died in Genoa on May 15, 1847. His heart is buried in Rome while his body rests underneath a giant round tower in Dublin's Glasnevin cemetery.

While O'Connell created modern Irish nationalism and designed the tactics of constitutional agitation used by the Irish and other peoples in the nineteenth and twentieth centuries, he left Repeal in a shambles. His alliance with the Whigs split the movement into Young and Old Ireland factions and destroyed what remained of an Irish party in the House of Commons. Inadequate returns from the Whig alliance, the failure of Repeal in 1843, and devastation by famine weakened the appeal of O'Connell's style of nationalism, leaving the field to Young Ireland's cultural version.

After Daniel O'Connell died, his son John inherited leadership of the Repeal Association, but not his father's charisma or political genius. While the Repeal Association was slipping into irrelevance, a tactical controversy between John Mitchel and Charles Gavan Duffy disrupted the Irish Confederation.

Mitchel, a Unitarian from Ulster and a barrister by training, first contributed to the *Nation* in 1842. Three years later, on Duffy's invitation, he joined its staff as assistant editor. With the other Young Irelanders he seceded from the Repeal Association in 1846. By 1847 Mitchel had lost confidence in the tactics of constitutional nationalism and in Young Ireland's goal of enlisting the Protestant gentry. He believed that the Ascendancy placed its property interests above Ireland. He argued that landlordism, a bulwark of the Union, should be destroyed, and that the property of Ireland should be distributed among its people. Mitchel insisted that taking up the agrarian issue was the best way for the Confederation to build a powerful nationalist movement.

Mitchel borrowed many of his ideas from James Fintan Lalor, a member of a prominent nationalist family. Lalor's father, Patrick, was active in the anti-tithe agitation of the 1830s. His younger brother, Peter, was a Repealer who later emigrated to Australia where he won acclaim as a labor leader and government minister in Victoria. James Fintan Lalor did not share his family's enthusiasm for Repeal. He believed that a solution to the land question deserved priority over the demand for an Irish parliament. In 1843 he wrote Peel to say that Repeal could be destroyed by concessions to the needs of tenant farmers.

Impressed with Lalor's intellect and his powerful journalistic style, Duffy invited him to voice his views in the *Nation* in 1847. In a series of letters, Lalor expressed his opinion that the land question was more important than Repeal, and argued that the only way Irish nationalism could retain mass support was by endorsing the cause of tenant farmers. He described moral-force agitation as an exercise in futility, and derided O'Connell's distinctions between legal and illegal protest. Lalor said that as long as the British government defined what was legal and illegal, constitutional nationalism would always be limited by restrictions imposed by its enemy. He suggested that Irish nationalism build its strategy around only one consideration, the best interests of Ireland, and recommended an agitation against rent payments to destroy landlordism and paralyze British rule in Ireland. Persuaded by Lalor's logic, Mitchel adopted a variation on his strategy in early 1848—a campaign against the payment of poor rates.

Strategies proposed by Lalor and Mitchel offended O'Brien's conservative landlord nationalism. He believed their radicalism would destroy the Confederation's hope of persuading Protestants to join the national movement. When Duffy agreed with O'Brien, Mitchel resigned from the *Nation* and took the dispute over nationalist tactics to the Confederation for a decision. To counter Mitchel, Duffy recommended the formation of an independent parliamentary party to publicize Irish grievances and convert British parliamentary and public opinion to the justice of Repeal. If the Irish party failed to make an impression on the British Parliament, and if British opinion remained hostile to Irish reforms, he said that Irish MPs should retaliate by obstructing British legislation in the House of Commons. Duffy proposed that while the Irish party was presenting Ireland's case at Westminister, nationalists at home should organize and use their franchise to win control over the agencies of local government. If Irish MPs were finally ejected from the Commons for practicing obstruction, he said that they could return to an Ireland under nationalist domination, and that Britain would eventually have to surrender to a united and disciplined national opinion capable of mobilizing effective passive resistance to the Union through its control of parliamentary representation, city corporations, Poor Law boards, and grand juries.

In contrast to Duffy's, Mitchel's plan was simple, direct, and revolutionary. He advised the Confederation to mobilize the people against rents and poor rates. After a long deliberation, a majority of the Confederation sided with Duffy. Mitchel resigned from the organization and began publishing his own weekly newspaper, *The United Irishman*. It advised readers to prepare for revolution by collecting and becoming proficient in the use of weaponry. Mitchel's editorials pleaded with nationalists to drive the British out of their country, to establish an Irish republic, and to abolish landlordism.

In February 1848, when Young Irelanders learned that French liberals and socialists had overthrown Louis Phillipe and established the Second Republic, they, like liberal nationalists in Belgium, Germany, and various parts of the Hapsburg empire, were caught up in revolutionary enthusiasm and optimism. Mitchel rejoined the Confederation, editorials in the *Nation* took on the same militant tone as those in *The United Irishman*, O'Brien and his colleagues tried to enlist John O'Connell and Irish conservatives in a national front, Young Irelanders made contact with friends of Irish freedom in the United States and the Chartists in Britain, O'Brien led a delegation to Paris to congratulate the leaders of the Second Republic and to secure their support and aid for an Irish revolution, and Confederate clubs throughout the country were ordered to gather arms and prepare for battle. While O'Brien was prepared to lead an uprising against British rule in Ireland, he had no intention of declaring war on property. His distrust of agrarian radicalism convinced Mitchel to leave the Confederation again.

Attempting to forestall revolution, British authorities arrested O'Brien, Mitchel, and Thomas Francis Meagher in May. When juries could not agree that they were guilty of sedition, the court released O'Brien and Meagher, but a packed jury, using a new treason felony law, convicted Mitchel, and a judge sentenced him to fourteen years' transportation. Meanwhile, plans for an insurrection stalled. Confederation leaders failed to win the cooperation of John O'Connell or the leaders of Protestant Ireland; the Catholic clergy remained hostile to Young Ireland; French republicans, anxious to win British acceptance of their new government, refused military aid to Irish nationalists; and Irish peasants, demoralized by hunger, disease, emigration, and the split in Irish nationalism did not have the means or the will to fight.

In July, however, the arrest of Duffy, government seizure of the *Nation* offices, and the suspension of habeas corpus pushed Young Ireland into rebellion. It had neither the materials nor the leadership for success. O'Brien was a sincere patriot and a brave man, but he lacked the necessary ruthlessness and was too committed to property rights to direct a peasant revolt against the Crown and the landlord establishment. The small number of peasants who answered O'Brien's call came with pikes to fight rifle-armed policemen and soldiers. During a brief July 29 engagement in Widow McCormack's cabbage patch in Ballingarry, County Tipperary, the army and constabulary easily routed this small, hungry, poorly-equipped army commanded by intellectuals full of zeal but lacking military experience.

By August 1848 some Young Irelanders were in prison awaiting trials that would end in sentences of death commuted to Tasmanian transportation. Others were on the run, looking for means of escape to France or the United States. In a time of crisis the Catholic priests and people of Ireland had rejected O'Brien and his colleagues, and the forces of the Crown had beaten them in battle, but 1848 was only a temporary defeat for Young Irelanders. They had lost a fight but in the long run won emotional and intellectual allegiances to Irish nationalism. The failures of 1848 became heroes for future generations of Fenians, Home Rulers, Gaelic Leaguers, and Sinn Féiners.

Over time, Young Irelanders proved that they were the most talented group yet to have served their country. Thomas D'Arcy McGee helped establish the federated Dominion of Canada and was a member of its cabinet. Duffy became prime minister of Australia's Victoria province. Thomas Francis Meagher became a brigadier general in the Union army in the American Civil War and was later named governor of the Montana territory; he drowned in the Missouri River on his way to take office. John Blake Dillon returned from exile in the United States to play a prominent role in Irish politics during the 1860s. John Martin, Mitchel's brother-in-law, cofounded the Irish Home Rule movement and the Irish parliamentary party in the 1870s. Other Young Irelanders organized the Irish Republican Brotherhood in Ireland and Britain and its Fenian Brotherhood counterpart in the United States. As a journalist in the United States, John Mitchel, a racist in contrast to O'Connell's cosmopolitan liberal nationalism, fought abolitionism and defended the Confederate cause in the Civil War. Voters in the 1870s twice elected him MP for Tipperary, but the government denied him his seat as a convicted felon.

After the 1848 fiasco, Duffy was the only prominent Young Irelander left in the country. Five times the government prosecuted him for sedition, but brilliant defense tactics by his attorney, Isaac Butt, and the inability of juries to reach a unanimous decision, enabled him to avoid transportation. After release from prison, Duffy revived the *Nation*. With new allies, Dr. John Gray, a Protestant who was part owner of the leading nationalist daily newspaper, *The Freeman's Journal*, and Frederick Lucas, owner and editor of the *Tablet*, a Catholic weekly, he set out to blend the ideas of Lalor and Mitchel with his own recommendations to the Irish Confederation.

Duffy and his friends proposed an independent Irish party in the British House of Commons primarily dedicated to the issue of tenant rights. They believed that an agitation that concentrated on agrarian grievances would unite the Protestant tenants of Ulster in common cause with Catholics of the same class throughout the country. They expected that a successful example of Catholic-Protestant cooperation would break down old barriers of suspicion and animosity, clearing the way for an inclusive Irish nationalism.

Encouraged by Duffy, Lucas, and Gray, representatives of tenant societies from all four Irish provinces began to discuss common goals and methods of achieving them. This dialogue produced the Irish Tenant League, which had the following stated aims: fair rents established by impartial evaluations, secure tenures for farmers who paid their rents, and the right of tenants when leaving to sell their interests in farms they had occupied. The existence of the Irish Tenant League encouraged a number of Irish MPs to join an independent Irish party. They promised their constituents to remain aloof from British parties and not to support any government unwilling to enact a comprehensive program of tenant right. The new party reached the summit of its influence in July 1852 when a general election returned forty-eight Irish MPs pledged to independent opposition and tenant right. But within a few months it began to disintegrate.

From the start, the independent Irish party lacked coherence: it was a coalition of the Irish Tenant League and the Irish Brigade. The Brigade, the "pope's brass band" to its detractors, was the response of a small group of liberal Irish MPs to Lord John Russell's 1851 Ecclesiastical Titles Bill, which threatened to prosecute and punish Catholic clergymen who took territorial church titles derived from the United Kingdom. It was a cheap effort by the prime minister to exploit no-popery anger following Pius IX's decision to create a diocesan structure for the Catholic Church in England.

Insulted by British Liberal courtship of prejudice, George Henry Moore, MP and father of the novelist George Moore, organized a small group of Irish parliamentarians to punish Russell by voting with the opposition in an effort to destroy the Whig government. The passage of the Ecclesiastical Titles Bill so aroused Irish-Catholic opinion that Moore decided to keep the Brigade in existence as an independent party. To give it constituency support, Brigade MPs organized the Catholic Defence Association of Great Britain and Ireland in August 1851.

Gray's *Freeman's Journal* endorsed the Brigade and the Catholic Defence Association. Duffy respected the talent and integrity of Moore but had doubts with regard to some other Brigade MPs. In August 1851, however, he assisted William Sharman Crawford, MP, the Ulster tenant-right leader and champion of a federal contract between Britain and Ireland, in completing an alliance between the Brigade and the Irish Tenant League. This arrangement seemed a good bargain for tenant righters. It gave the League powerful parliamentary representation without committing the nondenominational movement to the Catholic goals of the Brigade.

Shortly after the general election of 1852, two independent Irish party members, William Keogh and John Sadleir, both Brigade MPs, broke their pledge of independent opposition by accepting office in Lord Aberdeen's Peelite-Whig coalition government. Dublin's Catholic Archbishop, Paul Cullen, condoned their apostasy. Cullen was a close friend of Pius IX and had been rector of both the Irish and the Propaganda Colleges in Rome. In 1848 he had witnessed Giuseppe Mazzini's expulsion of Pius IX from Rome, and had rescued the Propaganda College by placing it under the protection of the United States government. The next year Pius IX appointed Cullen archbishop of Armagh and primate of the Catholic Church in Ireland. He succeeded Murray as Archbishop of Dublin in 1852. Cullen considered Duffy the Irish Mazzini, Young Ireland a local version of Young Italy, and the independent Irish party a vehicle for secular and revolutionary ideas. Instead of independent opposition at Westminster, Cullen preferred that Irish-Catholic politicians cooperate with the Aberdeen administration in an effort to win concessions for Catholicism, particularly in the area of education. He was happy to see two Catholics, Sadleir and Keogh, in office.

Duffy was convinced that the treason of Sadleir and Keogh, and the support of Cullen and other bishops for their defection, destroyed the independent Irish party. By 1855 he had lost confidence in the movement he had helped establish and in his ability to shape the future of Irish nationalism. Duffy sold the *Nation* to A.M. Sullivan, a young nationalist from County Cork, and sailed to Australia. As an old man, he returned to Ireland as Sir Charles Gavan Duffy, endorsed the Home Rule movement, and inspired Irish nationalism with books on Young Ireland, Thomas Davis, and the independent Irish party.

The defection of Sadleir and Keogh and the conduct of some

of the Catholic bishops did damage the independent Irish party, but there were other factors, just as important, that contributed to the demise of the Irish Tenant League and its parliamentary representation. Aberdeen's government attracted the support of Ulster tenant farmers. Memories of hardships faced together during the Great Famine fostered a temporary solidarity in the ranks of the Irish peasantry. But the population decline from death and emigration increased the size of Irish farms. This significant change in the agrarian economy, plus a series of good harvests and rising agricultural prices in the 1850s, improved the Irish standard of living in terms of diet and housing. Relative prosperity relieved the insecurities and cooled the anger of tenant farmers, especially in the north where they had better relations with landlords than in the other three provinces. With the horrors of the Famine fading into the background, ancient religious animosities reemerged and undermined the effort to create a united Irish opinion directed to the destruction of the manorial economic and social system.

The 1850s were also a time of landlord political resurgence. With the Catholic hierarchy split on political policy and tactics, the aristocracy and gentry were able to construct an effective organization that returned fifty-seven Conservative Irish MPs in the general election of 1859. The pro-Italian nationalism, anti-papal positions of Whig leadership contributed to this success. Cardinal Wiseman of Westminster and some Irish bishops encouraged Irish voters in Britain and Ireland to support Conservative candidates.

The independent Irish party's difficulty in finding suitable candidates aided the revival of landlord politics. The prohibitive expenses involved in contesting an election and then living in London without a salary while Parliament was in session made politics a vocation for the affluent. Most Irishmen in a position to pursue a parliamentary career were landlords hostile to peasant economic, political, and religious interests. Candidates prepared to gamble small fortunes to represent nationalist and tenant-farmer constituencies could not always be relied on to keep their pledges once separated from voters by the Irish Sea. Irishmen anxious to acquire status, prestige, and wealth were often willing to sell their allegiance in exchange for government office.

By 1858 only twelve MPs wore the independent Irish party label. A year later, it ceased to exist; most remaining members moved to the Liberal benches. In the 1860s a number of Irish Liberal MPs were active in the National Association, committed to government financial support for Catholic elementary, secondary, and university education, disestablishment of the Protestant Church, and tenant right. George Henry Moore and John Blake Dillon put the Association together and enlisted the support of Archbishop Cullen and other members of the Catholic hierarchy.

Under Cullen's leadership the Catholic Church in Ireland experienced what Professor Emmet Larkin has described as a "Devotional Revolution." Before the Famine, Catholicism in urban centers and in the Anglicized eastern parts of Ireland already had a spiritual resurgence manifested in parish missions, increased attendance at Mass, and interest in a number of devotional practices. But in the Gaelic-influenced, impoverished west, pagan superstition often competed with orthodox Catholic beliefs. During his Irish travels, de Toqueville observed that Irish Catholics, even in remote, rural areas, were more devout and consistent in their religious practices than those on the Continent. Still, many were not diligent in attending Mass. A shortage of priests and chapels, ignorance of post–Council of Trent (1545-63) Catholic dogmas, and a feeling of shame about wearing tattered clothes to religious services contributed to low church attendance.

Famine deaths and emigration not only eased pressures on the Irish agrarian economy, they also assisted a reformation in Irish Catholicism. The poorest, and therefore the most ignorant, segment of the Catholic population suffered most of the Famine casualties, and demographic change reduced the shortage of priests and chapels. In post-Famine Ireland it was easier for the clergy to instruct the laity, and a more affluent peasantry saw a connection between religious practice and social respectability.

Associations between Catholicism and nationalism were mutually beneficial. The struggle for civil rights had united Catholic Ireland behind O'Connell's leadership, and bishops and priests had been recruiting agents and lieutenants in the Emancipation and Repeal agitations. Through the course of the nineteenth century Catholic and national identities merged, intensifying each other. Catholic devotionalism became a visible sign of fervent Irishness. Despite the protests of those national leaders who have preferred a more inclusive view of Irishness, in no other country except possibly Poland have religion and nationality been so closely connected as in Ireland.

Building on Famine-induced population and economic

changes and the strong associations between nationality and religion, Cullen transformed Irish Catholicism. He ended public controversies among the hierarchy; recruited large numbers of priests, brothers, and nuns to serve the spiritual and educational needs of the laity; built churches and schools; encouraged Mass attendance, reception of the sacraments, and popular devotions; and made the Irish Church the most dedicated and obedient servant of Rome. Irish Catholics not only generously contributed to their parishes, they sent vast sums to Rome, and furnished priests, nuns, and brothers to the diaspora and remote British colonies. Ireland was a victim of colonialism, but the Irish Catholic Church was a vast spiritual empire.

Under Cullen the Irish Catholic Church was a more politically and socially conservative institution than in O'Connell's time. Although still closely tied to their peasant roots, the hierarchy and clergy were less inclined to lead and participate in populist agitations than the preceding generation. This has to be stated in qualified terms because in Ireland men of the cloth continued to be more politically active than Catholic or Protestant clergy in other countries.

A relative decline in nationalist involvements may have been the result of the Church's growing prosperity, increased clerical self-confidence, and a secure position of priestly leadership in the Catholic community. Another factor was Cullen's close contact and friendship with the pope. Pius IX's Rome was the most conservative capital in Europe. Close ties between Dublin and the Vatican decreased Gallicanism and increased ultramontanism in the Irish Church. Localism, however, would continue to influence the character of Irish Catholicism.

Because of his denunciation of Young Ireland and Fenianism and his hostility to Home Rule, a large section of nationalist opinion has viewed Cullen, made a cardinal in 1866, as a villain. In the bitter Christmas dinner episode in James Joyce's *Portrait of the Artist*, Simon Dedalus sarcastically referred to Cullen as "another apple of God's eye!" But when he worked with the National Association in the 1860s, Cullen revealed a concern for the economic plight of his people and showed a more flexible approach to politics than his reactionary friend, the pope. He was prepared to collaborate with Liberals at Westminster to achieve reforms for Ireland and, although he demanded government financial support for Catholic education, Cullen did endorse the principle of separation of church and state. But the ultramontane and anti-nationalist Cullen weakened the influence of the National Association by personal negotiations with British politicians, and by using English Henry Edward Cardinal Manning to exert pressure at Westminster. In addition, the Irish cardinal's excessive fear of Protestant proselytism, and his view that the interests of Catholicism and the welfare of Ireland were inseparable made him insensitive to the nationalist spirit of his own country and to important ideas, trends, and issues of the modern world.

The National Association worked closely with British radicals and Dissenters in the Liberation Society to disestablish the Protestant Church and to advance democracy by extending the franchise to the working class. The compact between Irish Catholics in the National Association and British Protestant radicals contributed to the passage of the Second Reform Bill (1867) and to the Irish legislation of the first Gladstone administration. British no-popery—revitalized by the 1870 Vatican Council, agrarian outrage in Ireland, and the reluctance of Irish Catholics to help the disestablishment movement in Britain—alienated further British Liberal support for Irish reform, but this in some ways ideologically incompatible Irish-Liberal alliance followed the precedent of the O'Connell-Whig connection and prepared the way for the later coalition between Liberals and Home Rulers.

Although the National Association included respected representatives of national and tenant-right interests and championed popular causes, it never succeeded in capturing the emotional commitment of most Irish Catholics. After the failure of constitutional and parliamentary efforts in the 1840s and 1850s, many Irish nationalists were ready to try physical force methods of liberating their country. Emigration played a major part in the opinion swing from constitutional to revolutionary nationalism.

The Famine institutionalized and hastened the pace of emigration as a safety valve for Irish poverty, with parents raising most of their children for export. From 1845 to 1891 over three million entered the United States, while many others crossed the Irish Sea to find employment in British cities. Unprepared psychologically or vocationally for industrial environments, they became the most underprivileged element in urban Britain and America. Irish immigrants did the dirty, hard work that Anglo-Saxons and Anglo-Americans were too proud or too weak to do. They built railroads, dug canals, mined coal, and washed dishes and scrubbed floors in the homes of the upper and middle classes. Anglo-Protestants in

Britain and in Boston, New York, and Philadelphia despised dirty, ignorant Irish papists, and British and American working classes hated them as cheap labor competition. Rejected by others, the Irish lived in miserable circumstances, producing many juvenile delinquents, petty thieves, mental cases, and alcoholics.

Since the Irish were among the worst victims of British industrialism, they made substantial contributions to Chartism in the first half of the nineteenth century, to the unskilled labor movement of the 1880s and 1890s, and to the spread of Syndicalism (a movement to place the "means and modes" of the industrial economy in the hands of labor unions through the technique of a general strike) and the growth of the Labour party in the twentieth century, but they were no more radical than the English, Scottish, or Welsh working classes. Because they were in a country with more social mobility and economic opportunity, in general Irish Americans were more conservative in their economic and social views than the Irish in Britain. They were significant in the development of the labor movement in the United States, but they placed a great deal of faith in the urban political machines they created and/or dominated to solve their problems.

But good times came slowly to Irish pioneers of the American urban ghetto. Anglo-Americans loathed them as a massive social problem polluting their cities; they detested them even more because they were Catholic. As in Britain, nativism in the United States was constructed on anti-Catholic foundations. Embittered Irish Americans channeled their sense of alienation into a fanatic hatred of Britain as the source of their misery in the old world and the cause of their exile to the new, where they again encountered poverty and prejudice.

In anti-British Irish nationalism, the diasporic Irish found psychological escape from the unpleasant realities of economic deprivation and slum dwelling. The myths of Irish cultural nationalism, taught by Young Ireland, gave them pride and identity. When faced with poverty and social inferiority it was consoling to dream of the past glories of the Irish race and to blame others for their present wretched condition. And it was both pleasant and exciting to believe that, though poor, the Irish were really more noble, moral, and spiritual than "materialistic, inhuman, and bloodthirsty Saxons." For the Irish in the English-speaking world, nationalism as well as religion was an opiate.

In 1858 James Stephens founded the Irish Republican Brotherhood (IRB); that same year John O'Mahony and Michael Doheny established its American counterpart, the Fenian Brotherhood. All three men were veterans of 1848. O'Mahony, a Gaelic scholar, named the American organization after the Fianna of ancient Irish sagas. Fenianism became the popular designation of republicanism in Britain and Ireland as well as the United States. The IRB was a secret revolutionary society dedicated to the establishment of a democratic Irish republic. Stephens was "head centre" of the Republican movement in Ireland and Britain; O'Mahony had the same title in the United States.

Stephens recruited bright young journalists who resented the O'Connellite and Young Ireland establishments blocking their paths to recognition; revolutionary republicanism gave them a podium and an audience. Thousands of enthusiastic young men enlisted in Fenian circles in Britain, Ireland, the United States, and Canada. In Ireland, the IRB provided recreational activities in a country where opportunities for social intercourse were extremely limited. In the United States, Fenian picnics with food, drink, games, and speeches offered entertainment for Irish working-class families. Fenianism recruited a substantial number of Irishmen serving in the British army, and during the American Civil War many Irish lads enlisted in the Union and Confederate forces in order to gain military experience, intending to employ it someday against Britain.

While the vast majority of republicans in Ireland, Britain, and the United States were from the industrial and agrarian working classes, Fenianism, unlike O'Connell's Catholic and Repeal Associations, the Irish Confederation, the independent Irish party, or the National Association, consciously ignored social and economic issues. But it did adopt the premise from O'Connell and Young Ireland that Irish nationalism was above religious or class differences. Fenians believed that a democratic republic would serve as a panacea for Ireland's ills.

John Martin and William Smith O'Brien, returned to Ireland from Australian penal exile, opposed the IRB, as did other forty-eighters. John Mitchel, Thomas Francis Meagher, and Thomas D'Arcy McGee criticized Fenianism in the United States, though Mitchel later changed his mind. A.M. Sullivan and his brother, T.D., in the *Nation* associated Fenians with agrarian terrorist organizations such as the Ribbon societies in a blanket condemnation of physical-force nationalism. But the most powerful enemy of Republicanism was the Cullen-led Roman Catholic hierarchy. Bishops attacked the secret character of the IRB and its revolutionary strategy. To Cullen, Fenians were dangerous secularists out to destroy throne and altar, radicals inspired by the excessively democratic and violent environment of the United States, and Irish disciples of the Italian physical-force nationalists, Mazzini, Camillo Benso Cavour, and Giuseppe Garibaldi. Kerry's bishop, David Moriarity, informed the laity that "hell isn't hot enough or eternity long enough" to punish IRB members.

From the original condemnation of the Fenians in 1858 until 1865, Cullen managed to keep his fellow bishops and Irish priests hostile to republicanism, though there were, of course, exceptions. Since most clerics came from tenant-farmer families, they shared the grievances and hatreds of their class. Some were bold enough to defy their superiors by giving prayers and sympathy to republicans. Father Patrick Lavelle, a Mayo priest, defied Cullen in 1861 by delivering a eulogy at the IRB-staged Dublin funeral of Terence Bellew McManus, a veteran of 1848 who had died in San Francisco. Lavelle's superior, Archbishop MacHale, who never went so far as to endorse the IRB but remained on good terms with Fenians and accepted their charitable donations, shielded him from Cullen's wrath.

The American Civil War interrupted Fenian activities, but when it ended American republicans told Stephens to prepare his followers for action. Men who had commanded Union or Confederate troops infiltrated Ireland to train IRB units for combat. American pressure forced Stephens to plan a rising for 1866, but a factional dispute in the United States cut off military supplies to Ireland. At their 1865 convention in Philadelphia, Fenians adopted a new constitution, substituting a president for head centre and making him responsible to a General Congress divided into a Senate and House of Delegates. President O'Mahony wanted to focus on an Irish revolutionary strategy, but Colonel William R. Roberts, the Senate leader, insisted that Irish Americans invade and conquer Canada, leaving Stephens and the IRB responsible for activities in Ireland. Rather than have his inadequately equipped followers face the superior weaponry of the army and constabulary, Stephens postponed the insurrection.

When a British spy in the offices of the *Irish People*, the IRB newspaper, supplied the government with incriminating documents, officials shut it down and arrested such prominent members of the staff as Charles Kickham, the Irish novelist, Jeremiah O'Donovan Rossa, founder of the Skibbereen Phoenix Society, which had merged with the IRB in 1858, Thomas Clark Luby, an amateur historian of some merit, and John O'Leary, friend of and nationalist inspiration for William Butler Yeats. Stephens also went to jail, but a young IRB member, John Devoy, the future leader of the Clan na Gael in the United States, arranged his escape. After his rescue, Stephens left for America, hoping to end the feud between O'Mahony and the Fenian Senate, and to persuade them to send guns and ammunition to Ireland. But Stephens was such a difficult personality that his presence encouraged rather than ended American Fenian dissension.

While Stephens was in the United States, British authorities took the IRB by surprise, transferring Irish soldiers serving in their own country to Britain, suspending habeas corpus, and arresting a number of prominent republicans. In futile gestures of defiance, republican units in various parts of Ireland took up arms against the British in March 1867. The Royal Irish Constabulary and the army easily defeated these small bands of poorly armed rebels.

With Fenians in prison, and their cause no longer a serious threat, even priests, much to Cullen's disgust, expressed sympathy for the brave if misguided heroes. An incident in England added to Catholic clerical and lay pro-Fenianism. In September 1867 an IRB unit in Manchester freed Irish-American Fenians Colonel T.J. Kelly and Michael Deasy from a police van in Manchester. During the incident someone shot and killed a constable. Authorities arrested three members of the rescue party, W.P. Allen, Michael Larkin, and Michael O'Brien, and tried them for murder. They admitted to being present when the incident took place but denied firing the fatal bullet. Anti-Irish hysteria surrounded the trial. Jurors found the prisoners guilty, and a judge sentenced them to death. With the execution of the "Manchester Martyrs" a wave of anger against British injustice swept over Ireland. Some bishops and priests were active in the Amnesty Association, which had been founded to obtain commutation of Fenian prison sentences. But Odo Russell, the British representative at the Vatican, with the support of Bishop Moriarity and with promises of benefits to the church in Ireland, persuaded Pius IX to issue a condemnation of the IRB. This created more pro- than anti-Fenian sentiment among Irish Catholics.

Deciding to take advantage of a more friendly climate of opinion and to increase their organizational efficiency, Fenians deposed Stephens and O'Mahony and restructured republicanism on both sides of the Atlantic. By 1870, however, Fenianism was retreating from the Irish stage, and Home Rule, a new expression of constitutional nationalism, was waiting in the wings.

Although Fenianism did not seriously challenge British rule in Ireland, it, along with the efforts of the National Association, persuaded William Ewart Gladstone, prime minister following the 1868 general election, to initiate Irish reform. Under his guidance, Whigs, Radicals, and Peelites finally coalesced into an effective Liberal party. Following in the footsteps of his mentor, Sir Robert Peel, Gladstone decided that it was expedient for the British government to subvert Irish nationalism by eliminating the grievances sustaining it. In 1869 he attempted to conciliate Irish Catholics by disestablishing the Irish Protestant Church, and the next year he pushed a Land Act through Parliament. This measure attempted to guarantee the security of tenant farmers by making landlords compensate them for improvements they made to the property and for the disturbance they suffered when evicted for any reason except nonpayment of rent. Gladstone believed that the expense of eviction would force landlords to think twice before clearing their estates. John Bright authored a clause in the act offering government loans of up to two-thirds of the purchase price to tenants who wanted to buy their farms.

Since the Land Act permitted eviction without compensation if rents were not paid, it failed as an instrument of tenant security. Landlords could raise rents and then evict if tenants were unable to pay. Since loan terms were unmanageable for most farmers, the Bright clause did not significantly increase the number of peasant proprietors. In fact, in the severe agrarian depression that began in the late 1870s evictions dramatically increased.

While inadequate as a means of solving the agrarian dimension of the Irish Question, the Land Act was a precedent. It broke down some resistance to government action in the area of private property, thus smoothing the way for meaningful legislation in the early 1880s. And the Bright clause pointed to the final solution of landlord-tenant conflict—peasant proprietorship. Because the Land Act was the first major interference by government with the traditional rights of property, it had implications for the British as well as the Irish. By expanding government responsibility in social and economic areas, the Land Act was a significant step in the evolution of British liberalism from its early nineteenth century laissez-faire start to its collectivist welfare-state agenda of the late nineteenth and early twentieth centuries.

Gladstone's efforts to solve the Irish Question were too timid to satisfy Irish nationalist opinion and too radical for the tastes of British Conservatives, who exploited his Irish policy to rally no-popery, anti-Irish prejudices against the Liberals. In addition, Gladstone's friendly intentions toward Ireland encouraged Catholic bishops to expect concessions in the area of denominational education.

Although he empathized with Irish-Catholic complaints that they were denied facilities and opportunities for higher education, as the leader of a party dependent on the votes of British Nonconformists and one that had just disestablished the Irish Protestant Church, Gladstone could hardly endow Cullen's Catholic University. In 1873 he proposed a compromise he believed would answer the demands of Catholics for higher education without contradicting the principle of separation of church and state in Ireland. His Irish university bill would have expanded Dublin University into a national institution with affiliated sectarian colleges. The university would have offered no lectures or examinations in controversial and divisive subjects such as theology, history, or moral philosophy. Affiliated colleges, however, would have been free to offer courses and certificates in these fields.

As opponents of nondenominational higher education since the Queen's Colleges debate of the 1840s, Catholic bishops rejected Gladstone's proposal as inadequate. They argued that without a government endowment, the Catholic affiliate within Dublin University could not academically compete with Oxford and Cambridge, two Protestant British universities, or with Trinity College in Dublin, another well-endowed center of Protestant studies. Influenced by the hierarchy's criticism, a number of Irish Liberal MPs voted against the university bill, defeating it, forcing Gladstone to call for a January 1874 general election. Expanded by the Reform Bill of 1867, and emancipated by the secrecy of the 1872 Ballot Act, partly the result of nationalist, priest, and landlord intimidation in Irish by-elections, the British electorate returned a Conservative majority to the House of Commons, and Benjamin Disraeli succeeded Gladstone as prime minister. In Ireland, the contest between Liberals and Conservatives was of minor importance compared to the return of fifty-nine MPs pledged to Home Rule.

4

Home Rule
1870–1880

Isaac Butt, Home Rule's founding father, was born in 1813, the son
of a Donegal Protestant vicar. While a brilliant student at Trinity
College he cofounded and for a time served as editor of the *Dublin
University Magazine*, the most intelligent conservative journal in nineteenth-century Ireland. As previously mentioned, in Butt's time the
DUM promoted Irish cultural nationalism as an alternative to the
political variety. After earning his degree in 1836, Butt stayed on at
Trinity to teach political economy and, at the same time, studied for
the bar at the King's Inn. In 1838 Butt resigned his academic position
to practice law. As a young Tory barrister, he championed Protestant
Ascendancy, no-popery causes. Butt's articulate argument against
the Irish Municipal Reform Bill before the House of Lords impressed
British and Irish Tories. He was one of the few Protestants serving
in the reformed Dublin Corporation, where he debated Repeal with
O'Connell in 1843.

Butt's defense of Protestant Ascendancy unionism was more
than narrow self-interest. He described himself as a Burkean conservative and an Irish patriot. Butt believed that the British connection
provided Ireland with an enlightened constitution that protected
property and political rights, and that the union of church and state
guaranteed that religious values would guide ordinary and political
conduct. He also was convinced that the Union promised peace and
stability, necessary conditions for the advance of the Irish economy
and standard of living.

Since Butt was raised and educated within the narrow confines of Protestant Ascendancy, he naturally shared its apprehensions concerning Catholic nationalism. He believed that Catholics were a superstitious and seditious rabble that threatened the Union, social order, enlightened religion, property rights, and cultural values. His conservative, Anglo-Irish Protestant attitudes motivated him to resist what he considered the advance of chaos and anarchy.

Butt's passage from unionism to nationalism actually began when he lectured in political economy at Trinity College. In opposing laissez-faire dogmatism, he insisted that the British government had a responsibility to foster a healthy Irish economy. Conservative commitments made him reluctant to suggest changes in the system of landholding; instead he recommended tariffs to protect Irish industry and agriculture. Butt's economic nationalism would eventually expand and take on new dimensions.

By the late 1840s Butt realized that Protestant Ascendancy posed a major threat to social stability and conservative principles of government. It provoked anger and discontent, driving the Catholic clergy and laity into the arms of demagogues preaching radical change. Butt decided that if religious and economic benefits were extended to Catholics without placing serious restrictions on the rights of property or the Protestant Church, the Union could be preserved. The Irish of diverse classes and faiths would work together for the progress of their country.

In an 1847 pamphlet, "Famine in the Land," Butt repeated criticism of British laissez faire, suggesting an alternative program of government relief: public works projects to provide employment and at the same time increase economic potential, expanded transportation facilities to stimulate industrial and agricultural production, and sponsored emigration to relieve the strain of overpopulation. Butt concluded by warning Britain that it could no longer depend on class and religious divisions in Ireland to preserve the Union. He said that the Famine was teaching Irish classes and creeds the value of cooperation. He predicted that if unity of feeling survived the existing crisis, and if British politicians persisted in ignoring the needs of Ireland, the Union would perish.

In 1848 Butt provided legal defense for Young Irelanders, blaming British misgovernment and economic policies for compelling them to rebel. He insisted that Repeal was a constitutionally valid objective. Butt argued that the government's response to the

Famine indicated that British politicians lacked the knowledge or competence to deal with Irish problems. He intimated that an Irish parliament dealing with local affairs might not be inconsistent with the spirit of unionism or a danger to the empire.

During their trials, Butt asked Duffy, Meagher, and O'Brien to endorse him for a seat in the House of Commons. Duffy and Meagher agreed on the condition that he declare himself a Repealer. Evidently Butt was not yet ready to take such an advanced position. Instead, from 1852 until 1865, he served as an undistinguished Conservative MP. His positions on Irish issues, however, did reveal an evolving nationalism. He endorsed tenant right, pressed for extensive railroad construction in Ireland, and defended Catholicism against the attacks of no-popery bigots. After his defeat in the general election of 1865, Butt returned to Dublin to practice law and write pamphlets on the land question and denominational education. A brief stay in debtors' prison gave him unexpected if uncomfortable leisure to write.

In analyzing the agrarian situation, Butt decided that secure tenures at fair rents, promptly paid, was a conservative solution that should satisfy both landlord and tenant. He also endorsed the appeal of Catholic bishops for government funds for Catholic schools. Butt insisted that Irish public opinion supported religious education as a way to preserve Ireland from the radical and secular ideas permeating Britain and threatening the spiritual values of the United Kingdom. Butt's conservative reform views led him to propose the dual establishment of Catholicism and Protestantism in Ireland.

At considerable personal expense and inconvenience, Butt again came to the defense of Irish rebels during the 1867 Fenian trials, increasing his popularity and prestige in nationalist circles. After the trials, he served as president of the Amnesty Association, which had some success in commuting Fenian sentences.

By the late 1860s Butt had lost confidence in the Union, deciding that the differences between industrial Britain and agrarian Ireland were too extreme to be reconciled in a common legislature. He feared that British social, political, and economic radicalism would spread to and corrupt Ireland. Butt determined that it was now time for conservatives to take the helm of Irish nationalism and steer it on a constructive course. He and George Henry Moore concluded that since the success of the North in the American Civil War had made federalism popular in British intellectual and some political circles, leading to the North American Act, which established the Dominion of Canada, perhaps it was a key to the solution of the Irish Question. Moore died in early 1870, leaving Butt the task of putting the idea of a federated United Kingdom into motion.

On the evening of May 19, 1870, forty-nine prominent Dubliners, most of them Protestant merchants, met at the Bilton Hotel to discuss Ireland's future. Butt summoned the gathering to exploit a perceived shift in Irish conservative opinion encouraging the possibility of collaboration between Catholics and Protestants in an agitation to restore the Irish Parliament. Angered by the disestablishment of their church, frightened by the implications of the proposed Land Act, and troubled by the unhealthy condition of the Irish economy, Protestant leaders, especially those from the business class, denounced the economic, religious, and political consequences of the Union. Some demanded an Irish parliament to cope with unique local problems.

Convinced by Butt's eloquence and logic, the meeting unanimously adopted two resolutions: the first called on the British government to approve an Irish parliament with complete control over Irish affairs; the second established the Home Government Association (HGA) to promote self-rule. The HGA held its first meeting at the Dublin Rotunda on September 1, 1870. As planned, it began as a relatively small, private organization dedicated to uniting all classes and religions behind an effort to create public opinion in Britain and Ireland favorable to a federal arrangement between the two islands. Members were screened for admission and paid a pound annually as dues to cover operating expenses and the costs of publications. The HGA invited members of Dublin trade unions to become associate members for a yearly shilling. For every twenty associates, unions could delegate a regular member to attend Association meetings. Branches of the HGA emerged in various parts of the country.

According to Butt's Home Rule plan, the Irish parliament of Lords and Commons would have jurisdiction over local resources and revenues. Westminster would retain authority over such common interests as colonial affairs, foreign policy, and imperial defense. The federal contract would not alter either the prerogatives of the Crown or the principles of the constitution. In order to attract the support and calm the fears and suspicions of the Protestant upper classes, the

HGA endorsed all existing religious and property rights, and promised not to discuss issues not directly related to self-government.

In his 1870 book, *Irish Federalism*, Butt told Irish and British conservatives that Home Rule would prevent rather than encourage radical excesses in Ireland. He predicted that when the Irish enjoyed the benefits of self-government they would cease rebellious activities and become the most loyal supporters of the Crown and constitution in the empire. He said Irish Catholics, influenced by their church to distrust radical democratic ideologies, under normal circumstances would follow conservative leadership. If these assurances were inadequate to satisfy sceptics, Butt reminded his readers that a hereditary, largely Protestant and conservative Irish House of Lords would block radical proposals emanating from a democratic, mostly Catholic, House of Commons.

Butt directed *Irish Federalism* at British and Irish conservatives. And what he said was true: an Irish House of Lords could block Irish reform. But he hoped for something better. Like O'Connell, he believed that a Dublin parliament would be Irish in sentiment and point of view, and thus respond to Irish opinion. In time, he thought, even Irish peers would submit to the mood of the country and would fulfill their obligations to people who looked to the aristocracy for justice, mercy, and leadership.

From the start the HGA enjoyed successes. The Dublin Corporation, Poor Law boards, town councils, tenant right organizations, and many newspapers endorsed its program. Local branches of the HGA in England and Scotland multiplied so rapidly that in 1873 it was found necessary to create the Home Rule Confederation of Great Britain, with Butt as president. Many Confederation leaders and members were Fenians with more energy and devotion for Irish nationalism than members of the HGA. Their main task was the mobilization of the Irish vote in British cities behind candidates sympathetic to Home Rule.

From January 1871 to August 1873, Irish voters returned eight Home Rulers to the House of Commons in by-elections, and six Irish Liberals already in Parliament declared that they were federalists. These victories were offset by the inability of the HGA to win the approval of the Protestant aristocracy and gentry or the blessing of the Catholic hierarchy. Butt made a special effort to enroll Protestant landlords in the HGA. He told them that tenant farmers were prepared to accept their political guidance; he also warned them that this might be their last opportunity to reach a settlement with their Catholic neighbors. He cautioned Protestants that if they obstructed efforts to achieve an Irish parliament, they could expect little respect for their religion or property in a Home-Rule Ireland.

In reaction to Gladstone's Irish policy, some Protestants did become Home Rulers. Fondly recalling the Irish Protestant nation of the eighteenth century, they thought that their interests might receive more respect in a revived Irish legislature, dominated by the upper classes, than in a Liberal-controlled British Parliament. When early enthusiasm cooled to sober reflection, many of them decided that there was a wide gap separating the ambitions of Irish Catholics and their own concerns. Now they were dealing with tenant farmers who could use the suffrage and the secret ballot to establish a peasant democracy. Perhaps, they decided, it would be better to rely on the protection of the British Parliament with its strong Protestant Conservative representation than on Catholic promises of moderation and good will. After the initial fervor of the spring and summer of 1870, few Protestants joined the HGA, and many of those initially enrolled ceased to take an active part. According to the *Nation*, in 1871 Protestants were two-fifths of the HGA membership and had a majority of three on its sixty-one man Executive Council. In June 1872 the *Nation* reported that in the recent election for the Executive Council, Protestants cast only one-third of the ballots and Catholics had a majority of seven on the Council. Alfred Webb, a Quaker official of the Association, advised nationalists to abandon hope of "attaching any large number of our Protestant fellow countrymen."

While Home Rule propaganda concentrated on wooing non-Catholics, Butt and his colleagues understood the necessity of securing the good will of Catholic bishops and priests. This meant weaning them away from their admiration for Gladstone. Hoping that he would endow a Catholic university, the Irish hierarchy feared that Home Rule nationalism would antagonize the Liberal leader, alienating him from the issue of Catholic education. When invited to join the HGA, many of the hierarchy and clergy said they would not participate in any movement dominated by anti-Catholic Protestants using Home Rule to undermine clerical influence with the people and to attack a Liberal government anxious to extend justice and friendship to Ireland.

Because the Catholic hierarchy was cool to Home Rule, not many priests applied for HGA membership. From 1870 to 1873 only two in Cullen's Dublin archdiocese joined the Association, and one later withdrew. The names of twenty Protestant and only twelve Catholic clergymen appeared on an 1870 *Nation* list of HGA members. Some prominent politicians also avoided contact with a movement frowned on by the hierarchy. Home Rule by-election candidates often met clerical opposition. Some priests were hostile to Butt when he successfully contested Limerick in 1871. Joseph Ronayne, victorious in a Cork city by-election, encountered the resistance of a number of clerics. Rowland Blennerhassett, a Protestant landlord, managed to win a Kerry seat despite the antagonism of Bishop Moriarity. Joseph Biggar, however, suffered defeat in Derry because the bishop, Francis Kelly, and his clergy campaigned for the Liberal candidate, split the nationalist vote, and thus guaranteed a Conservative victory. Although Home Rule candidates usually surmounted clerical opposition, the bitterness of the contests did nothing to reconcile the Catholic hierarchy to federalism.

After the House of Commons rejected the Irish university bill, HGA officials tried to exploit the bishops' dissatisfaction with Gladstone's proposal. In pronouncements condemning it, several prelates did advocate Home Rule as an initial step in the direction of denominational education. A few went further by complimenting the program and leadership of the Association. This apparent softening in the hierarchy's attitude encouraged a number of priests to endorse federalism.

Many Home Rulers interpreted election victories and the conversion of Catholic priests to their cause as signs that the HGA had succeeded in educating Irish opinion on the merits of federalism. Now was the time, they said, to replace the Association with an organization open to public participation. Twenty-five thousand signatures, including those of twenty-five MPs, appeared on a requisition calling for a national conference to discuss and plan the future of Home Rule.

On November 18, 1873, the national conference convened in Dublin's Rotunda. During four days of meetings, nine hundred delegates approved resolutions supporting a federal contract between Britain and Ireland, insisting that nationalist MPs were responsible to their constituents and future national conferences, and substituting the Home Rule League for the Home Government Association. Anyone paying one pound in annual dues and willing to accept the resolutions of the national conference could become a League member. Later, to provide Home Rule with more popular support, and to increase the income of the League, Butt borrowed an O'Connell tactic by creating associate memberships for a shilling a year.

In three years Butt had done much to revitalize Irish nationalism after the failure of Repeal in the 1840s, of the independent party in the 1850s, and of the Fenian movement in the 1860s. Reactions to Gladstone's Irish policy assisted Butt's effort to convince Irish opinion that federalism would be the fulfillment of its aspirations. When Irish farmers realized that the Land Act would not result in secure tenures at fair rents, and when the Catholic clergy discovered that Gladstone had no intention of conceding their education demands, they moved into the ranks of Home Rule. Although the timid platform of the HGA offered no solutions to education and agrarian questions, priests and farmers were ready to use federalism as an outlet for their frustrations. They seemed to accept the Association's idealistic assumptions that an Irish parliament would be able to harmonize conflicting class, economic, and religious interests.

Unfortunately, the HGA did not succeed in reconciling Irish Catholics, Anglo-Irish Protestants, Ulster Presbyterians and other Nonconformists. Nor was there, when considered realistically, much chance of resolving religious differences in the Ireland of the 1870s. Members of other sects were still too suspicious of Catholic motives to abandon their parochialism, siege mentality, and dependence on the British Parliament for protection in what they considered a hostile environment. Perhaps if the Land Act had proved more successful in increasing the security of tenant farmers, or if the Catholic hierarchy had been less determined to win government funds for their schools, a Catholic-Protestant alliance outside Ulster, where Protestants and Presbyterians were hopelessly hostile to Catholicism and nationalism, might possibly if not probably have resulted. But without the land and education issues Home Rule could never have enlisted the support of the Catholic priests and people. And it was far more important for a nationalist agitation to have the allegiance of the Catholic majority than the Protestant minority.

Butt's nationalist career peaked with the election of fifty-nine Home Rule MPs in the 1874 general election. This group met in Dublin and organized the Irish Home Rule parliamentary party, with Butt as chair. Party objectives, rules of conduct, and parliamentary strategy reflected his moderate inclinations. Home Rule MPs had to vote as a unit only on self-government. On other issues they could act as their consciences and/or interests dictated. Butt rejected Charles Gavan Duffy's concept of a completely independent, strongly disciplined Irish party voting as a block on all legislation touching Ireland. He said that Home Rule MPs were not of one opinion on British, imperial, or even Irish matters, and that independent opposition would create the impression that they were Liberal allies. He also believed that tight discipline would force the party to have definite positions on land and religion, convincing Irish Protestants that Irish nationalism could not be separated from Catholicism and agrarian radicalism.

Aware that by appeasing Protestant Ireland he risked alienating Irish Catholics, Butt urged Home Rule MPs as individuals, not as party members, to support his efforts to amend the Land Act, reform Irish suffrage, and promote denominational education. His please-all strategy was too complex. How many nationalists or unionists would distinguish between the actions of individual Home Rule MPs and their party program?

Conciliation best describes Butt's parliamentary policy. He was convinced that the conservative principles underlying federalism, and the good manners and courtesy of the Irish party at Westminster would finally persuade British MPs to consider the case for Home Rule with an open mind. He instructed his colleagues to conduct themselves as gentlemen in the Commons, always respecting its traditions and procedures. He also advised them to display their loyalty to the Crown, their willingness to share the burdens of empire, and their admiration for the principles of the British constitution.

The results of the 1874 election and the formation of the Irish party excited optimism among Irish nationalists. By 1876, however, cynicism had replaced hope, and many considered the Irish party just another collection of opportunists exploiting nationalism to improve their own prospects. The failure of the party to meet the expectations of 1874 can be attributed to the unsatisfactory quality of its members, Butt's leadership inadequacies, and the miscalculations of his parliamentary strategy.

Like the Repeal party of the 1830s and 1840s, and the independent Irish party of the 1850s, the Home Rule party of the 1870s suffered from less than mediocre talent. As previously discussed, financing an election campaign and providing for maintenance in London during parliamentary sessions were beyond the means of most sincere nationalists. This left the political field to men long on cash but short on integrity and talent. The brief interval between the national conference and the 1874 general election made it impossible for the newly formed Home Rule League to exert much influence over the selection of candidates. Consequently, constituencies had no choice but to accept men who in many cases adopted federalism only to gain or retain seats in the Commons. Once elected, they neglected parliamentary duties and made light of Home Rule commitments. Absenteeism was directly responsible for the defeat of two Irish franchise reform bills and weakened the party in other important tests of strength.

Butt's leadership deficiencies encouraged party apathy. While a skilled debater, a brilliant framer of legislation, and a popular figure at Westminster, he was timid in parliamentary combat, reluctant to enforce party discipline, and, due to financial problems, negligent in regard to his duties. Butt's money woes necessitated frequent absences from the Commons when his ability and experience were needed.

Butt's conciliation policy failed. The logic of federalism did not impress British MPs. They considered it another Irish attempt to destroy the United Kingdom and disrupt the empire. The Irish party's refusal to take stands on issues outside Home Rule and the freedom of action of its members irritated all shades of Irish opinion. Despite Butt's denial, Protestants were sure that Catholicism, agrarian radicalism, and nationalism were an inseparable trinity. Catholics insisted that tenant right and religious education were intrinsic to the objectives of nationalism. They found it difficult to give their enthusiasm to a movement that divorced political from social, economic, and religious imperatives.

Criticisms of Home Rule MPs and their party began during the parliamentary session of 1874 and had become widespread when Parliament adjourned in 1876. Tenant right leaders and advocates of denominational education accused Home Rule MPs of insincerity in pressing their grievances. Some suggested the abandonment of federalism for an agitation more sympathetic to Catholic and agrarian interests. T.D. Sullivan, editor of the *Nation* while his brother A.M. held a seat in the Commons, was critical of the Irish party's conciliatory parliamentary policy. He advised it to employ obstruction as a proper response to the indifference British politicians displayed toward Ireland. Sullivan's suggestion was a major topic of newspaper debate in the summer of 1876; most of the nationalist press preferred obstruction to conciliation.

During the August 1876 Dublin convention of the Home Rule Confederation of Great Britain, delegates criticized the apathy and tactics of Home Rule MPs. They passed a two-part resolution: the first expressed loyalty to Butt, the second demanded a more disciplined, active party that would pursue an aggressive policy at Westminster. Butt assented to the resolution, committing himself and the party to a more determined course of action. This promise was made under duress, and Butt, by his subsequent conduct in the Commons, indicated that he had no intention of complying.

During the 1877 parliamentary session, the obstructive tactics employed by Charles Stewart Parnell and Joseph Biggar captured the attention and interest of Irish nationalists. Parnell, a Wicklow Protestant landlord, had won a seat for Meath in an 1875 by-election. During his first two years at Westminster he seldom spoke but was always present for debates and votes. Parnell had been impressed by Joseph Biggar's experiment with obstruction during the parliamentary session of 1875. Biggar, a Belfast Protestant provision merchant who later became a Catholic, had been a member of the IRB and sat on its Supreme Council until expelled in 1877 for his Home Rule commitment. In the 1874 general election, nationalist voters in County Cavan elected him their MP. The next year he delayed passage of an Irish coercion measure by reading long passages from parliamentary blue books. Biggar's conduct outraged Benjamin Disraeli, the prime minister, and other Conservatives. It also disgusted Butt, who insisted that Home Rulers should act like gentlemen and play by the accepted rules of the parliamentary game.

In 1877 Parnell and Biggar, assisted by a handful of colleagues, impeded the government's agenda with motions to adjourn or to report progress, and with amendments to almost every bill on the docket. Some of the amendments were quite constructive, but they necessitated long discussions, seriously delaying the legislative timetable.

Many British newspapers and periodicals depicted Parnell and Biggar as uncouth Irish ruffians. Butt described their tactics as insubordination that threatened the existence of the Irish party. He condemned obstruction as a negative tactic that would intensify anti-Irish sentiment in Britain by encouraging a conviction that the Irish were incompetent to govern themselves.

Parnell and Biggar denied that their diligent attendance in the Commons, frequent motions, and numerous amendments constituted an attempt to paralyze the machinery of government. They described their actions as an effort to insure adequate discussion of important issues at convenient times. Parnell argued that if conscientious devotion to duty delayed the legislative schedule, it was proof that the British Parliament should share its complex burdens with subordinate assemblies.

Parnell rejected Butt's thesis that reason could persuade British politicians to render justice to Ireland. He said that Liberal and Conservative MPs seldom took the time to evaluate Irish claims, no matter how well presented. According to Parnell, all that really counted in the Commons was party strength, and the Irish party was weak in numbers and morale. He insisted that Ireland could achieve Home Rule only with the support of one of the British parties. To win this support he suggested intimidation rather than reason. Parnell advised his party colleagues to present Parliament with a clear choice: Home Rule for Ireland or persistent Irish interference in British and imperial affairs. He said that if this active parliamentary policy failed to achieve self-government, then the Irish might as well abandon all confidence in constitutional methods.

Obstruction or conciliation? That was the issue debated by Butt, Parnell, and their partisans in newspapers, nationalist organizations, meetings of the Irish party, tenant right societies, and on political platforms in Ireland and Britain. Butt fought with unusual energy but with little effect. Slowly but surely Parnell gathered the support of national opinion. Newspapers praised the man who dared to defy the House of Commons and recommended his parliamentary policy to other Home Rule MPs. A growing number of Butt's friends in the party advised him to compromise his quarrel with Parnell by adopting a more vigorous parliamentary strategy. For the most part, it was the despised absentee and Whig elements of the Home Rule parliamentary party that remained loyal to Butt.

Parnell's strongest support came from the Irish in Britain. In 1877 the Home Rule Confederation elected him instead of Butt as its president. In Ireland, Parnell's supporters successfully pressured the Home Rule League to call another national conference to decide the question of obstruction or conciliation. When the conference assembled in January 1878, it decided to retain Butt as party leader, but instructed him to unify and energize Home Rule MPs.

In appreciation of Butt's courtroom efforts on behalf of Fenians and his work with the Amnesty Association, quite a few IRB members joined the Home Government Association, the Home Rule

League, and the Home Rule Confederation of Great Britain. In the United States, the Clan na Gael, founded by Jerome J. Collins in 1867, superceded a faction-ridden Fenian Brotherhood humiliated by a series of failed Canadian invasions. After his release from a British prison in 1871, John Devoy came to the United States and became a journalist, finally settling in New York. He joined the Clan na Gael and became its dominant personality. In 1877 the Clan formed an alliance with the IRB, establishing a joint Revolutionary Directory. The Clan was better organized and more secret than the Fenian Brotherhood. Its membership also was more middle class and socially and politically prominent. In many ways the Clan represented an Irish-American nationalism moving away from the bitterness of alienation toward a search for respectability. Experiencing economic mobility, many of the Irish in the United States were puzzled when other Americans continued to reject them socially. They concluded that their low status reflected Ireland's colonial bondage and decided that they would elevate Irish America by liberating Ireland.

At first the Clan rejected Home Rule because of its trust in constitutional and parliamentary methods and its refusal to completely reject the British connection in favor of a democratic republic. Since Irish America financed republicanism in Ireland it was able to influence IRB policy. Clan leaders notified Charles Kickham, president of the IRB Supreme Council, that his organization must stop its federalist collaboration. He complied and expelled Home Rulers from the IRB.

In the late 1870s some Clan leaders took another look at Home Rule. Parnell's and Biggar's activities at Westminster suggested to them that a parliamentary party led by a man of Parnell's determination using obstruction as a weapon might achieve significant results. Devoy, John Boyle O'Reilly, another IRB exile and editor of the *Boston Pilot*, and others in the Clan were convinced that Britain would become involved in the Russo-Turkish war on the side of the Turks. They believed that perhaps Parnell and his friends, backed by Irish America, could exploit Britain's preoccupation with a Balkan war to extort concessions for Irish nationalism. They hoped to repeat the victory of 1782 when Britain, frightened of a French invasion, submitted to armed Ireland's demand for an extension of Irish parliamentary sovereignty.

While Clan leadership was pondering the possibilities of a

working arrangement with Parnell, Patrick Ford, editor of the New York–based *Irish World*, Irish America's most influential newspaper, argued (like James Fintan Lalor before him) that the way to energize Irish nationalism was by emphasizing economic issues. Ford's populism described the Irish in Ireland and the Irish in America as victims of vicious economic systems. Agrarian capitalism exploited Irish tenant farmers; industrial capitalism enslaved the Irish-American working class. Ford urged Clan leaders to stop theorizing about revolutionary strategy and to mobilize the Irish masses by emphasizing a war on landlordism in Ireland and the exploitation of labor in the United States.

Ford's tactics fit the times. A severe agricultural depression in Ireland, the result of foul weather and the importation of cheap American grains into the United Kingdom, had brought about the worst misery since the Great Famine. The situation was particularly bad in the underdeveloped west, but suffering existed in all parts of the country. Emigration and eviction figures rapidly increased.

Devoy's willingness to collaborate with Parnell, combined with Ford's strategy to mobilize Irish opinion behind a struggle to exterminate landlordism, created the "New Departure." This was a two-point program for bridging the gap separating the Irish masses from republicanism. Devoy and his colleagues decided to support an agitation for peasant proprietorship as a stratagem to instill and mobilize nationalist passion among tenant farmers suffering from the agricultural depression. They hoped that a republican commitment to tenant-farmer interests would not only attract their loyalty, but might also lead to an alliance with those Home Rule MPs still enjoying public favor. According to the New Departure blueprint, when tenant farmers became fervent nationalists, and when a significant portion of the Irish party committed to complete separation from Britain, the stage would be set for action. MPs would initiate the struggle for independence by insisting on immediate Home Rule. When the British Parliament rejected their demand, they would withdraw from the House of Commons and establish a provisional government in Dublin. All Ireland would stand ready to support it with arms supplied by the Clan na Gael. Wedded to the original IRB strategy of avoiding religious and class conflict, Kickham, O'Leary, and some other Irish Fenians did not warm to the New Departure.

In October 1878 the Clan offered Parnell specific terms for an alliance, including "abandonment of the federal demand and substitution of a general declaration in favor of self-government"; vigorous agitation of the land question on the basis of peasant proprietorship, while accepting concessions to abolish arbitrary eviction; an Irish party united on all Irish and imperial questions pursuing an aggressive parliamentary policy; and "advocacy of all struggling nationalities in the British Empire and elsewhere."

While not as interested in or as sympathetic to tenant farmer problems as Butt, Parnell recognized the value of combining agrarian and Home Rule agitations. He also understood the importance of Irish-American financial support, but he was reluctant to conclude a compact with the Clan on its terms because such an arrangement might persuade the Catholic hierarchy to oppose his bid to control the Home Rule movement. While waiting for a more appropriate and favorable opportunity to reach a mutual relationship with American republicans, Parnell and his colleagues in the active wing of the Irish party joined forces with agrarian radicals. During the fall of 1878 they spoke at a number of tenant right meetings. At one, John O'Connor Power, MP for Mayo, repeated Lalor's words, "the land of Ireland for the people of Ireland," which became the cry of the National Land League.

Although Parnell and the Clan did not complete a formal pact until 1879, Butt was convinced that one already existed, and that it was intended to destroy Home Rule. In the autumn of 1878 he made a final effort to preserve conservative nationalism in a manifesto to the Irish people. Butt's treatise warned that obstruction would lead to the expulsion of Home Rule MPs from the House of Commons, the disfranchisement of nationalist voters, the resurgence of physical force nationalism, and, inevitably, bloody defeat on the battlefield.

Because his parliamentary conduct in 1878 alienated Irish nationalists, few heeded Butt's warning. In exchange for the Intermediate Education Bill providing government scholarships for students in Catholic secondary schools, Butt promised to support the Conservative government's foreign and imperial policy. True to his bargain, and consistent with his pro-empire personal convictions, Butt defended Disraeli's actions at the Congress of Berlin against Liberal criticism. When Parliament convened in December 1878 to deal with the crisis in Afghanistan, he blocked the efforts of other Home Rule MPs to submit an amendment to the Queen's Speech that asked for a redress of Irish grievances. Butt said that it would embarrass the government during a period of international tension.

He insisted that Home Rulers should be patriotic supporters of Crown and empire.

Nationalist newspapers were dumbfounded that a parliamentary champion of Irish nationalism would defend and support Tory imperialism. Even Butt's warmest friends in the press, those who took his side against Parnell, disowned him for encouraging "a government avowedly hostile to the claims of Ireland."

On February 4, 1879, in an atmosphere of suspicion, disillusionment, and controversy, the annual meeting of the Home Rule League took place. T.D. Sullivan gave notice of two resolutions he intended to submit for approval. The first censured Butt for personally negotiating with the government on the Intermediate Education Bill, a violation of the party pledge of 1874; the second demanded increased activity and consistent attendance in the House of Commons from Home Rule MPs. Butt persuaded Sullivan to withdraw his censure motion, but he suffered a defeat when the second resolution passed by a margin of eight votes. A depressed and weary Butt left the meeting on the arm of his son, Robert. Death spared him further humiliation. A few weeks after the League meeting, he became ill, never recovered, and died of a stroke on May 5, 1879.

A majority of Home Rule MPs elected William Shaw, a successful Cork banker and Nonconformist clergyman, as Butt's successor as chair. Under his direction the party failed to improve its parliamentary performance. Meanwhile, Parnell was preparing to test his strength at the next general election. In October 1879 he assisted Michael Davitt in launching the National Land League. Davitt, a released Fenian prisoner, had gone to the United States in 1877 on a Clan-sponsored speaking tour. While there he converted to the New Departure, returning to Ireland to head its agrarian phase. In August 1879 he founded the Land League of Mayo, dedicated to peasant proprietorship. Three months later it evolved into the National Land League. Realizing that a Protestant landlord and leader of the active wing of the Irish party would make a better front man than himself, Davitt generously and shrewdly stepped aside and invited Parnell to become Land League president. The offer was accepted and worked out well for Parnell and the League.

From January to March 1880, while in the United States soliciting funds for the war on landlordism, Parnell completed an alliance with the Clan na Gael on his own rather than their terms. For the next ten years the vast majority of Irish-American nationalists would serve Parnell and Home Rule rather than revolutionary republicanism. He returned from his triumphant tour just in time for the March general election. Parnell personally contested and won three seats, deciding to represent Cork. When all the returns were in, Irish voters had elected sixty-one Home Rule MPs, most supporting Parnell. On April 26, 1880, in an election for chair, he defeated Shaw by twenty-three votes to eighteen. Shaw and his supporters refused to accept Parnell's leadership. They sat as independent nationalists working with Liberals. Parnellites replaced most of them in the 1885 general election.

Although the Butt-led Home Rule movement failed to achieve significant victories, the period 1870-80 was more than just a false start or a prelude to a more glorious era of nationalism. Despite his weakness of character, his gentleness, his limited view of independent opposition, and his naive respect for the British political tradition, Butt made a major contribution to the development of Irish nationalism. He articulated the Home Rule demand, created public opinion to support it, and organized an Irish party to achieve it. For all of its many weaknesses and failures, in quality and quantity of membership the 1870s Irish party was the best representation that Irish nationalism had yet had at Westminster. Home Rule MPs publicized Irish grievances, introduced reform measures, and, in some instances, interested British Liberals in Irish causes.

Had it been successful, Butt's brand of federalism would have put an end to those class and religious hatreds dividing Ireland; it would also have eased the centuries-old tensions that warped Anglo-Irish relations. Unfortunately, Butt's political realism did not match his good intentions. Psychologically, Anglo-Irish Protestants and Ulster Presbyterians could not cooperate in a nationalist movement with Catholics. They could not overcome hysterical fears that a Catholic peasant democracy, lusting after Protestant property and political influence, would dominate an Irish Parliament and impose dreaded popery on the land. Distrust of Catholics and class and property self-interests firmly committed non-Catholics in Ireland to a British rather than an Irish identity. On the other hand, after experiencing centuries of exploitation, Catholic tenant farmers could not have had much confidence in a Protestant landlord-sponsored nationalism.

British politicians rejected Butt's arguments for Home Rule

for the same reason they had O'Connell's demands for Repeal. To British parliamentary and public opinion, Irish independence, no matter how restricted, was a knife pointed at the heart of the British empire, a repudiation of traditional property interests, and a Catholic tactic to establish religious ascendancy in Ireland. Home Rule bucked a tide of imperialism that Conservatives successfully employed to attract British voters.

While less intellectual and experienced than Butt, Parnell had clearer insight into the true nature of British politics and the real, not mythological, possibilities of Irish nationalism. He was aware that Irish Protestants and Nonconformists would not easily embrace Home Rule, and that nationalism must be grounded on Catholic enthusiasm and Irish-American dollars. Parnell observed that British MPs voted in conformity with British needs and party discipline, and that they were not swayed by logical and reasonable arguments. Before making concessions to Irish nationalism, they had to be convinced that it would serve British and party interests. In order to impress British politicians with its determination and to compensate for its lack of numbers, Parnell decided that the Irish party needed inflexible discipline, and that it must retaliate for British indifference to Ireland. His strategy was based on a simple but effective formula: if the British Parliament denied freedom and reform to the Irish people, the Irish party would deny the British people effective government. Discipline and a determination, if necessary, to sabotage vital British and imperial legislation would compel British leaders to see the potential danger of Irish discontent and force them to negotiate with Irish nationalism.

Obstruction, however, proved even more important as an effective tactic to capture the confidence of Irish nationalism. To sustain popular enthusiasm and obtain funding for Home Rule, Parnell endorsed agrarian radicalism and negotiated an alliance with the Clan na Gael. Eventually this compact between the parliamentary party, agrarian agitators, and Irish Americans achieved security of tenures at fair rents and finally peasant proprietorship for Irish farmers. And it won Irish nationalists a broader suffrage, increased authority in local government, and expanded educational opportunities. It also extracted a Home Rule commitment from the Liberal party. Parnell and the Home Rule movement he revived and modified from 1910 to 1914 would come as close to achieving the Irish hope of self-government as constitutional methods permitted.

5

Home Rule
1880–1906

When Parnell took command of the Irish party he was, as president of the National Land League, directing an agrarian agitation that bordered on insurrection. The League's ultimate goal was peasant proprietorship, but it was prepared to accept secure tenures at fair rents as an intermediate step. Generously endowed by Irish America, in March 1880 the League had over £20,000 available to aid victims of evictions.

In a September 19, 1880, speech at Ennis, County Clare, Parnell told tenants to hang on to their farms and not to pay unjust rents. And he advised against physically punishing the land-grabbers who occupied the farms of evictees: "I wish to point out to you a very much better way—a more Christian and charitable way, which will give the lost man an opportunity of repenting. When a man takes a farm from which another has been evicted, you must shun him on the roadside when you meet him—you must shun him in the streets of the town—you must shun him in the shop—you must shun him on the fair-green and in the market place, and even in the place of worship, by leaving him alone, by putting him in a moral Coventry, by isolating him from the rest of the country, as if he were the leper of old—you must show him your detestation of the crime he has committed."

Land Leaguers followed Parnell's advice. All over Ireland they refused to pay what they considered excessive rents and first applied his suggestion of socially isolating the agents of landlordism on a

Mayo estate under the management of Captain Charles Cunningham Boycott. Boycotting became an effective weapon during the land war, and Irish-American workers borrowed and varied it in their struggle against industrial capitalism.

Relatively prosperous times in the 1850s, 1860s, and 1870s had multiplied the numbers and increased the income of shopkeepers in Irish towns. This group had close kinship and economic ties with tenant farmers, and some rented land themselves. The agricultural depression of the late 1870s threatened to destroy this marginal rural bourgeoisie, motivating many of its members to become local Land League officials. Fenians also played important mobilizing and leadership roles in the land war.

Irish landlords, British politicians, and conservative journalists described Land League activities as a revolutionary class war against the rights of property and saw Ireland as a country in a state of anarchy. During the agrarian struggle, militants burned the hayricks of unpopular landlords and maimed their cattle. They also boycotted and inflicted physical punishment on landlord agents and farmers who dared to occupy farms of evicted tenants. In response, the government used the Royal Irish Constabulary, and sometimes soldiers, to evict stubborn tenants from their holdings.

Following the Liberal victory in the general election of 1880, Gladstone returned as prime minister. Ireland's agrarian situation convinced him that Parliament had to alter landlord-tenant relations in that country. He introduced a bill to compensate evicted tenants, but the House of Lords rejected it. Gladstone then responded with a carrot-and-stick approach to the Irish land crisis. Liberals passed a coercive Peace Preservation Bill in an attempt to halt violence, and introduced a Land Act providing for fixity of tenure at fair rents and for a tenant's right to sell his investment in the farm. With the queen's influence, the House of Lords approved the Land Act in late August 1881. In addition to establishing de facto dual ownership of Irish land and clearing the way for peasant proprietorship, it was a devastating blow to the remnants of laissez-faire economic dogma. Conservative foes pointed out that Gladstone's emergency legislation for Ireland established dangerous precedents for Britain.

Instead of receiving the Land Act with expressions of gratitude, Parnell complained that it did not cover tenants in arrears. But the main reason Parnell did not support the Liberal measure on its second reading involved tactics. He did not want to be responsible for legislation that might prove to be flawed in execution, and he wanted to be free to press for amendments and further land reform. To Parnell, mobilizing tenant farmers for the land war was the first step in a long march toward Home Rule. Therefore, he could never accept any British concession as completely satisfactory. He always had to push for more until Irish nationalism reached its final destination.

After the Land Act became law, Parnell urged the Land League to pursue the case for tenants in arrears, and to demand that rent-establishing tribunals respect tenant interests. Gladstone lost patience with the continuation of agrarian agitation and applied provisions of the coercion bill to Parnell and a few of his lieutenants. When the government imprisoned them in Dublin's Kilmainham jail, Parnell retaliated with a no-rent manifesto. Since influential members of the Catholic hierarchy and clergy opposed it as a violation of legitimate property rights, the manifesto had little effect. Imprisonment, however, increased Parnell's stature as a national leader, and encouraged rather than retarded violence in rural Ireland. In April 1882 Gladstone decided that for the sake of Irish tranquility and the best interests of the United Kingdom as a whole, the government must negotiate with Parnell. In the unofficial "Kilmainham Treaty" Gladstone promised to settle the arrears question and to suspend coercion; Parnell agreed to issue a public statement accepting the Land Act as "a practical settlement of the land question," and to collaborate with the Liberals in efforts to forward Irish reform. The government released the Irish leader and his lieutenants on May 2, 1882.

Brutal Dublin murders four days later prevented Gladstone from fulfilling his part of the Kilmainham bargain. The Invincibles, republican extremists with Irish-American connections, stabbed to death Lord Frederick Cavendish, chief secretary for Ireland and the husband of Gladstone's niece, and T.H. Burke, the undersecretary, as they strolled in Phoenix Park. When Parnell heard the horrible news he believed that the assassinations were an attempt to discredit him and Home Rule. He seriously considered leaving politics, but on the advice of Gladstone changed his mind. But the Phoenix Park murders provoked such an anti-Irish backlash in Britain that Gladstone had to back away from further Irish reforms, and Parnell understood his predicament.

Since the land war had enlisted mass support and enthusiasm

for Irish nationalism, Parnell decided that it was time to consolidate and discipline the unruly forces he led and direct their attention to Home Rule. In 1882 he substituted the Irish National League and the Irish National League of Great Britain for the Home Rule League and Home Rule Confederation. Delegates from local branches of the INL joined with representatives of the Catholic clergy in county and city conventions to select Home Rule general and by-election candidates. The branches and the conventions gave the Home Rule movement a democratic image and spirit, but in reality the Irish party determined candidate selection. Its MPs chaired and usually persuaded conventions to select party-preferred candidates. Home Rule MPs residing in England dominated the Irish National League of Great Britain, using it to mobilize the Irish vote in British cities to serve the interests of Home Rule.

Since the Land League contained many Fenians antagonistic to parliamentary methods and Home Rule, Parnell was not unhappy when the government outlawed it in 1881. But agrarian agitation continued under the auspices of Anna Parnell's Ladies Land League until 1882 when her brother abolished it as an obstacle to nationalist unity. With the land war concluded, Parnell applied leftover funds in the Land League treasury to Home Rule purposes. A continuing flow of money from the Irish National League of the United States and from Irish nationalists in Britain and Ireland also assisted Parnell's work. With considerable financial resources at its disposal, the Irish party, unlike its predecessors, did not have to depend on opportunists. It could select dedicated and talented young men from all classes of society, pay their election expenses, and, if necessary, provide them with a stipend for serving their country at Westminister. An efficient election machine, a substantial treasury, the secret ballot, and household suffrage (the product of the 1884 Reform Bill) resulted in the return of eighty-six Home Rule MPs in the 1885 general election.

Home Rule successes, like Catholic Emancipation's victory, further polarized Catholics, Protestants, and Nonconformists in Ireland. Some Ulster Protestant and Presbyterian tenant farmers had joined the Land League, but when the agrarian movement headed down the path of Home Rule, they withdrew, placing their loyalty to the British connection before class solidarity. As the Irish party grew stronger, the Liberal party, which had once had a respectable following among Catholic and non-Catholic farmers, virtually disappeared in Ulster. Catholics voted Home Rule; Protestants and Presbyterians supported the Conservative party, the champion of Protestantism, the Union, and the empire.

Under Parnell's direction, Home Rule MPs became a tightly knit unit. Before their acceptance as candidates, they had to promise to vote together on all issues. Under the supervision of Parnell and his chief lieutenants, a parliamentary committee of sixteen formed party policy. During the 1880s the Irish party was the most disciplined in the House of Commons, and its front benches probably contained as much talent as those of the Liberals and Conservatives. Irish party discipline and funding were instrumental in shaping Britain's modern party system.

With a cohesive, well-financed, relatively large Westminster representation, Parnell could abandon obstruction, a tactic rendered almost useless by changes in House of Commons rules. His new strategy was based on a balance of power. Home Rule votes in 1885 dismissed the Liberals from office. After Conservatives pledged not to reapply coercion, to introduce a land purchase scheme, to investigate the possibility of extending local self-government, and to appoint a viceroy sympathetic to Irish issues, Parnell agreed to support a minority administration headed by the Marquess of Salisbury, before and after the general election of 1885. Because he had more confidence in Randolph Churchill, the bright young champion of Tory democracy, than in the cold personality of Joseph Chamberlain, a possible heir apparent to Liberal leadership, Parnell had another reason for selecting a Salisbury over a Gladstone government. To a considerable extent, Conservatives fulfilled their bargain. Salisbury appointed Lord Carnarvon, a believer in a mild form of Home Rule, as lord lieutenant, and Conservatives enacted the Ashbourne Act, which appropriated £5,000,000 for land purchase at 4 percent interest with a forty-nine-year repayment period.

Although Parnell gained much for Ireland from his arrangement with Conservatives, Gladstone was prepared to offer more. In December 1885, through his son Herbert, he announced his conversion to Home Rule as the best possible solution to the Irish Question. Perhaps this was an honest conviction, but Gladstone had practical reasons for seeing merit in Irish self-government. He needed the votes of Irish party MPs in the Commons because of Conservative imperialism's appeal to a large portion of the British electorate. After Gladstone announced his adherence to Home Rule, Conservatives retreated from their effort to conciliate Ireland, made preserving the Union the main plank in their party platform, and introduced an Irish coercion bill. Parnell responded by replacing a Conservative with a Liberal government.

Gladstone began his third administration supported by an Irish nationalist-British Liberal alliance in the House of Commons that transformed both British politics and Irish nationalism. The alliance limited the independence of the Irish party by wedding the fate of Home Rule to Liberal fortunes, and it ideologically defined and clarified British party politics. Before the Parnell-Gladstone connection the Whig landed aristocracy element in the Liberal coalition prevented an uncompromising commitment to political, social, and economic reform, tarnishing the party's image as a vehicle of progress and retarding its efforts to capture the loyalty of the recently enfranchised working class. This problem was solved when Whigs rejected Gladstone's commitment to Home Rule, seceded from the Liberal party, defined themselves as Liberal Unionists, and eventually found their way to the Conservative benches. There they were at home with people who shared similar views concerning class distinctions, property rights, and the integrity of the empire. By pruning Whigs from the Liberal fold, Home Rule emphasized social, economic, and imperial issues rather than hereditary allegiances as the focus of British party differences. Their association with Irish nationalism made it easier for Liberals to commit to democracy and social change in other areas. Since the vast majority of Home Rule MPs were sympathetic to extensive social reforms and the triumph of democracy, their alliance with British Liberalism served mutual interests.

The Irish party did not necessarily embrace British Liberalism's total package. Representing a predominantly Catholic country, it could not accept secular views of education. As spokesmen for an agrarian country, Home Rule MPs were more interested in the problems of Irish tenant farmers than in those of British or Irish industrial workers, and, unlike most British Liberals, they were not passionate free-traders. Home Rulers did not share the Liberals' evangelical conscience or zeal. They did not consider alcohol a vice, and criticized Liberal sin taxes. Since brewing and distilling were important Irish industries, they naturally influenced Irish-party views on the subject of drink. When it came to the support of causes associated with human freedom and dignity, Home Rule MPs often were in advance of a majority of Liberals. The destruction of the House of Lords and the creation of a democratic suffrage had been goals of Irish nationalism since O'Connell's time. Irish nationalist MPs spoke up for the rights of people who lived in underdeveloped parts of the empire, and some sympathized with the women's suffrage movement. In general, the Irish party was friendly to the communally and democratically conscious New Liberalism that was replacing the old individualistic version.

The Irish-Liberal alliance was a bonanza for Conservatives, giving them Whig defectors from the Liberal party, and providing them with another opportunity to exploit anti-Catholic British nativism. Instead of competing with Liberals on social issues, they could play on public anxieties with such slogans as "Home Rule is Rome Rule," and by implying that Irish self-government would eventually destroy the empire as well as the United Kingdom.

When the British economy began a post-1870 decline, factory workers and miners in Scotland and Wales were more interested in bread-and-butter issues than in Ireland or the empire. Therefore, until the advent of the Labour party, the Celtic fringes of Britain remained loyal to the Liberals, but the growing strength of Irish nationalism persuaded Protestants and Presbyterians in Ireland and members of the established church in rural England to identify with the Conservatives. In order to emphasize the issue of Home Rule, exploit no-popery, demonstrate a commitment to the empire, and attract the allegiance of Liberal party secessionists, Conservative leaders rechristened their party "Unionist."

In many ways, Parnell's Irish party fulfilled Charles Gavan Duffy's independent Irish party strategy. Parnell had exploited tenant grievances in order to revive Irish nationalism and create an Irish influence in the Commons. From another perspective, the Home Rule effort was something less than what Duffy projected. It did not persuade Protestants and Presbyterians to make common cause with Catholics, and the ramifications of the Liberal alliance restricted the independence of the Irish party. After 1886 the success of Irish nationalism depended on British Liberalism, and Parnell and the Irish party were in somewhat the same relationship to it as O'Connell and his Repeal party were to Whiggery in the 1830s.

On April 8, 1886, Gladstone introduced the first Home Rule (Government of Ireland) bill. It provided for an Irish executive and Parliament with control over local affairs, but Westminster remained in charge of matters concerning foreign and imperial policy, the Crown, peace and war, customs and excise, the post office, coinage and legal tender, and trade and navigation. Technically, the Irish parliament was to have only one house divided into two orders; the smaller was designed to represent property and was partly elective, the larger was wholly representative. Each order had a suspensory veto over legislation. Gladstone intended the smaller, more conservative order to protect the various interests of the non-Catholic minority. Irish MPs would not sit at Westminister unless it became necessary to revise the provisions of the Home Rule bill. The Dublin government would appoint Irish judges and the Irish Exchequer would pay their salaries. Ireland also was obliged to contribute to the costs of empire. Decisions from Irish courts were subject to appeal to the Privy Council in London, which could also decide on the constitutionality of bills passed by the Irish parliament.

Irish party MPs opposed certain provisions of the bill: British control over customs, the imperial contribution, the temporary Westminster jurisdiction over the Royal Irish Constabulary, and voting by orders in the Irish Parliament. They expressed their criticisms, but voted for and praised the bill during its first and second readings because they knew that Whig opposition threatened its passage and, therefore, Gladstone needed their support.

A number of British MPs argued that since the British government would collect and spend 40 percent of Irish taxes, it would be unfair to deny Ireland representation in the Imperial Parliament. Conservatives attacked the bill as a concession to Irish extremism and a danger to British security. They also insisted that the Union was necessary to the empire's survival. But division within Liberal ranks delivered the fatal blow to the Home Rule bill. Lord Hartington led the Whig opposition, and Joseph Chamberlain, leader of the Radical contingent in the party, convinced that Home Rule threatened the empire and bitter because Gladstone had given him a minor position in the Cabinet, also rejected the bill. On June 8, 1886, at the close of the second reading debate, ninety-three Liberals, most of them Whigs, voted against Gladstone and put him and his Irish allies in the minority, 343 votes to 313.

Gladstone dissolved Parliament and took the Home Rule issue to the British electorate. Conservatives used no-popery, anti-Irish opinion against Liberals. Cynically playing the "Orange Card," Lord Randolph Churchill exploited Irish Protestant hatred of Catholics. Visiting Belfast, he coined the slogan "Ulster will fight and Ulster will be right" to encourage armed resistance to any Home Rule bill that Parliament might pass. Election results gave Conservatives 316 seats, Liberal Unionists 78, Home Rule Liberals 191, and Irish nationalists 85. With the support of Liberal Unionists, the Conservatives formed a government with Salisbury as prime minister.

In 1893, in his fourth and final administration, Gladstone introduced a second Home Rule bill. This time he attempted to eliminate one of the criticisms of the first: Ireland would have representation at Westminster during discussion of Irish and imperial questions. The second Home Rule bill passed through the Commons, but the Lords crushed it. Gladstone wanted to dissolve Parliament and fight an election on the issue of the Lords' veto power, but other Liberal leaders disagreed. This and other conflicts with his colleagues convinced the old man to resign as prime minister and party leader. Lord Rosebery, lukewarm on Home Rule and hot on empire, replaced him. During the crisis in Parliament, and in the Liberal party over the second Home Rule bill and the Lords' veto, the Irish party's influence was considerably weaker than in the 1880s. In December 1890 Home Rule MPs and Irish national opinion had split into Parnellite and anti-Parnellite factions.

In late 1889 Parnell was at the height of his popularity in Ireland; he had even won the respect of a considerable portion of British opinion, the result of a confrontation with the *Times* of London. In 1887 the traditionally anti-Irish newspaper published a series on Parnellism and crime, asserting that the Irish leader and other members of his party were responsible for violence and agrarian outrage in Ireland. In one article the *Times* reproduced a letter with Parnell's signature condoning the 1882 Phoenix Park murders of Cavendish and Burke.

The *Times'* attack on Parnell's integrity intensified British antagonism to him and Home Rule. Seemingly indifferent to British opinion, Parnell ignored the charges, but a former colleague turned opponent, F. Hugh O'Donnell, who was also mentioned in the articles, sued the newspaper for libel. During the trial, the *Times'* attorney produced more incriminating letters allegedly authored by the Home Rule leader. Parnell decided to move against the newspaper, though he had no confidence in the justice of British courts and juries in regard to matters Irish. He asked the government to create a parliamentary committee of inquiry to investigate the authenticity of the letters. Salisbury denied his request but did appoint a committee of three judges to investigate all of the charges against Irish nationalism. The hearing revealed that the *Times*, in good faith, had bought the letters from Richard Pigott, a Dublin journalist with a shady reputation. In February 1889, Parnell's counsel, Charles Russell, demonstrated that the *Times'* letters were counterfeit. After the brilliant cross-examination that revealed the truth, Pigott, the forger, left for Spain and committed suicide in a Madrid hotel room. The *Times*, that most respectable newspaper, was in disgrace. Irish opinion rejoiced that its leader had evaded and exposed a vile Unionist plot, and many Britons, with their notions of justice and fair play, also believed that a foul conspiracy involving the *Times*, the Conservatives, and the Liberal Unionists had victimized Parnell. Following the exposure of Pigott's duplicity, Home Rule and Liberal MPs gave Parnell a standing ovation when he entered the House of Commons.

On December 24, 1889, about ten months after the Parnellism and Crime Committee inquiry, Captain William O'Shea, one-time friend of Parnell and former Irish party member, sued his wife Katherine for divorce on grounds of adultery and named the Home Rule leader as co-respondent. Mrs. O'Shea had been Parnell's paramour since 1880, and Liberal leaders were aware of the relationship; she had been their go-between in negotiating the Kilmainham Treaty. A number of Home Rule MPs also knew that Katherine O'Shea was Parnell's lover. This had been made clear in 1886 when Parnell backed O'Shea for a Galway seat even though he refused to take the Irish party pledge. But in the Victorian period there was a great deal of difference between a quiet relationship and a public scandal. A messy divorce case had destroyed the promising career of Sir Charles Dilke, Gladstone's likely successor as Liberal leader.

When O'Shea first announced his intention to divorce his wife because of her physical intimacy with Parnell, the Irish party chair told his colleagues that the trial would prove that his long romance was honorable. Many Irish nationalists believed that the divorce case, like the *Times'* accusation, was a Unionist plot to discredit Home Rule and its leader. A number of Irish public bodies passed resolutions endorsing Parnell, and the divorce matter dropped from general discussion for ten months.

During the November 1890 divorce hearing, O'Shea testified that Parnell had come into his home as a guest and had taken advantage of his hospitality by seducing his wife. He said that for ten years Katherine and his so-called friend had continued to deceive him, resorting to all sorts of subterfuges to carry on their adulterous association. Historical evidence indicates that O'Shea and his wife were on bad terms before she met Parnell, that the captain was aware of their relationship, and that he had received an allowance from her and a seat in Parliament from Parnell for his compliance. For some time Katherine had intended to divorce William and marry Parnell but had hesitated to do so while her aunt, Mrs. Benjamin Wood, was alive. Wealthy Mrs. Wood provided the O'Sheas with a considerable income; had she known about her niece's relationship with Parnell, she might have cut off the allowance and disinherited her. O'Shea had kept quiet to protect his income. When Mrs. Wood died in 1889, Katherine planned to use £20,000 of her inheritance to purchase a divorce from her husband. Legal obstacles temporarily tied up the estate, causing O'Shea to suspect that his wife was reneging on their bargain. In vengeance, he sued for divorce. Since it was the only way to get rid of O'Shea and to become man and wife, Parnell and Katherine finally decided not to contest the case. As a result, the judge granted O'Shea his divorce and awarded him Katherine's children, two of whom were Parnell's. O'Shea's uncontradicted testimony left British opinion with a sordid portrait of the Irish party chair.

Early Irish nationalist reactions to the trial and judgment favored Parnell. The Irish National League confirmed his leadership, but Michael Davitt, in the *Labour World*, asked him to resign as party chair, and Cardinal Manning of Westminster advised Gladstone to repudiate the Home Rule leader. Manning, who viewed the Irish party as an advocate of Catholic causes throughout the United Kingdom, often acted as an intermediary in negotiations between Gladstone and Irish bishops. He disliked Parnell, and told members of the Irish hierarchy that they should not tolerate a Protestant in charge of Irish nationalism. Manning saw the divorce scandal as an opportunity to destroy Parnell and increase the Catholic bishops' influence over the Home Rule movement.

British Liberals were dependent on votes from Nonconformists, who issued an ultimatum to Gladstone: disassociate your party from the Irish adulterer and home-wrecker or suffer the consequences at the next election. The Irish party had scheduled a November 25 meeting to elect its chair for the coming parliamentary session. The day before, Gladstone informed John Morley, his closest friend and advisor on Irish policy and intended chief secretary for Ireland in the next Liberal government, and Justin McCarthy, Irish party vice-chair, that Parnell would have to step down for the sake of the Irish-Liberal alliance and for the good of Home Rule. Morley failed to see Parnell before the meeting, but McCarthy delivered the message. Parnell ignored it, McCarthy didn't mention his Gladstone conversation to other Home Rule MPs, and they, in ignorance of the issue at stake, unanimously reelected "the Chief" as chair. When on the following day Gladstone made public his position, many in the Irish party forced Parnell to summon a second meeting to reconsider his leadership. From December 1 through December 6, in committee room 15 of the House of Commons, the Irish party debated whether they should retain or depose the man who had raised Irish constitutional nationalism from the ashes, achieved considerable reform legislation for Ireland, and maneuvered the Liberals into a Home Rule commitment.

If Parnell had been a farsighted, selfless, dedicated patriot, logic would have demanded a gracious abdication as party chair to save the Liberal alliance and Home Rule. He still would have been a powerful Irish party voice, and, after a few years of public penance, he might have been able to resume its leadership. But Parnell's intense pride and lust for power did not groom him for self-sacrifice. Ruthlessness and ego had made his political fortune as they had shaped the Home Rule movement. Parnell believed that he was the leader of the Irish nation not through election but by right of conquest over Butt and apathy, and he was not going to abandon his position at the dictate of the British puritan Nonconformist conscience or its public spokesman, William Ewart Gladstone.

In committee room 15, Parnell's most articulate supporter, John Redmond, argued that if Home Rule MPs deposed their leader at Gladstone's command, the Irish party would publicly surrender its independence and exist as a Liberal satellite. Parnell told his colleagues that if they were going to sell him out, they had better make sure that Gladstone offered them a generous Home Rule measure as the price. Parnell's opponents replied that when Parnell consummated the alliance with Gladstone, the fortunes of the Liberal and Irish parties became indistinguishable, and that Home Rule's fate rested on the former's appeal to British voters. British liberal opinion had spoken, Gladstone had no choice but to listen and obey, and the Irish party had no option but to depose Parnell and elect a new leader.

On December 6 Justin McCarthy, followed by forty-four of his colleagues, left committee room 15. They assembled in another place and elected McCarthy party chair. Parnell was left with twenty-seven followers. During the debate over Parnell's leadership, some prominent Irish party members were soliciting funds in the United States. Among them, William O'Brien and John Dillon could not return home. If they did, the government would arrest them for their roles in the Plan of Campaign, an 1886-90 agrarian agitation attempting to settle rents through collective bargaining. Although they were two of Parnell's chief lieutenants, O'Brien and Dillon, along with most of the American delegation, agreed that political necessity dictated his resignation.

Refusing to abandon his leadership without a struggle, Parnell appealed over the head of the party to the people, thus inviting Irish Catholic bishops and priests to play a decisive role in his retention or rejection. Since British Nonconformists and other Protestants had denounced Parnell as a public sinner, an enemy of the sanctity of marriage, and thus unworthy of political influence, the Catholic hierarchy and clergy, which had always placed a high premium on sexual morality, could hardly appear to be less principled than "heretics" on the other side of the Irish Sea. On December 4, during the committee room 15 discussions, the bishops, emphasizing the moral equation rather than the Liberal alliance, issued a manifesto asking Irish Catholics to reject Parnell. Their position did not influence Home Rule MPs, who made a political rather than a moral decision, but it did have an impact on the minds of Catholic Ireland.

In 1891 Parnell put his prestige on the line in three by-elections. He had never exerted himself more vigorously or courageously than he did while campaigning for his candidates. In addressing friendly and hostile audiences, Parnell projected an inclusive Irish nationalism uniting Catholics and non-Catholics, tenant farmers and landlords, employers and employees under the umbrella of a secular, liberal, democratic Irish state. He also appealed to Fenians by saying that if parliamentary efforts failed physical force might be necessary to emancipate Ireland from British rule.

Representing affluent large farmers and members of the middle class, Timothy Healy, MP, Parnell's most prominent and vicious opponent, proposed a much more conservative and Catholic version of a self-governing Ireland. Despite his liberal, tolerant, and progressive nationalist appeal, and his overture to republicans, Parnell was defeated by a combination of the political realities of the Liberal alliance, the opposition of the Catholic hierarchy and clergy, and the influence of the Irish party majority. His candidates lost all three elections, and he ruined his health campaigning in the cold and damp of Ireland. On October 6, 1891, Parnell died in Brighton of rheumatic fever with his wife Katherine at his bedside. Following a large and emotional Dublin funeral procession, his friends buried him close to O'Connell in Glasnevin cemetery. The dead "Uncrowned King of Ireland" left behind a shattered Irish party, a disillusioned and divided Irish national opinion, and the powerful myth of a martyred messiah—one that would inspire future generations of young people, particularly writers and poets.

From the defeat of the first Home Rule bill in the summer of 1886 until December 1905, Liberals were in power less than three years (August 1892-February 1895). Lord Salisbury was the Unionist prime minister from 1886 to 1892, and then again from 1895 to 1902. His nephew, Arthur J. Balfour, succeeded him. As chief secretary for Ireland from 1887 to 1891, Balfour designed Unionist Irish policy. For a time while he was prime minister, his brother, Gerald, served as chief secretary.

Salisbury and the Balfours agreed that primitive and volatile Irish Catholics were too irresponsible to completely manage their own affairs and that Home Rule would result in an anti-Protestant Dublin parliament, threaten Britain's security, and lead to the dissolution of the empire. Dominant in the Unionist party coalition, Conservatives continued to encourage British and Irish Protestant anti-Catholicism as a weapon against Home Rule and its Liberal supporters. They also rallied property interests behind the Unionist standard by identifying the Irish-Liberal alliance with radical democracy and socialism.

But the Unionist government's Irish policy was not solely based on repression of Irish nationalism and preservation of the status quo. Balfour, a tough chief secretary, believed that Ireland had to be cowed into subservience by a long period of resolute government. Because of his extensive use of a severe 1887 Crimes Act to suppress agrarian agitation and outrage, Irish nationalists referred to him as "Bloody Balfour." That name, however, was an unfair estimate of his approach to the Irish Question. In the twenty-year period dominated by the Unionist party, Balfour balanced coercion with conciliation. He believed Irish nationalism was a synthetic movement that would collapse if British legislation improved the economic well-being of its constituency.

Balfour's Irish program was more than what his brother, Gerald, described as an effort "to kill home rule with kindness." He and Salisbury wanted to pacify Ireland so that British attention and resources could focus on United Kingdom and imperial imperatives without the continual distraction of the Irish Question. They also needed to reassure Liberal Unionist coalition colleagues who were sympathetic to reform in Ireland that, short of Home Rule, the government would address Irish discontent. And they wanted to make sure that, though divided by religion (Anglican and Nonconformist) and by class (tenant farmer and landlord, industrial capitalist and worker), Ulster non-Catholics would remain under the inclusive banner of Unionism.

As both chief secretary and prime minister, Balfour introduced or encouraged legislation dealing with land, poverty, economic development, and local government in Ireland. Unionist land bills dealt with tenant security and with peasant proprietorship culminating in the 1903 Wyndham Land Act, which provided landlords with a 12 percent cash bonus to encourage them to sell off their estates. The government offered tenants low-interest rates on loans and a sixty-eight-and-one-half-year repayment period. In 1909, a Liberal administration amended the Wyndham Act to compel sales in certain instances. Land purchase proved to be the final solution to the agrarian dimension of the Irish Question: it created close to two hundred thousand peasant proprietors who possessed about half of the country's arable land.

To cope with Ireland's poverty and low standard of living, Unionists, under Balfour's guidance, established a number of important agencies and introduced many productive programs. The Congested Districts Board (1891) functioned in the most depressed parts of the country, mostly in the west, employing government subsidies to develop cottage industries (spinning and weaving), fishing, and agriculture, and inaugurate extensive programs of technical and agricultural education. The Board consolidated many small farms into efficient agricultural units, placed poor farmers on these plots, and taught them to work the land with competence. In addition to the Congested Districts Board, Balfour attempted to energize Ireland's economy with public works projects that constructed railway lines and roads, built bridges, and drained water-saturated bog land. These activities provided considerable employment as well as economic development in the country. In 1899 Chief Secretary Gerald Balfour created the Department of Agricultural and Technical Instruction for Ireland to supervise agricultural and technical education, fisheries, prevention of animal and plant disease, the National Library, and the National Museum, and after 1905 the geological survey.

A Unionist government, constantly warning against Liberal socialist tendencies, was operating welfare state projects in Ireland far in advance of anything yet attempted in Britain. Perhaps peasant proprietorship, the Congested Districts Board, and the Department of Agriculture and Technical Instruction delayed modernization by perpetuating agrarianism and discouraging industrialism, but most experts agree that they did raise the Irish standard of living and provide new economic opportunities. Balfour's effort was probably the most intelligent, successful, and humane product of British rule in Ireland during the nineteenth century.

While unrelenting in their opposition to Home Rule, Unionists did make a major concession to the Irish demand for self-government. Stripping the Protestant gentry-dominated grand juries of all fiscal and administrative powers and responsibilities, the 1898 Local Government Act transferred these duties to popularly elected urban, rural, and county councils that women as well as men could vote for and serve on. These new instruments of government gave the Irish as much local authority as enjoyed by the British. Unionists intended the various councils to substitute for an Irish parliament. Instead, the experience of managing local affairs provided a training ground for Home Rule and raised nationalist expectations.

Balfour's Irish policy encouraged contacts between some progressive Protestant Unionists such as Lord Dunraven and consensus building nationalists such as William O'Brien. Dunraven believed that the process of planning and passing the Wyndham Land Act established a precedent for solving all Irish problems in a conciliatory and cooperative manner. His 1904 Irish Reform Association proposed the creation in Ireland of financial and legislative councils with extensive powers as an alternative to Home Rule. Dunraven invited Sir Anthony MacDonnell, the undersecretary for Ireland, to assist him in drafting a devolution proposal. MacDonnell, formerly of the

Indian civil service, a Catholic liberal with an Irish party MP brother, did not enjoy the complete trust of ultra-Unionists. When they learned that he had helped author Dunraven's devolution scheme, they raised cries of outrage, forcing George Wyndham, the chief secretary, to resign.

Ulster Unionists were not satisfied by Wyndham's downfall or by the government's denial that it was entertaining passage of Dunraven's scheme. They feared that the Dunraven-MacDonnell proposal indicated that, despite its denials, the government might be softening in its opposition to Home Rule. Their response was to form the Ulster Unionist Council, established in 1905 with Walter Long, MP, as chair. This group became the staunchest champion of unionism and a constant pressure on British Conservatives to maintain a steadfast hostility to Irish nationalism. Irish Protestant and British ultra-Unionism's intimidation pressured the government to put the brakes on progressive unionism in Ireland.

When Unionists left office in December 1905, only the university education question remained of the economic, social, and religious issues that conceived, birthed, and nourished Irish nationalism. Nevertheless, Unionist reform measures did not silence the Home Rule demand. The Balfour-Salisbury view of Irish nationalism as a mere reflection of economic and social discontent was a superficial assessment of the situation. In contrast, Gladstone understood that Irish nationalism had assumed an identity independent of its originating and sustaining grievances, and that it could only be satisfied by some concession of legislative independence. Conservative refusals to consider an Irish parliament and exploitation of religious and property prejudices to strengthen unionism made a final settlement of the Irish Question more difficult for both Britain and Ireland.

6

The Crises of
Home Rule Nationalism
1906–1914

After a long period of negotiations, in 1900, John Dillon, Justin McCarthy's successor as anti-Parnellite leader of the Irish party in the Commons, graciously stepped aside, and John Redmond, commander of the small Parnellite minority, became chair of a reunited party. As part of the arrangement, William O'Brien's United Irish League replaced the Irish National League as the Home Rule organization. The UIL was conceived in 1898 as a movement in the west to buy out wealthy graziers and distribute their land among farmers. By 1901 it had almost a thousand branches. Irish party unity increased its influence at Westminster, lifted nationalist morale, and made it easier to solicit funds for Home Rule activities at home and from the diaspora. But the Irish party never again attained the prestige and popular favor that it had enjoyed in Parnell's time.

The divorce scandal, followed by the party split, disillusioned some nationalists and made others cynical about politics. They could not transfer to Redmond the same kind of affection or commitment they had given to Parnell. And by 1900 the bloom of youth had left the Irish party: energetic and militant young men who followed Parnell in the early 1880s had become middle-aged, respected politicians. While their devotion to Home Rule remained, the compromise, give-and-take character of parliamentary politics had tempered their enthusiasm and passion. Irish party MPs had served their constituents well, forcing Liberals to endorse Home Rule, and Conservative as well as Liberal governments to pass significant legislation improving and reforming the Irish situation. Nationalist voters appreciated these successes, and if the party was not the bright political light that it had once been, it still enjoyed their overwhelming support. Home Rule MPs, however, had become so involved with parliamentary routine that they began to lose touch with the people they represented. When they started to think like British politicians, they became insensitive to undercurrents in Irish life.

In many ways Redmond was an excellent party chair. His colleagues admired him and he graciously listened to and considered their suggestions. At Westminster, his intelligence and effective debating skills earned him the respect of British politicians. With few exceptions, such as his opposition to women's suffrage, Redmond had a liberal disposition. He also was a man of courage and integrity; both qualities had been tested and proven in the 1890s when he defended Parnell and, at great personal sacrifice and risk, remained loyal to his memory. On the negative side, Redmond had a serious flaw for a leader of Irish nationalism: like Isaac Butt, he had too much respect for things British—their Parliament, constitution, institutions, and code of conduct. Redmond also shared Butt's admiration for and pride in Ireland's contributions to the empire. When not in the House of Commons, whether in London or at his home in Wicklow, Redmond was a shy introvert who enjoyed his privacy and the companionship of a few close friends. He relished parliamentary activity but not public meetings or the demagoguery essential to the leader of a popular cause, one that depended on the enthusiasm and financial generosity of nationalists at home and abroad.

Home Rule's emphasis on political and economic issues did not prove emotionally or psychologically satisfying to all Irish nationalists. In the 1880s and 1890s cultural nationalism was reactivated by more than the Parnell divorce scandal, the cynicism and disillusionment caused by the split in the party, or the stodginess of the Home Rule agenda. The Gaelic scholarship of Sir Samuel Ferguson and Standish O'Grady, two Protestant unionists, stimulated considerable interest in Ireland's culture and history. Revived cultural nationalism also responded to the social-Darwinist, Anglo-Saxon racism that had joined anti-Catholicism as part of British nativism. In Britain, academics, journalists, newspaper and periodical cartoonists, and Unionist politicians depicted Irish Catholics as an inferior, simian-featured, irresponsible, irrational, and emotional subspecies incapable of managing their own affairs. Replying to these insults,

Irish cultural nationalists claimed the inheritance of an ancient high culture that made them spiritually superior to materialistic Anglo-Saxons. They said that Gaelic virtue survived in the lifestyle of the peasantry and in the Irish language.

Following in the tradition of Young Irelanders, a new generation of cultural nationalists insisted that political independence was not their country's most pressing need. They wondered what would be accomplished if Ireland had her own legislature but its people remained British in mind and spirit. They said that de-Anglicization was essential for true sovereignty, insisting that Ireland must develop a historical self-consciousness, an awareness of its own language and traditions—it had to recover its own soul. Cultural nationalism inspired three significant movements: the Gaelic League, the Gaelic Athletic Association, and the Literary Revival.

Since Young Ireland's time there had been efforts to preserve the Irish language where it existed, resuscitate it where it was dying, and restore it where it had perished. In 1893 Eoin MacNeill, an Ulster Catholic scholar, and Douglas Hyde, the son of a Roscommon Protestant clergyman and a graduate of Trinity College, founded the Gaelic League. Hyde, its president, was raised in an Irish-speaking district. He learned the language and cultivated the literature and traditions of the people. He devoted his life to restoring Irish as the voice of the people, and in 1889 published the first in a number of volumes of translations of Gaelic stories and poems. After 1908 both MacNeill and Hyde held chairs in University College, Dublin, a branch of the new National University of Ireland. In pressing for the de-Anglicization of their country, they demanded that Irish be honored as the national language. The Gaelic League was dedicated to this objective and to the study and publication of Gaelic literature. It also encouraged and promoted the development of contemporary writing in Irish.

Some of the most militant Gaelic Irelanders, such as D.P. Moran and W.P. Ryan, were journalists who had learned their profession in London. They were lonely in an alien, anti-Irish environment and became contemptuous of English culture and manners. Gaelic organizations in the British capital became their refuge. They returned to Ireland determined to advance the theory and the reality of an Irish Ireland, but their British experiences made them friendly to an economically modernized as well as a Gaelic Ireland.

By 1903 there were over five hundred branches of the Gaelic

League. Members learned the language, read Irish literature, played Irish music, sang Irish songs, and danced Irish dances. On their annual holidays they traveled to Irish-speaking districts in Waterford, Donegal, West Cork, Kerry, Connacht, and the Aran Islands to polish their language skills in conversations with native speakers, and to absorb Gaelic traditions at their peasant roots. Like Miss Ivors in James Joyce's "The Dead," Gaelic Leaguers often were intolerant of people indifferent to the language, reviling them as "West Britons."

While sympathetic to Home Rule, Hyde attempted to keep the Gaelic League independent of politics. To him legislative independence was of secondary importance to cultural sovereignty. Distressed that sectarianism and political factionalism stood in the way of cultural cohesion, Hyde wanted the League to unite all shades of religious and political opinion in an Irish-Ireland commitment. Some Home Rule MPs saw the League as competition for the affections—and thus the financial contributions—of nationalists, but practical considerations forced an Irish party endorsement of its work and objectives.

The Gaelic League appealed to the middle class in cities and large towns. Cultural nationalism came to small towns, villages, and rural parishes in the form of the Gaelic Athletic Association. In 1884 Michael Cusack, the model for the Citizen in Joyce's *Ulysses*, founded the Association at Thurles, County Tipperary. Archbishop Thomas William Croke of Cashel, in giving it an episcopal blessing, ridiculed such English sports as lawn tennis, polo, croquet, and cricket as alien and not "racy of the soil." He urged Irish lads to participate in the games of their ancestors: hurling, football, running, leaping, hammer throwing, and wrestling, and lassies to play camogie, a version of field hockey.

The GAA spread through Leinster, Munster, Connacht, and Catholic areas of Ulster with parishes and counties organizing hurling or football teams and sometimes both. Like the Gaelic League, the GAA fostered intolerance to things British. In order to maintain control over the young and to isolate them from foreign influences, it banned those who played English games from the Association.

Gaelic League and GAA versions of cultural nationalism eventually spread to the diaspora, but they did little to interest the rest of the Western world in the Irish Question. Most people outside the United Kingdom thought of Ireland as a country with an unfortunate history and legitimate grievances against British rule, but it was too insignificant to merit serious attention or concern. Its economic development was retarded, its culture was primitive, and its citizens failed to make significant contributions to art or literature. Ireland's chief city, Dublin, once a flourishing eighteenth-century capital, was now a seedy, dull, provincial town.

Then, suddenly, in the late nineteenth century, dreary little Dublin became a major center of literary and theatrical activity. The Literary Revival took inspiration from the language movement and scholarly investigations into pre- and early-Christian Irish history and culture. Most of the prominent figures in the Revival were Anglo-Irish Protestants such as William Butler Yeats, John Millington Synge, George Russell, and Lady Gregory. Rejecting the class, religious, and political prejudices of their background, they embraced cultural nationalism, condemning British rule as an obstacle to the appreciation of distinct, creative, and significant native traditions. Like Gaelic Leaguers and members of the Gaelic Athletic Association, Anglo-Irish writers attempted to restore ancient cultural values by recalling their virtues to the youth of their time.

Parnell fascinated Yeats and his friends. For young writers combating various forms of "tyranny"—British political and cultural influences, and a provincial, puritanical society—Parnell symbolized resistance to colonialism and the popular conventions that destroyed him. To many of the literati, Parnell was a classic tragic hero brought down at the height of his power, and an Irish messiah "crucified" by those he came to liberate. In using and expanding the Parnell legend, writers attempted to prepare the way for another savior—perhaps one of themselves—who would rescue Ireland and, through the Celtic genius, the rest of Western civilization from Anglo-Saxon materialism. In glorifying the simple, unsophisticated Irish peasant and attacking British urban industrialism, the writers adhered to the message of Thomas Davis and the *Nation*. They believed that rural Ireland contained the necessary spiritual energy to revive Irish civilization. Tillers of the soil had not sold their "racial" souls to foreign materialistic influences. They preserved the folk tradition, the belief in supernatural forces—pagan as well as Christian—and the language.

Not all Irish writers were romantic or sentimental. Synge, a Yeats protege friendly to Home Rule, refused to subordinate his talents or his view of truth to the myths of cultural nationalism. His earthy peasant characters, in contrast to the ethereal creatures of

Yeats's early years, introduced realism and surrealism into the Irish theatre. James Joyce, a product of urban middle-class Catholic Ireland, stayed apart from the literary and language movements and, by embracing exile, also rejected the creed of cultural nationalism. He believed that Ireland could only achieve salvation by a candid examination of the national conscience.

Although they both expressed cultural nationalism, there were considerable tensions between the Gaelic League and the Revival. The former had a narrow and more inclusive view of what was Irish. It insisted that a true national literature must be expressed in the native language. Many League members refused to see literature as the expression of free, artistic genius. Instead, they viewed it as an auxiliary of nationalism, and writers as agents of the cause. In contrast, Yeats and his friends believed that while writers must be knowledgeable about and sensitive to Gaelic culture and traditions, and draw on them for subject material, as artists they had an obligation to interpret Irish life in an independent and aesthetic way. They also asserted that they could express a native mood and cultural spirit in English, a more expansive and flexible literary language than Irish, and one with a wider reading audience.

The conflict between the "provincial" views of the League and the more "cosmopolitan" attitudes of the Revival was evident in the Abbey Theatre riot over Synge's 1907 *The Playboy of the Western World*. The play offended the sensitivities of Irish-Ireland Gaelic Leaguers, who felt that Synge's earthy and rowdy West-of-Ireland peasants were not a true representation of Gaelic cultural values and that they cast Ireland in a bad light.

In the late nineteenth and early twentieth centuries, with the influx of middle-class Catholics and the support of the Catholic Church, the non-Literary Revival dimensions of cultural nationalism became increasingly exclusive. Until that time, Catholic secondary schools, particularly the Jesuit variety, had little interest in Irish cultural nationalism. Curricula and athletic programs (rugby and cricket) imitated those in English public schools. Many Catholic secondary-school students and those attending universities looked forward to employment in the British civil service at home, in Britain, or in the empire. Toward the end of the nineteenth century, a shortage of civil service appointment opportunities and anti-Catholic discrimination in the selection process blocked mobility for the sons of the Irish Catholic middle class. Disappointment and disillusionment led them into Irish cultural nationalism as an outlet for their ambition and talent and gave them hope for a better future.

With the exception of D.P. Moran, editor and publisher of *The Leader*, who insisted that "Gaelic" and "Catholic" were pretty much synonymous terms, almost all early Gaelic Leaguers rejected sectarianism and, like Young Irelanders, wanted to include Irish Catholics, Anglo-Irish Protestants, and Ulster Presbyterians under a common national identity. There were Catholic priests active in the Gaelic League, but at first most bishops and priests interpreted Irish-Ireland as a rival to Catholic Ireland. W.P. Ryan, editor of *The Irish Peasant*, agreeing with such Protestant critics of Catholic influence as Horace Plunkett and Filson Young, complained that authoritarian, conservative, fatalistic, other-worldly Catholicism impeded the liberation and modernization of Ireland. He said that Catholic puritanism encouraged emigration by making life in the country dull and monotonous.

Despite the inclusive views of liberal Catholic Gaelic Leaguers such as Ryan, it was almost inevitable that Irish-Ireland and Catholic Ireland would meld in a religious-cultural marriage. The overwhelming majority of Gaelic League and Gaelic Athletic Association members was Catholic; with few exceptions, Protestant and Nonconformist Ireland rejected the Gaelic tradition as Catholicism in disguise and clung to British identity. Despite early hostility, the hierarchy came to realize that Catholic Ireland and Irish-Ireland were not inherently contradictory and that they shared common goals. Both despised British urban industrial culture and wanted to prevent its spread into Ireland. Catholic leaders decided to exploit the Anglophobia of cultural nationalism and to divert its original goal of a religiously pluralistic but culturally monolithic Ireland into an essentially Catholic Ireland.

With the exception of George Russell (A.E.), the leaders of the Revival were not involved with specific economic, social, or political issues. Though they played a significant role in the national awakening and deserve some credit for its triumphs, their contribution has often been exaggerated. In one of his poems, Yeats pondered whether his words had sent young men off to die in Easter Week 1916, but those of Thomas Davis probably more directly captured their imaginations. And there were other inspirational ingredients contributing to Ireland's early twentieth-century wars of liberation: the Republican tradition of 1798, 1848, and 1867; the memory of

Robert Emmet; social injustices that produced syndicalism in the labor movement; tactical mistakes by the Irish party; and the insensitivity of British politicians.

But the Revival did put its stamp on Irish cultural nationalism, and its writers, unlike Young Ireland propagandists, were great artists. The quality of their creative endeavors was unsurpassed in other countries. For the first time in centuries, Ireland made a significant literary contribution to Western civilization. Through the works of Revival writers, sophisticated and influential people in Britain, on the Continent, throughout the empire, and in the United States learned of Ireland's culture, traditions, grievances, and demand for freedom. During the 1919-21 Anglo-Irish War, world opinion finally convinced British politicians that they must extend a measure of independence to Ireland.

Friction between the various expressions of cultural nationalism probably stimulated rather than discouraged intellectual excitement and energy in Dublin during the two decades preceding World War I. Sinn Féin, the brainchild of journalist Arthur Griffith, also contributed to the period's vitality.

In 1898 Griffith began to express Sinn Féin ("we-ourselves") self-determination theories in *The United Irishman*. In doing so, he synthesized a variety of sources: his study and interpretation of Hungarian history; the writings of Jonathan Swift, Thomas Davis, and John Mitchel; a strategy that Charles Gavan Duffy proposed to the Irish Confederation; the protectionist economic theories of Friedrich List; and some of O'Connell's ideas and experiments during the Repeal agitation of 1843. Griffith endorsed Gaelic League and GAA efforts to de-Anglicize Ireland. He was a republican, but he did not believe that Irish nationalist opinion shared that conviction, and he was certain that Ireland could not succeed in establishing a republic through revolution. Therefore, Griffith suggested a compromise, a dual monarchy based on the example of Austria and Hungary.

Griffith asked the Irish party to admit that its attempt to win Home Rule at Westminster had failed, and to follow the example of Francis Deak, the Hungarian nationalist who in 1867 refused to recognize the sovereignty of the Austrian legislature. As Duffy recommended in 1847, Griffith advised Irish nationalist MPs to leave Westminster and establish a Dublin parliament. He predicted that it would have the loyalty of local government boards and agencies, and could set up its own justice system modeled on O'Connell's successful experiment with arbitration courts. Faced with a de facto Irish government and a determined passive resistance to their continued rule and occupation, the British would retreat from Ireland, Griffith believed, and would recognize Irish independence. Then the two islands would be joined only in common allegiance to the same monarch. Griffith insisted that since sovereignty had to be economic as well as cultural and political, after independence the Irish government would pass legislation protecting native industries.

Griffith's Sinn Féin vision contained a provincialism and intolerance that flourished in extreme forms of cultural nationalism. He praised the work and the goals of the Gaelic League and the Gaelic Athletic Association, but was suspicious of the Literary Revival. Like John Mitchel before him, Griffith's Irish nationalism contained no empathy for other persecuted people. He was antisemitic and unsympathetic to nonwhite victims of colonialism. Griffith was one of the most malicious attackers of Synge's *Playboy*, sharing the stance of Young Ireland and the Gaelic League that writers and intellectuals must subordinate their genius to the aims of Irish nationalism. He said that literature should help create a sound nationalist opinion, publicize Irish grievances, and justify self-government. In his opinion, when writers presented Irishmen or Irish life as less than ideal, they insulted their country and weakened the national effort. Not too many years later, cultural nationalists abused Sean O'Casey for his Abbey Theatre interpretation of life in Dublin tenements.

Prior to World War I, Sinn Féin was not a serious rival to the parliamentary party. But its program attracted the interest of some intelligent and dynamic young people who had become disenchanted with the style of the party and filled with a desire to do something for Ireland. Sinn Féin also caught the attention of the Irish Republican Brotherhood. At the start of the twentieth century, IRB membership was small, but the quality of the organization exceeded the quantity of its followers. The IRB had active centers in Dublin and British cities and close ties with the Clan na Gael in the United States, and it recruited intelligent and dependable talent. Appreciating the possibilities of cultural nationalism, the IRB infiltrated the Gaelic League and the GAA. Republicans also joined Sinn Féin when it became an official organization in 1905, persuading Griffith to drop dual monarchy as the official objective and to substitute an open policy in regard to the form of government that would follow the end of British rule. Few in numbers but strong in conviction, Irish Republicans were on the move, and by 1914 were in a good position to determine the direction of Irish nationalism if the Irish parliamentary party faltered.

Labor militancy was another example of a slowly changing Irish social, economic, political, and intellectual climate. Early twentieth-century Dublin had more poverty-related problems than any other United Kingdom metropolis, problems that were typical of those in other Irish cities. One-third of the population lived in slum tenements, most unfit for human habitation. Surplus labor meant large-scale unemployment. Employers took advantage of the situation by paying wages far below British standards. Subhuman living conditions, inadequate diets, unemployment, and low wages encouraged alcoholism, prostitution, and other vices, and resulted in a high death rate, with tuberculosis and infant diseases as major killers.

James Larkin, a Liverpool-born Catholic with an Ulster family background, and a socialist with syndicalist leanings, made a valiant effort to give dignity and financial security to the lives of the Irish urban poor. In 1908 he organized the Irish Transport and General Workers Union. Four years later the ITGWU had about ten thousand members representing a wide variety of skills and occupations. Through tough negotiations, an iron will, and the use of strikes, Larkin won a series of major victories, increasing wages and improving working conditions.

In August 1913 the ITGWU struck William Martin Murphy's Dublin United Tramway Company. Murphy, owner of the *Irish Independent* newspaper, the wealthiest man in Ireland with extensive economic interests in Britain and the empire as well as family and ideological connections with the conservative Catholic Tim Healy Home Rule faction, decided to destroy Larkin's influence. He organized an Employers' Federation Limited against the IGTWU. By September 1913, it had locked twenty-five thousand workers out of their jobs. The strike and lockout lasted until January 1914, when finally the employers' combination, the hostility of the Catholic hierarchy, and the reluctance of British trade unions to continue financial support forced strikers back to work, often on stringent anti-union terms. During the strike, pro-capitalist, anti-organized labor Arthur Griffith constantly abused Larkin and the ITGWU in the *United Irishman*, as he had previously lambasted Synge.

After workers were forced to submit to their bosses, Larkin

left for the United States to raise funds for his union's depleted treasury. While there he organized copper workers in Montana, helped found the American Communist party, and, during the Red Scare of the 1920s served three years in Sing Sing prison for his activities and convictions.

The strike offered insights into the character of the Irish Question and added fuel to a growing revolutionary spirit in nationalist Ireland. The decision of the British Trades Union Congress to limit its support of Larkin indicated that national prejudices were stronger than class loyalties. The gulf that divided the British and Irish working classes exposed the lack of understanding that most of the British had for Ireland and the Irish. The failed strike and the indifference of British labor to economic and social injustices in Ireland influenced Irish workers to become more nationalistic and sympathetic to physical force. Many believed that only a revolutionary expulsion of the British would clear the way for a transformation of Irish society.

Shifts in the British political situation fostered dissatisfaction in some Irish circles with the parliamentary party. Following the defeat of the second Home Rule bill, Liberals reconsidered their commitment to Irish nationalism. Many decided that it would be wise to de-emphasize Home Rule as a major or immediate objective. They believed that Joseph Chamberlain Radicals and Whig imperialists who had left the Liberal party over the Irish-Liberal alliance could be persuaded to return by a platform combining social reform and commitment to empire.

Irish attitudes as well as British political considerations alienated post-Gladstone Liberal leaders from Home Rule. Considerable pro-Boer support in Ireland during the South African War (1899-1902) offended chauvinist British public opinion and the imperialist wing of the Liberal party. And the Irish party's decision to take a more independent stance in the Commons also strained relations with Liberals, thus encouraging their retreat from Irish nationalism.

In the 1906 general election Liberals won an overwhelming victory at the polls. Since they had a large majority in the Commons, they did not need Irish party support, and while they did not totally repudiate Home Rule, their policy fell far short of Irish self-government. As a Home Rule substitute, the Liberals in 1907 offered the Irish party a bill that proposed to establish a council in Ireland composed of elected and appointed members, with the lord lieutenant as an ex-officio member. With a generous government grant, the council would have had the power to coordinate and control the efforts of various agencies in Ireland. Henry Campbell-Bannerman, the Liberal prime minister, told Redmond that the Irish council bill would provide Irish nationalists with an opportunity to prove to the British that they were capable of governing themselves, setting the stage for Home Rule. The Irish party chair did not approve of the devolution scheme, but he presented it to an Irish convention that emphatically rejected it as an inadequate response to the self-government demand.

Although the council bill was an affront, Liberals did make two significant concessions to the demands of Irish nationalism. Responding to the Catholic education lobby, in 1908 the government settled the longstanding university controversy by establishing the National University of Ireland, with constituent colleges in Cork, Dublin, and Galway. University College, Cork and University College, Galway were the former Queen's Colleges; University College, Dublin originated in Cullen's Catholic University. Belfast's Queen's University remained as an independent institution. In 1909 the government improved the 1903 Wyndham Land Act, increasing funds for land purchase, sometimes requiring land sale and, in general, speeding the process of peasant proprietorship.

In placing the Irish Question on a back burner, Liberals decided to appease British appeals for radical social reform that had been building since the post-1870 decline in Britain's industrial economy. In 1906 the massive Liberal victory and the election of twenty-nine members of the newly formed Labour party illustrated public anxiety and discontent. Reacting to public opinion and the challenge of socialism, Liberals legislated a program designed to alleviate many of the social security burdens of the working class. It provided old age pensions, health insurance, unemployment compensation, employers' liability, and labor exchanges. This legislation necessitated large expenditures at a time when taxpayers were also financing the expansion and modernization of the British navy to meet the threat of German jingoism and militarism.

Searching for new revenue sources, Lloyd George, chancellor of the Exchequer, borrowed ideas from Fabian socialism. He recommended substantial duties on the unearned income of landed property, higher income taxes for the wealthy, and, to please the

Nonconformist element in his party as well as to raise revenue, increased taxes on liquor and tobacco.

Unionists lacked sufficient numbers in the Commons to halt the advance of the welfare state or to resist the Liberal attack on wealth and property, so they used their majority in the Lords to subvert the government's program. In violation of established tradition that the Commons decides financial matters, the peers capped off a series of vetoes by rejecting Lloyd George's budget, thus precipitating a grave constitutional crisis. Liberal leaders decided to use this rash defiance of election returns and constitutional precedent to abolish the absolute veto of the upper house. Although the budget's heavy duties on liquor injured important brewing and distilling interests in Ireland, the Irish party viewed the Lords as the major barrier to Home Rule, and was more than eager to help the Liberals limit its power. Labour MPs objected to the hereditary House of Lords as a citadel of property and a barrier to a planned and classless society. They joined the Irish in supporting the Liberals in a parliamentary battle for popular sovereignty rather than hereditary prerogatives.

In January 1910 Herbert Asquith the late Campbell-Bannerman's successor as prime minister, took the issues of the budget and the veto to the country. Election returns (275 Liberal, 273 Unionist, 82 Home Rule, and 40 Labour MPs) shattered Liberal complacency. Why did the same electorate that had given Liberals a 224–seat advantage over the Unionists in 1906 reduce that lead to 2 only four years later, especially after the government had provided an extensive program to relieve poverty, and had announced its intention of eliminating the most glaringly undemocratic feature of the constitution? Did many middle-class and rural Liberal voters object to the collectivist character of the government's welfare program and the means of financing it through taxes on property? Did members of the working class resent paying more pennies for their pints and smokes? Did the increased Labour vote and representation in Parliament mean that trade-union leaders considered the government's welfare legislation inadequate? Was the House of Lords more popular with the public than the government suspected? Were Britons apprehensive concerning German naval and military power and the international crises that seemed to push Europe closer to war? In such an emergency did they trust Unionists more than Liberals? There is evidence to indicate that all of the above questions figured in the minds of British voters, but it is also true that the Irish Question played a significant role in the Unionist revival. Although Liberals played down the Home Rule issue in their election addresses, their opponents emphasized that a successful assault on the Lords would be followed by a Liberal effort to dissolve the Union.

In November 1910, after the Lords attempted to avoid catastrophe by passing the budget, Asquith, consulted with the new king, George V, and decided to ask the electorate for a second opinion on the Lords' veto. This time voters returned 272 Unionists to match an equal number of Liberals, and the Asquith ministry found itself deeper in bondage to its Irish and Labour allies, who controlled 84 and 42 seats respectively. More accurately, the Irish party had the allegiance of 75 MPs; 9 others referred to themselves as independent nationalists and followed the leadership of either William O'Brien or Tim Healy.

During the second 1910 election campaign, Home Rule received as much attention as the House of Lords. Speaking in Dublin, Asquith promised that Home Rule would follow a diminished power of the peers. Unionists responded by describing him as Redmond's pawn. They warned British voters that the fate of the United Kingdom and the empire was tied to that of the Lords.

In 1910 British voters unwittingly provided the Irish party with the balance of power. English, Scottish, and Welsh constituencies, voting either Liberal or Labour (and in Liverpool for T.P. O'Connor of the Irish party), gave Home Rule a 315 to 254 majority (18 Unionist MPs came from Ireland, 16 from Ulster, 2 from Trinity College). Still, the Unionist surge in these elections indicates that a large number of Britons retained their fanatic opposition to even a minimal degree of Irish independence.

After considerable prodding from the Irish and Labour benches, the government introduced a bill in February 1911 limiting the power of the Lords to a three-session or two-year suspensive veto over legislation passed by the Commons. When the peers realized that the king, if need be, would honor his pledge to Asquith and pack the Lords with Liberals to secure passage of the Parliament Act, they bowed to the inevitable, clearing the way for Home Rule. In delivering a fatal blow to their old enemy, the Lords, Irish nationalist MPs helped remove a formidable obstacle to the evolution of social and political democracy in Britain.

On April 14, 1912, Asquith introduced the third Home Rule bill. It was a mild federal proposal placing local affairs in the hands of a Dublin parliament consisting of a popularly elected lower house, with a set number of representatives from each of the four Irish provinces, and a senate, nominated in the first instance by the Crown and subsequently by the Irish executive. To protect its imperial interests, Ireland would retain a small delegation at Westminster. The bill restricted the Irish parliament from legislating on questions involving finance, foreign affairs, religion, and police powers. It guaranteed Protestant rights in a number of ways: Ulster would be overrepresented in the lower house of the Irish parliament, the appointed senate would contain many Protestants, and the Dublin government could not endow or show favoritism to any religion.

Redmond, with the clear support of Irish nationalist opinion, accepted Asquith's moderate Home Rule offer as a settlement of Irish claims to legislative independence. Even Sinn Féin moderated its criticism of the parliamentary party, and for a time a truce existed between various factions within Irish nationalism. Anglo-Irish Protestants and Ulster Presbyterians, however, were opposed to Home Rule, and they would be the decisive factor in determining its Westminster fortunes.

During the eighteenth century, Protestants and Presbyterians were the vanguard of Irish patriotism. Their volunteer army forced Britain in the 1780s to concede free trade and a significant extension of Irish parliamentary sovereignty. In the 1790s they created the Society of United Irishmen, which spearheaded the insurrections of 1798. During the parliamentary and national debates over the Act of Union, many, probably most, Anglo-Irish Protestants and Ulster Presbyterians opposed the British connection. For quite a few the motive was more sectarian than patriotic. They feared that a United Kingdom parliament would be more responsive to Catholic claims of equality than the Protestant parliament in Dublin. But there were others, such as Henry Grattan, who sincerely believed that the Irish could solve their problems without British intervention, and that Catholics as well as Protestants should be part of an Irish nation-state.

Following the Act of Union, Anglo-Irish Protestant and Ulster Presbyterian patriotisms gradually faded into insignificance as a British replaced an Irish identity. When linen factories and shipyards began to flourish in northeast Ulster, that part of the province became an extension of the British industrial complex. Non-Catholics in the north treasured the economic advantages of the Union, and their organization, the anti-Catholic Orange Order, once an opponent of the British connection, emerged as its staunchest defender.

With the rise of Irish-Catholic nationalism, an outgrowth of the Emancipation agitation, Protestants and Nonconformists decided that only the British tie could save their religious, political, and property rights from the ambitions of a Catholic peasant democracy. Throughout the nineteenth and into the twentieth century, they functioned as the British garrison in Ireland. Tory governments rewarded them by guaranteeing their monopoly on economic, political, and social power, and by protecting the privileged position of the established church. British Conservatives manipulated Irish Protestants, Presbyterians (even more anti-Catholic than members of the Church of Ireland), and other Nonconformists as pawns in resisting concessions to Irish nationalism. Lord Randolph Churchill encouraged British Unionists to "play the Orange Card" in opposing Home Rule.

Theoretically, Irish nationalism, both constitutional and physical force factions, rejected sectarianism and insisted on an inclusive Irish identity. Rejecting faith and fatherland notions, most Catholics had no hesitation in accepting Protestant nationalist leaders such as Butt, Parnell, and Hyde. But since the seventeenth century, except for the relatively brief period of eighteenth-century Protestant patriotism, religious and national identities have been inseparable in the Irish historical experience. The association between the two was much more a Protestant and Nonconformist than a Catholic decision. But Irish and British Protestant and Nonconformist resistance to Emancipation and Peel's effort to reconcile Catholics to the Union through concessions increased Catholic awareness that their religion and nationality were linked in the eyes of their enemies. Cullen's "Devotional Revolution," with its strong anti-Protestant tone, and its insistence that Catholicism was the key to a true Irish identity, also widened the Irish sectarian gulf.

Defensive no-popery unionism and Cullen's militant Catholicism made it difficult, if not impossible, for Catholics and non-Catholics to cooperate in efforts to promote the progress of their common country. Protestants and Nonconformists subordinated the general welfare of Ireland and, in the case of farmers and urban laborers, class interests to sectarian solidarity, leaving the landed aristocracy and big businessmen in charge of Irish unionist opinion. Of course there were exceptions. Thomas Davis, Sharman Crawford, Isaac Butt, Charles

Stewart Parnell, William Butler Yeats, and Douglas Hyde demonstrate that not all Protestants were motivated by narrow religious and economic interests.

Despite Protestant and Presbyterian efforts to resist the pressures of Irish-Catholic nationalism, Whig, Liberal, and even Unionist attempts to pacify Ireland gradually undermined Protestant Ascendancy, and transferred ownership of land to the peasantry and control of local government in Leinster, Munster, Connacht, and parts of Ulster to Catholics. Each government concession to Irish nationalism strengthened the Irish Protestant and Nonconformist conviction that only the Union could protect their minority rights.

Irish nationalist orthodoxy rejected the idea that Ulster non-Catholics constituted a separate cultural nation. They argued that divisions between north and south, Catholics, Protestants, and Presbyterians, unionists and nationalists were products of British engineering to prevent an independent, united Ireland. Only a few men such as Arthur Clery, professor of property law at the National University, and Walter McDonald, professor of theology at Maynooth, argued that the same logic that justified Home Rule for Catholic Ireland also applied to Protestant and Nonconformist Ulster. Clery suggested a partition strictly in conformity to religious cultures that would have resulted in less than a four-county unionist north.

After John Redmond announced Irish nationalist acceptance of Asquith's offer, Irish Unionist leaders Sir Edward Carson and Sir James Craig made it clear that since the Lords' veto no longer stood in the way of Home Rule, they were prepared to preserve the Union with physical force. They rejected the Home Rule bill as detrimental to the interests of Irish non-Catholics, and said that they would not consent to any legislation that severed the religious, economic, cultural, and patriotic ties that bound them to Britain or forced their submission to a Dublin parliament dominated by Anglophobe papists determined to discriminate against a helpless religious minority.

Carson and Craig demonstrated that they were not bluffing. In September 1912 they led Ulster Protestants and Nonconformists in signing a Solemn League and Covenant binding Irish unionists to resist Home Rule with every means at their disposal. Soon an Ulster Volunteer Army began drilling under the command of Lieutenant General George Richardson, KCB, and on September 23, 1913,

Ulster unionists announced plans for a Carson-headed provisional government to go into effect the day the Home Rule bill became law.

Instead of repudiating this threat of armed resistance to an act of Parliament, Andrew Bonar Law, leader of the opposition, and other British Conservatives MPs gave an unqualified endorsement to Carson's attack on constitutional government. They promised considerable British support for any Irish loyalist effort to defeat Home Rule and Irish nationalism. In British conservative circles, treason became fashionable. Conservative newspapers and periodicals, especially Irish nationalism's old nemesis, the *Times* of London, fervently endorsed Ulster's defiance of the constitution; so did the popular poet, Rudyard Kipling. A.V. Dicey, Oxford's distinguished professor of constitutional law, provided an academic apologia for Ulster unionist threats of civil war. Waldorf Astor and Lord Rothschild contributed large sums of money to the Ulster Volunteers. Bonar Law and many other British Conservatives in the Unionist fold hoped that they could manipulate the Ulster crisis into another general election. Balfour, the former prime minister, represented a Conservative faction not emotionally attached to Ulster loyalists but prepared to "play the Orange card" to preserve the Union by defeating the Irish-Liberal alliance.

From 1912 through 1914, as Home Rule made its stormy way through Parliament, events in Britain and Ireland confirmed fears that the government could not enforce Home Rule in northeast Ulster without risking civil disorder. Ulster Volunteers continued to increase in numbers and improve in warlike efficiency. A successful April 1914 gunrunning operation supplied them with rifles and ammunition. Asquith's administration feared the possibility that army officers would refuse to move against Ulster rebels.

Under the existing military system, most officers came from the same social background that provided Unionist party leadership and shared the opinions and prejudices of their class. Under the British system of government, however, the army is theoretically nonpolitical, and is expected to carry out government orders without questioning their validity. In designating suppression of rebellion in Ulster as an exception to this obligation, British military officers permitted themselves a luxury denied enlisted personnel. Labour MPs and Irish and British labor leaders complained that if the government used enlisted men from the working class as strike breakers, officers should not be exempted from enforcing laws offensive to their class sympathies.

During this period many in the upper echelons of the military establishment conspired to defeat the parliamentary process. Lord Roberts, chief of staff, recommended Richardson to Carson as commander-in-chief of the Ulster Volunteers and later congratulated the Irish unionist leader on the success of the gunrunning operation. Sir Henry Wilson, Ulster Protestant director of military operations, advised Carson and Craig to persist in their opposition to Home Rule. And he consulted with Bonar Law on ways in which Unionist MPs could amend the Army Appropriation Bill to prevent the use of military force against the Ulster Volunteers. Prominent Conservative politicians and army leaders were encouraging rebellion in the army at a time when it appeared that a major war might break out on the Continent, a war that would probably involve Britain since it was heavily committed to France. The unreliable state of the army was made clear to all in March 1914, when officers stationed at the Curragh, County Kildare, announced that they would resign their commissions rather than lead troops against the Ulster Volunteers. Because Asquith was reluctant to weaken Britain's military strength in a period of international tensions, the officers escaped punishment.

While pro-Home Rule British opinion was lukewarm, anti-Catholic, anti-Home Rule British opinion was fanatic. Public meetings, newspaper and periodical editorials, sermons from Church of England and Ireland and Nonconformist pulpits, petitions to Parliament, and a pattern of Unionist by-election victories indicated that many Britons were willing to support Ulster resistance, even to the point of civil war.

Confronted by potential armed rebellion in Ulster, "treason" in the army, pro-Unionist, anti-Catholic opinion in Britain, and waning Liberal strength in the Commons, Cabinet members such as Winston Churchill and Lloyd George recommended concessions to Ulster. As early as 1913, they suggested that non-Catholic sections of the province be excluded from the Home Rule settlement. And by 1914, Asquith openly admitted that partition was the only feasible alternative to civil war. Churchill commented: "Orange bitters and Irish whiskey will not mix." Two questions remained: how much of Ulster would remain outside the jurisdiction of the Irish Parliament, and for how long?

Asquith obtained Redmond's consent to a six-year, post-pleb-iscite exclusion for any Ulster county (presumably Armagh, Antrim, Derry, and Down) indicating a preference to maintain the British connection. In theory, this amounted to a temporary compromise between the nationalist and unionist positions. In reality, most likely it would mean permanent partition and a major concession, if not a surrender, by Redmond. Before six years passed there would be at least two general elections, and political trends indicated a Unionist victory at the polls in 1915. A Unionist majority in the Commons could and no doubt would then permanently exclude the four Ulster counties from the jurisdiction of the Irish parliament.

Hoping to kill Home Rule for any part of Ireland, Carson, a Dubliner, stubbornly demanded permanent exclusion from the be-ginning for all nine Ulster counties, an outrageous claim since at the last election the province had sent a seventeen-to-sixteen nationalist majority to Westminster, and Catholics outnumbered Protestants in five of the nine counties as well as the cities of Derry and Newry. At the king's request, negotiations on the principle of exclusion of at least part of Ulster took place at Buckingham palace in July 1914. Since Carson and Redmond could not agree on time limits and boundaries, the conference concluded without a settlement. Asquith could go no further in his effort to appease Ulster without encourag-ing a dangerous reaction in nationalist Ireland.

By late 1913, as they observed Ulster loyalist defiance and military preparations, the pro-unionist stance of prominent military figures, anti-Irish Catholic rallies in Britain, a series of Liberal by-election defeats, and Asquith's willingness to partition their country, Irish nationalists became apprehensive and restless. They worried that although Home Rulers had played and won the parliamentary game, the British were going to change the rules and deny victory to the Irish party. Perhaps, some decided, nationalist Ireland should imitate unionist Ulster by physically demonstrating to Britain that it would not be denied self-government.

During the 1913 ITGWU strike and subsequent lock-out, James Connolly, Larkin's colleague, created a small Citizen Army to protect workers from police brutality. In the autumn of 1913, a committee representing Home Rule, Sinn Féin, and republicanism formed an Irish Volunteer Army in Dublin. The IRB played an important role in creating and administering the organization, but

Eoin MacNeill, chair of the Volunteer council, never really understood the importance of its minority IRB faction.

MacNeill and most of his colleagues had no intention of
initiating a war of independence, but they were determined to
defend Ireland's right to Home Rule against the unconstitutional
intimidation of Ulster and British unionists. While most Irish Volunteers hoped that they would win legislative independence without
disturbing the peace by strengthening Liberal resolve, the IRB
element wanted more than Home Rule and an opportunity to prove
their love of country in battle.

Initially, Redmond considered the Volunteers a nuisance and
a threat to constitutional nationalism, but when he finally realized
that Asquith might compromise Home Rule to appease Carson and
anti-Irish British opinion, he changed his mind. In July 1913, by
threatening to form a rival organization, Redmond persuaded Volunteer leaders to permit the Irish party to nominate half of their
executive committee. In January 1914 the Irish Volunteers had only
ten thousand or so recruits, but Redmond's patronage increased
enlistments to over fifteen thousand a week and multiplied Irish-
American donations. The United Irish League of America promised
him that the Volunteers would have all the money they needed to
defend Home Rule.

In the early summer of 1914 Asquith faced an inescapable
dilemma. Home Rule had to be carried in some form or the Liberals
would forfeit the Irish alliance and control of government. A Home
Rule settlement that did not guarantee a permanent partition of
Ireland would provoke insurrection in Ulster; one that did would
encourage rebellion in nationalist Ireland. In either case, civil war
would engulf Britain and Ireland. Asquith did have two other alternatives: he could call another general election (though all the signs
indicated that the results would still keep him a prisoner of the Irish
and Labour parties), or he could resign and surrender office to the
Unionists. Since Bonar Law could not command a Commons majority, he would not be able to govern without the cooperation of Asquith
and other moderate Liberals. A national coalition might have been
able to steer Britain through the Home Rule crisis, but it would have
alienated not only Irish but also Labour MPs and some of their own
party from the Liberals. By the summer of 1914 parliamentary
government was not functioning, and politicians found themselves
at the mercy of forces not responsible to the House of Commons.

Since nationalists and unionists could not agree on partition, Asquith decided to proceed with the original plan for a six-year exclusion of the four northeast counties. He reasoned that six years would demonstrate the success or failure of Home Rule for the rest of Ireland and, in the meantime, voters would have at least one and probably two opportunities to express their wishes on an all-Ireland parliament. Liberal peers presented Asquith's proposal as an amending bill in the Lords, but the Unionist majority modified it to include all of Ulster on a permanent basis, and sent it to the Commons.

Asquith scheduled a debate for July 27 on the amending bill. With Redmond's approval, he attempted to please Carson and British Unionists by eliminating the six-year time limit. Bloodshed in Dublin postponed the debate. On Sunday, July 26, a company of Irish Volunteers unloaded a cargo of arms from a yacht near Howth, north of Dublin. The anti-Redmond faction in the Volunteers had purchased the guns in Hamburg without his knowledge. The assistant commissioner of police and a battalion of the King's Own Scottish Borderers blocked the Volunteers' return to Dublin, demanding a surrender of weapons. While the front ranks of the Volunteers held off soldiers with rifle butts, those in the rear drifted away with their guns. Frustrated Borderers returned to the city in a touchy mood. As they marched down Bachelor's Walk, a sidewalk crowd shouted insults, and some of its members threw stones. Suddenly, a few Borderers lost control and fired into the crowd, killing three, wounding thirty-six.

The next day in the Commons, Redmond asked for a delay on the amending bill debate so that the government could investigate the Bachelor's Walk incident. In his speech, he wondered why the Ulster Volunteers could publicly display their smuggled arms, while military force was employed against the Irish Volunteers? It was an excellent question, and the government could not provide a satisfactory answer. Instead, as usually happens in these cases, the politicians found scapegoats. Because David Harrel, the assistant commissioner of the Dublin police, admitted that sending soldiers to disarm the Irish Volunteers was illegal, a judicial committee of inquiry censured him and the commanding officer of the Borderers.

The delay in the amending bill debate and Austria's declaration of war on Serbia, which were followed by massive mobilization by all the great powers and Germany's declarations of war on Russia and France, turned the attention of the Commons and the British public away from Ireland toward the Continent. When the foreign secretary, Sir Edward Grey, informed Parliament on August 3 that Germany's threat to Belgian neutrality and Britain's commitments to France made probable a war against the Central Powers, John Redmond, with patriotic enthusiasm, announced that nationalists in the south would join unionists in the north to defend their country. British MPs cheered the leader of Irish nationalism, the successor to O'Connell and Parnell, as a patriotic defender of British interests, which in 1914 he sincerely believed represented freedom and civilization.

When Britain joined France and Russia against Germany and Austria-Hungary, Asquith, to win approval of and support for the war effort from both nationalist and unionist Irelands, pushed Home Rule through Parliament, but suspended its operation for the duration of hostilities. Then, he said, the government would take up the Ulster issue. World War I might have saved Britain from the devastation of civil war but at a terrible cost. Neither British nor Irish party politicians realized that the 1912–14 Home Rule crisis so altered Irish nationalism that the final solution to the Irish Question would not be achieved in the British Parliament. Carson's effort to preserve the Union through physical-force intimidation, British Conservative support for Ulster loyalist fanaticism, and British Liberal weakness in the face of Conservative-backed Ulster defiance created a mistrust of British integrity in nationalist Ireland and an atmosphere of violence that would reignite revolutionary Irish republicanism, destroy the United Kingdom, and partition Ireland. Bullets, grenades, and world opinion, not Irish or British ballots, would decide Ireland's future.

7

The Rose Tree
1914–1922

*There's nothing but our own red blood
Can Make a right Rose Tree.*

William Butler Yeats
"The Rose Tree"

John Redmond believed that Ireland's participation in a moral crusade against German authoritarianism and militarism and in defense of the integrity of small nations such as Belgium would convince Britain that it deserved Home Rule and demonstrate its will and capacity for self-government. Redmond urged Irish Volunteers to enlist in the British army, but Sinn Féiners perceived the conflict between Britain and Germany as a power struggle for empire and not a contest between good and evil. They pointed out that it was Britain not Germany that conquered, occupied, and oppressed Ireland. And they told Irishmen to stay home and prepare to fight for Ireland's cultural and political sovereignty.

In August 1914 only 12,000 of the 180,000 Irish Volunteers rejected Redmond's view of the war. Those that accepted it took the name National Volunteers, and many enlisted in the British army. Eoin MacNeill, professor of early Irish history at University College, Dublin, remained chief of staff of the minority Irish Volunteers. He continued to be unaware of the strong IRB influence in the organization.

MacNeill intended the Irish Volunteers as a defensive rather than an offensive force, a reminder to Britain that Ireland was determined to have Home Rule. But shortly after the start of hostilities on the Continent, the Supreme Council of the IRB decided that it should take advantage of Britain's preoccupation with the war, and created a Military Council to plan a rebellion. IRB leaders reasoned that even if an insurrection failed, there was a good chance that it would earn Ireland a voice in postwar peace talks. Patrick Pearse, IRB director of organizations, barrister by training, poet by inclination, and master of St. Enda's, a school teaching all subjects in Irish, was the link between the Military Council and the Irish Volunteers.

The Clan na Gael joined the revolutionary scheming. John Devoy received a commitment from the German ambassador in Washington that his government would aid a rebellion in Ireland. Sir Roger Casement, reared in a strict Ulster Presbyterian setting, also entered the conspiracy. Before converting to Irish nationalism, Casement, as a member of the British foreign service, earned a knighthood for exposing the brutal treatment of natives in the Congo and South America. He was in the United States when the world war began, but he left for Germany to obtain material support for a rising and to recruit Irish prisoners of war for a brigade to fight the British. Germans did not take Casement seriously, and only a few Irish POWs joined the brigade. Other IRB envoys made more of an impression in Berlin and were able to obtain solid guarantees of guns and ammunition.

Pearse and two other poets in the IRB, Joseph Mary Plunkett and Thomas MacDonagh, did not consider victory the ultimate purpose or objective of the coming rebellion. In their poetry they spoke of Ireland's need for a blood sacrifice to redeem Irish nationalism from the apathy, compromise ethic, and West Britonism of Home Rule politics. They promised that if brave young men shed their blood and sacrificed their lives for Irish freedom, the fire of nationalism, dampened into embers by parliamentarianism, would blaze again. They said that the first martyrs would inspire others to complete their mission and eventually drive the British out of the country, liberating it from the cultural and political corruptions of Anglicization.

After James Larkin left for the United States in October 1914, James Connolly, an Irish-Catholic socialist sympathetic to syndicalist tactics, took command of the Irish Transport and General Workers Union and its small, 200–member, well-disciplined Citizen Army. Independent of the IRB Military Council, he also was planning a rebellion. At first, blood sacrifice did not inspire Connolly's revolutionary purpose. He was confident of success, convinced that a Dublin-commenced rebellion would spread throughout the country and that the British, caught by surprise, tied down on the Western

Front and reluctant to destroy property in Ireland, would evacuate their oldest colony, leading to an Irish socialist republic.

In the first year of the Great War, most Irish nationalists remained loyal to Redmond, Home Rule, and the Irish party, and enthusiastically supported Britain against the Central Powers. But events in 1915 began the process of disenchantment. Lord Kitchener, secretary for war, did much to undermine the Irish party and its leader. Hostile to Irish-Catholic nationalism, he refused to woo its support for the war effort. While permitting Ulster Volunteers to enlist as a separate division with their own officers and emblem, the Red Hand of Ulster, Kitchener would not let the National Volunteers join as a unit with their own Catholic officers and insignia, the gold harp on a green field. For the most part, Anglo-Irish and British Protestants commanded Irish Catholics fighting on the war's various battlefields. Kitchener's calculated insult to Catholic Ireland curtailed enlistments in Leinster, Munster, and Connacht. Heavy Irish casualties in the 1915–16 Gallipoli campaign increased antiwar feelings, and also discouraged Catholic Irishmen from joining the British armed forces.

Heavy casualties on the Western Front and at Gallipoli and the prospects of a long, bloody war dampened spirits in Britain as well as Ireland. In order to raise morale and cement national unity, Asquith invited Unionists and Irish party leaders to participate in a coalition government in 1915. Loyal to nationalist principles, Redmond refused to participate in a British administration, but Carson, Bonar Law, and F.E. Smith (later Lord Birkenhead)—old and fanatic enemies of Home Rule—did join the government. Since the situation did not augur well for the postwar future of Home Rule, Irish nationalists responded negatively to an Orange-tainted British government.

Irish Volunteers and the Citizen Army drilled in the mountains and held public reviews in city streets. Sinn Féin and the IRB organized anti-recruiting campaigns; their newspapers preached Irish-nationalist neutrality in the conflict between the Allies and the Central Powers. To avoid a repetition of the July 1914 Bachelor's Walk incident, British authorities in Dublin Castle permitted the drilling and parading, but jailed or deported some Sinn Féiners and republicans, and closed down what they considered extremist nationalist newspapers. Most reappeared under new names.

Without informing the Supreme Council, the IRB's Military

Council finally selected a date for revolution, Easter Sunday (April 23), 1916. Considering that blood sacrifice ideology melded revolutionary theory with symbols of Christian redemptive theology, the choice of Easter Sunday for the resurrection of Ireland, after the long passion of British conquest and occupation, was no coincidence. Pearse and his associates persuaded Connolly to join the Military Council, and the Germans promised to land guns and ammunition during Holy Week on Ireland's southern coast. Pearse then persuaded MacNeill to call for a general review of all Volunteer units with full military equipment on Easter Sunday; he did not inform MacNeill that the general review would turn into a rebellion. Plunkett helped forge a British government document indicating that the authorities were preparing to raid the headquarters of the Irish Volunteers, the Citizen Army, Sinn Féin, and the Gaelic League, and to arrest their leaders. The Military Council used this document, which may have represented British intentions, to psychologically prepare MacNeill and the Volunteers for a defensive war without revealing its total strategy for Easter Sunday.

On Holy Thursday, Bulmer Hobson, an Ulster Quaker, a former member of the IRB's Supreme Council, a strong supporter of the Gaelic language movement, and a founding member of the Irish Volunteers, discovered the Military Council's plan for an Easter rebellion and told MacNeill. They agreed that blood sacrifice would be a futile gesture endangering the prospects of self-government. MacNeill continued to insist that the Volunteers existed as a defensive force exhibiting Ireland's determination to be free, and that it could only be used as an army of liberation if Britain reneged on its pledge of Home Rule. He also said that initiating a rebellion without a chance of success was an "immoral" waste of life. Hobson complained that the Military Council was violating the IRB's 1873 convention decision that insisted on prior majority support from the Irish people for any rebellion. He described Pearse and his friends as a cabal unrepresentative of either the IRB or Irish nationalism.

To prevent Hobson's strong persuasive powers from stopping Easter arrangements, Sean MacDermott, a member of the Military Council, pulled a gun on his old friend and had him detained until the rebellion began. After Pearse told him that German equipment was on the way, MacNeill decided it was too late to prevent the rising and turned control of the Volunteers over to the Military Council.

Rebellion plans began to unravel on Good Friday morning

when constables arrested Casement in Kerry after he came ashore from a German submarine with the intention of telling nationalists to call off the ill-fated rebellion. That afternoon, when a German ship, the *Aud*, arrived off the Kerry coast, no Volunteers appeared to unload her cargo. While she waited, British warships intercepted the vessel, and the captain scuttled her, sending obsolete Russian rifles and ammunition, captured on the Eastern Front, to the bottom of the sea. When the news of these disasters reached Dublin on Holy Saturday, MacNeill, convinced that the rebellion would fail, canceled Volunteer orders to mobilize and march on Easter Sunday.

Although he knew that few Volunteers would be available, Pearse decided to proceed with the rising, his mind fixed on blood sacrifice. He hoped that events in Dublin would inspire the rest of the country to take up arms. Connolly also was determined to lead the Citizen Army into action. Pearse seems to have convinced him that a few must offer their lives to redeem the many. Accepting a redemptive theological-ideological justification for the rising, Connolly wrote: "Without the shedding of blood there is no redemption." But he still entertained a small, naive hope that a capitalist British government would not destroy private property in order to subdue Irish rebels.

On Easter Monday a force of 1,528 rebels, 27 of them women auxiliaries, marched through the streets of Dublin, and seized the General Post Office and other strategic buildings. Rebels lowered the Union Jack from the post office flagpole and in its place hoisted a tricolor: green for the Catholic tradition, orange for the Protestant, and white for the theoretical bond of love between them. From the post office balcony Pearse read a document:

POBLACHT NA h-EIREANN
THE PROVISIONAL GOVERNMENT
OF THE
IRISH REPUBLIC
TO THE PEOPLE OF IRELAND

It proclaimed the "Irish Republic as a Sovereign Independent State." In addition to blood sacrifice and Gaelic cultural nationalism, the proclamation articulated an inclusive view of Irish nationalism, a commitment to liberal democratic values, and some of Connolly's socialist ideals. In part, the document read: "We declare the right of the people of Ireland to the ownership of Ireland and to the unfettered control of Irish destinies, to be sovereign and indefeasible." The document went on to say that "the Republic guarantees religious and civil liberty, equal rights and equal opportunities to all its citizens, and declares its resolve to pursue the happiness and prosperity of the whole nation and all of its parts, cherishing all the children of the nation equally, and oblivious of the differences carefully fostered by an alien government, which have divided a minority from the majority in the past." Copies of Pearse's statement were posted throughout Dublin.

From Monday until they surrendered on Saturday, the rebels held off the police and the army, quickly reenforced from Britain. Vicious and intense fighting claimed many casualties: 508 people were killed (300 civilians, 132 soldiers and policemen, and 76 members of the Volunteer and Citizen Armies); 2,520 were wounded (2,000 civilians, 400 soldiers and policemen, and 120 rebels). Connolly was wrong: "Britannia's sons with their long range guns" bombarded the city and by fire and shell destroyed many buildings, turning much of Dublin's main thoroughfare, Sackville (now O'Connell) Street, into rubble.

Easter Week did not inspire many Irish people to join the fight for freedom. While rebels bravely but hopelessly engaged the British army and the Dublin Metropolitan Police, many Dubliners took advantage of the chaos to loot shops, and at Westminster Redmond condemned the rising as a German plot involving a fanatic and misguided small minority. "Respectable" Irish opinion considered Pearse's Volunteers and the Citizen Army as "hooligans" and dirty traitors. Since many Irish nationalists had husbands, sweethearts, brothers, sons, and friends fighting in France, they condemned what they first interpreted as a "stab in the back." When British soldiers marched rebel prisoners to jail, people lining the way cursed, jeered, and spat at them.

Engaged in a life-or-death struggle with Germany, Britain reacted in anger and vengeance against "treason" in Dublin. The government's decision to mercilessly punish Irish rebels turned out to be a dreadful mistake. Over a period of ten days, military tribunals tried and executed fourteen rebel leaders, including Pearse, Connolly, Plunkett, MacDonagh, and other signers of the Easter Monday proclamation. (The British tried and executed another rebel in Cork, and later did the same to Casement in Britain.) Although he was badly wounded in the post office, soldiers strapped Connolly to a chair and shot him. The authorities imprisoned more than two thousand Sinn Féiners and republicans, many without trials.

Easter Week 1916 transformed Irish nationalism, steering it away from constitutionalism in the direction of physical force. The republic, the bullet, and the grenade replaced Home Rule, the ballot box, and parliamentary debates as the goal and route of Irish nationalism. Executions of "traitors" in time of war is common, but the court-martials and firing-squad executions made it clear that Britain had substituted sadistic revenge and terror for justice. And the imprisonment of so many men, without normal legal procedures, seemed cruel and arbitrary. Within a few weeks the "dirty traitors" of Easter Week became gallant martyrs and national heroes. Irish homes displayed their pictures, and Irish people bought, read, and quoted their speeches and poems. The British made Pearse's case: blood sacrifice did convert nationalist apathy into passion. As Yeats wrote shortly after the rising, "A terrible beauty is born."

Irish nationalism's changing mood compelled Westminster politicians to reassess their Irish policy. In 1916 they were trying to persuade the United States to enter the war on Britain's side, but Irish America, a powerful force in the ruling Democratic party, allied with German America, insisted on neutrality. Asquith assigned Lloyd George, who soon replaced him as prime minister, the task of pacifying Ireland. Lloyd George decided on an immediate application of the third Home Rule bill with the exclusion of six Ulster counties until a postwar Parliament could determine the extent and duration of partition. Unionists objected to the plan because it did not insure that the six counties would always remain British, and Redmond withdrew his blessing when he became convinced that Lloyd George intended a permanently divided Ireland.

When immediate Home Rule proved politically inexpedient, the government attempted to cool the Irish situation by releasing republican prisoners. One of the returnees was Eamon de Valera, a mathematics teacher who had commanded Volunteers in Boland's flour mill, blocking the route of British reinforcements marching from Kingstown to central Dublin. His unit was the last to surrender. A military tribunal had sentenced him to death, but British and Irish reactions against further executions and de Valera's technical American citizenship (he was born in New York) saved his life. As the only surviving Easter Week commandant, de Valera returned to Ireland a hero, the popularly recognized leader of republican nationalism. With other released republicans, he set out to reorganize the Volunteers and to challenge the Irish party. Before the end of the war, under a Sinn Féin label, they won seven by-elections, and then refused to take their seats at Westminster.

When the United States entered the war in the spring of 1917, President Woodrow Wilson, a strong Anglophile with an Ulster Presbyterian heritage, hostile to Irish-American ethnicity but aware of its power in the urban wing of the Democratic party, told the British that enlisting maximum American energy and enthusiasm behind the Allies would be difficult as long as the Irish Question remained unresolved. To satisfy Wilson, and to revive Irish support for the war, Lloyd George, now prime minister, decided at Redmond's suggestion to approve an Irish Convention representing all shades of opinion—Sinn Féin, Home Rule, and unionist—to work out an acceptable Home Rule proposal.

Sinn Féin rejected Redmond's invitation, but southern unionists attending the Convention were prepared to cooperate in an effort to create a limited Irish legislature. Ulster unionists, however, encouraged by their British colleagues, disrupted unity efforts. Redmond was so generous in his willingness to make concessions to Irish Protestants that he antagonized some important Catholic nationalists, including members of the church hierarchy. The Convention held its first session in July 1917 and concluded in an April 1918 stalemate. A month before the Convention adjourned, Redmond died of complications following a routine gallstone operation. Exhaustion and disillusionment contributed to his death.

By late 1917 the war on the Western Front was going badly for Britain and France, and the future looked bleak. Brutal trench warfare had taken the lives or wounded millions of soldiers, creating a serious troop shortage. Reacting against unrestricted German submarine warfare, the United States had entered the war in April, but the British and French calculated that it would take a considerable length of time for Americans to mobilize their manpower and resources. Meanwhile, with the Bolsheviks in Russia ready to make peace, Germany could concentrate its total army on the Western Front. Desperate for canon fodder, in April 1918 Parliament authorized Lloyd George to draft Irishmen into the British army. Immediately, the Irish party left the Commons and joined Sinn Féin,

Catholic bishops and priests, and trade unions in a common front against conscription.

Negative Irish reactions to a draft strengthened republicanism, hastened Volunteer reorganization, and goaded Britain into a strict coercion policy. Authorities deported many Sinn Féiners, and sent others, including de Valera, to prison, but, due to the unexpectedly quick American impact, the war concluded before Britain applied conscription to Ireland.

The December 1918 post-Armistice general election resulted in victories for the Coalition government in Britain and for Sinn Féin in Ireland. Republicans won seventy-three seats to six for the Irish party and twenty-six for the Unionists. But these figures exaggerate the republicanism of Irish nationalism. Because of Sinn Féin intimidation, Home Rulers did not contest a number of constituencies. In those that they did challenge, only 69 percent of the eligible voters cast ballots, and just 47 percent of them voted Sinn Féin. By extending the suffrage to men over twenty-one and women over thirty, the 1918 Representation of the People Act increased the Irish franchise from 701,475 in 1910 to 1,936,673. Since 1918 election results showed an actual gain in votes for the Irish party in contested constituencies, it seems that older voters tended to stay with Home Rule while republicanism captivated younger electors. But election contests were not clearcut generational clashes. Many of the local branch leaders of the United Irish League, the Irish party's constituency base, switched over to Sinn Féin when it became evident after 1916 that republicanism was the political wave of the future. Their skills and experience were valuable assets in Sinn Féin's development.

Refusing to sit at Westminster, Sinn Féin MPs met in Dublin and established an Irish parliament, Dáil Eireann, which attempted to govern in the name of the Irish Republic. It created arbitration courts to supersede the British legal system, a board to settle industrial disputes, and a land bank to make loans to people wishing to purchase farms; it also sent delegates to the Versailles Peace Conference to plead the case for Ireland's independence. Refusing to antagonize his British ally, the great apostle of national self-determination, Woodrow Wilson, ignored Irish delegates. This snub offended Irish America, costing the president support for his League of Nations and for his party in the 1920 election.

In February 1919 Michael Collins, who did most to revive the Volunteers, and his close friend, Harry Boland, another member of the Sinn Féin executive, engineered de Valera's escape from Lincoln Gaol in England. After his return to Ireland, the Dáil elected de Valera its president in April. In June he left for the United States to raise money for the Republic, remaining there until December 1920, collecting a considerable sum but dividing Irish America in a feud with Devoy and another powerful Clan na Gaeler, Judge Daniel Cohalan. The quarrel was largely a conflict of personalities, but it also involved different views of Irish nationalism. Like many Irish Americans, Devoy and Cohalan were more fanatically anti-British than the Irish in Ireland. They considered de Valera's suggestion that Ireland would accept a Monroe Doctrine for the British Isles in order to appease British security anxieties a contradiction of Irish sovereignty.

While de Valera was in the United States, Arthur Griffith served as acting president of the Dáil. Collins was in charge of finances, but he retained his rank and duties as adjutant general and director of organization for the Volunteers; Cathal Brugha was minister of defense and Volunteer chief of staff. There was friction between Brugha and Collins; perhaps the former was jealous of the latter. Collins' brilliant intelligence network, his daring escapes, and his dashing personality made him a popular hero and overshadowed the more pedestrian efforts of Brugha.

In January 1919 Sinn Féin's passive resistance to British rule evolved into a shooting war, forcing Britain to strengthen the Royal Irish Constabulary, the main target for rebel attacks, and to increase the size of the army serving in Ireland. In March 1920 the British government began recruiting ex-servicemen in England and sending them to Ireland to supplement the beleaguered RIC. Because of a uniform shortage, they wore dark green caps with khaki shirts and pants. Because of this color combination, Irish nationalists referred to them as the Black and Tans or just Tans. Later in 1920, Britain recruited former army officers to serve as a special RIC auxiliary force.

During the Anglo-Irish War, the Irish Republican Army (the new name of the Volunteers) adopted guerrilla tactics. Men in civilian clothing ambushed lorries, assassinated "spies" and "informers," attacked and burned RIC barracks, shot soldiers, policemen, Tans, and Auxiliaries, then quickly melded into the civilian population, which sheltered and refused to inform on them. British officials described IRA guerrilla tactics as murder, but they were the only practical way for a small nation limited in resources and population to fight a war of liberation against a world power.

Court-martial tribunals tried captured republicans. Frequently torture was used to try to elicit confessions and information. British security forces met terror with terror in a policy of reprisals. They burned, looted, and occasionally murdered. To focus international attention on Ireland's struggle for freedom, some rebel prisoners went on hunger strike. Terence MacSwiney, lord mayor of Cork, died of starvation in England's Brixton prison on October 25, 1920. At his mayoral inauguration ceremony, he had articulated the theme and purpose of Irish martyrdom: "It is not those who inflict the most but those who suffer the most who will conquer." The courage and sacrifice of hunger strikers provided powerful ammunition in Sinn Féin's propaganda campaign.

The ambiguity and complexity of the situation limited British efforts to cope with the Dáil and the IRA. Since it refused to recognize the existence of the Irish Republic, Britain was technically involved in a police action to put down rebellion. Because Westminster politicians could not afford to admit that they were fighting the Irish nation by waging a total war for victory, they attempted a limited campaign against Sinn Féin and the IRA that they hoped would not jeopardize a future peaceful settlement with the Irish people.

World and British opinion also fettered Lloyd George's government. Black and Tan and Auxiliary reprisals damaged Britain's image and shocked a growing number of its people. Prominent clergymen in the Anglican church, notably the archbishop of Canterbury, Asquith Liberals, and Labour party MPs condemned British policy in Ireland and demanded a negotiated settlement. They argued that IRA terror tactics did not justify barbaric retaliation from representatives of a country that had recently fought a war defending the self-determination of small nations. Constant pressure from the pulpit, opposition benches in the Commons, and the left-wing press insisted on a self-government solution to the Irish Question.

Reacting to anti-government British and world opinion, Lloyd George in 1920 attempted to end the Anglo-Irish War with the Better Government of Ireland Bill. It created two Irish Parliaments—one for the six northeast counties of Ulster and one for the rest of the country and a Council of Ireland composed of representatives from both legislatures. By administering services delegated to it by both Parliaments, the Council of Ireland was supposed to function as a bridge leading to a United Ireland. The Better Government of Ireland Bill also placed some Irish nationalist and Unionist MPs in the British Parliament.

By 1920 British opinion was pro-Home Rule, but the 1912-14 constitutional crisis, Easter Week, and the Anglo-Irish War had moved Irish nationalism far beyond that point. While 1920 elections produced a Unionist Parliament and government in six-county Ulster, nationalists in the other twenty-six counties used the ballot box to reassert republican commitments. The war went on with its ambushes, assassinations, burnings, lootings, and murders. "Bloody Sunday," November 21, 1920, is a prime example of the vicious quality of the Anglo-Irish War. On that day, Collins had twelve men shot, some in front of their wives; eleven were British counter-intelligence officers. In retaliation, the Auxiliaries and the RIC strafed a Gaelic football crowd at Croke Park, Dublin, killing twelve, including a woman, a child, and a football player, and wounding sixty others. "Bloody Sunday" exemplified the brutality of reprisals, increasing and intensifying British opposition to Lloyd George's Irish policy. Failing to solve the Irish Question with Home Rule and partition, or with physical force, the prime minister had to bargain directly with de Valera. In July 1921 they agreed on a truce as a preliminary step to negotiations.

London conversations between the British and Irish leaders were fruitless. The wily, pragmatic Welshman could not communicate with the Irish republican. When Lloyd George tried to discuss specific terms, de Valera replied with lectures on Irish history. But the prime minister did make it clear that he was ready to concede dominion status with the following reservations: Britain would continue to maintain naval and air bases in Ireland and recruit Irishmen for her armed forces; Ireland would have to limit her army in conformity with the British military establishment, maintain free trade relations with Britain, and contribute to the British war debt. De Valera rejected the offer as too restrictive on Irish sovereignty. When Lloyd George threatened a resumption of the war, the Irish leader agreed to take the British offer back to the Dáil for discussion.

Although the Dáil, on his recommendation, rejected Lloyd George's offer, de Valera told General Jan Smuts of South Africa among others that he realized that Britain would never concede the republic and that he was prepared to accept something less. Believing the door still remained open for a compromise settlement, Lloyd

George scheduled an autumn conference in London. In a puzzling decision still debated among Irish nationalists, de Valera announced that he would not go, and the Dáil selected Griffith to head the delegation accompanied by Collins, George Gavan Duffy, Robert Barton, and Eamon Duggan. Barton's cousin, English-born and -educated Erskine Childers, went along as one of the secretaries to the Irish delegation. Childers was author of the superb spy novel *The Riddle of the Sands*, captain of the *Asgard*, which carried guns to the Volunteers at Howth in 1914, a British naval intelligence commander in World War I, and an uncompromising republican. The envoys were commissioned to negotiate and conclude a treaty with the British government, but were ordered not to sign any agreement unless the Dáil first approved the contents. When Griffith and his fellow negotiators left Dublin, they had no clear definition of what would be an acceptable settlement.

Historians supporting de Valera's decision to remain in Dublin have said that he was of more use there restraining hotheaded republicans such as Brugha and Austin Stack and controlling the tempo of the London negotiations. Since the Irish envoys would have to refer all offers to the Republic's Cabinet for discussion and approval, they could not cave in to British pressure. Critics hostile to de Valera have suggested that he did not go to London because the British would not concede a republic, and he wanted to use Collins, his rival in popularity, as a scapegoat for frustrated Irish expectations.

When London deliberations began in October, the Irish delegation, experienced in combat but not in diplomacy, confronted a British team familiar with all the nuances of politics and negotiations—Lloyd George, Austen Chamberlain, Lord Birkenhead, and Winston Churchill. Lloyd George was willing to be flexible, but he was the leader of a coalition government dominated by anti-Irish Unionists. This political reality limited the concessions he could make. Irish envoys were caught between the exigencies of British politics and Irish republican fanaticism.

Lloyd George resubmitted his offer of dominion status in the form of an Irish Free State, but two issues emerged as major obstacles to a final settlement: the oath of allegiance to the British monarch and the status of the six counties in the northeast. Instead of concentrating on the most important—and to the British most embarrassing— issue, partition, the Irish delegation focused on the abstract oath of allegiance. Lloyd George told them that it had to be part of an Irish Free State constitution. As an alternative to an oath-bound dominion status, Irish envoys offered de Valera's idea of external association. According to this formula, the Irish republic would belong to the British Commonwealth and recognize the Crown as its head. Following World War II, Britain yielded external Commonwealth association in regard to such republics as India and Pakistan, but in 1921 this was too advanced a notion for acceptance. Instead, Lloyd George offered to let the Irish design an oath of allegiance that would not be any more demanding than those in other dominions, and would emphasize primary allegiance to the Free State rather than to the Crown.

When Irish envoys informed Lloyd George that they could not consent to a permanently divided Ireland, he replied that Sir James Craig, Northern Ireland premier, had the support of the British Unionist majority at Westminster in his refusal to accept the jurisdiction of a Dublin parliament. As a compromise, the prime minister suggested a Boundary Commission to survey six-county loyalties before drawing a final border between the two Irelands. He led Griffith, Collins, and the others to believe that the Boundary Commission, basing its decision on the will of inhabitants, would award the Irish Free State Fermanagh and Tyrone and perhaps parts of South Down, South Armagh, and Derry City. Lloyd George told them that such a large territorial transfer would eventually doom an economically unfeasible Northern Ireland and lead to national unity. Irish envoys accepted the Boundary Commission as a plausible solution to the partition issue.

During a pause in the London negotiations, the Irish delegation returned to Dublin. Under pressure from republican extremists Brugha and Stack, de Valera rejected dominion status with an oath of allegiance to the Crown and insisted on external association as a maximum compromise. But in early December, Lloyd George impatiently decided to intimidate the inexperienced Irish diplomats into signing an agreement. He issued an ultimatum: dominion status or all-out war. Griffith, whose original Sinn Féin program was constructed around the principle of dual monarchy, had no objection in principle to dominion status. Michael Collins, in a position to know, was convinced that the IRA and war-weary Irish civilians were not prepared for a resumption of hostilities, and he considered the British offer a major concession. Lloyd George's ultimatum might have been a bluff, but Irish republicans were in no position to call it. With heavy hearts and many doubts, the envoys signed an agreement with the British government on December 6, 1921, establishing the Irish Free State as a dominion within the British Commonwealth.

From December 14, 1921, to January 7, 1922, the Dáil debated the Anglo-Irish Treaty. De Valera led the opposition, insisting that when Griffith, Collins, and the others signed it they betrayed the Republic that had been duly established on Easter Monday 1916. Collins replied that Lloyd George's offer was the best deal that Irish nationalism could expect, and that a continued military effort would not improve the situation. He also emphasized that dominion status was far more than previous nationalist movements asked for, and that it could be a beginning rather than an end to the quest for national sovereignty. Surprisingly, considering the importance it would later have, the Treaty debate paid scant attention to partition. Irish republicans were more concerned about the metaphysics of the oath of allegiance than they were about the harsh reality of a divided Ireland. And no doubt Boundary Commission prospects diminished the significance of the six-county issue in many minds. Some of the most passionate opponents of the Treaty were female members of the Dáil—the widows, mothers, and sisters of men who gave their lives for the Republic. They spoke of the Free State as a bitter betrayal of the "martyred" dead. After all the speeches were made and the vote was taken the Dáil ratified the Treaty sixty-four to fifty-seven.

After his defeat, de Valera resigned as president of the Dáil, and its members elected Griffith as his successor. Within a few weeks, British officials transferred the instruments of government to Free State authorities and, except for naval bases at Cobh, Lough Swilly, and Berehaven ("the Treaty ports"), began to evacuate three provinces in a country they had occupied for almost eight hundred years.

In a June general election, 80 percent of Irish voters preferred pro-Treaty Dáil candidates. The 20 percent who opposed the Treaty, insisting that the Republic was inviolate and that the majority had no right to be wrong, were prepared to wage civil war. Although de Valera preferred persuasion, his words incited violence. On St. Patrick's Day 1922, he warned that the Free State would lead to fratricide. In the republican scheme of things, de Valera remained legitimate president of the Republic, and Griffith and Collins were pretenders, British pawns operating a colonial enterprise, but the IRA shoved politicians such as de Valera aside and took up the gun.

In April 1922 Rory O'Connor, a prominent IRA commandant in the Anglo-Irish War, led a republican occupying force into the Four Courts, the hub of Ireland's legal system. Westminster politicians, especially Winston Churchill, warned Collins that unless the Free State army evicted O'Connor, the British would have to do so. On June 26 Collins ordered government troops using British-provided canons to shell the Four Courts, commencing the Civil War.

Most Anglo-Irish War heroes such as O'Connor, Liam Mellows, Ernie O'Malley, Sean Russell, Tom Barry, Harry Boland, Erskine Childers, and Cathal Brugha fought for the Republic. Devoted republican women, represented by Cumann na mBann, rallied behind rebel troops, and many suffered imprisonment. IRA bravery and commitments could not compete with superior Free State numbers and equipment. Many Irishmen who fought in the British army in World War I contributed their experience and expertise to the government army. But the main difference between the Anglo-Irish conflict and the Civil War was the response of Irish opinion. Since a large majority of the Irish people were pro-Treaty, were tired of debating the metaphysical, almost theological, implications of the oath of allegiance, and wanted to get on with the business of constructing a viable nation-state, guerrilla tactics no longer worked. Anti-Treaty rebels could no longer depend on a sympathetic public to shelter them. Trade union spokesmen, the Labour party, and the Catholic hierarchy condemned republican violence and endorsed the Free State.

The Civil War placed a heavy human and financial burden on the Free State. More than 600 people lost their lives, and 3,000 were wounded (compared to the 752 dead and 866 wounded in the much longer Anglo-Irish War). It cost the government about £17,000,000 to defeat the rebels, a sum that would have been better invested in agriculture, industry, and social services. In addition, the Civil War deprived Ireland of valuable leaders. On August 22, 1922, Griffith died of a heart attack. Ten days later an ambush in County Cork took the life of Michael Collins. His one-time close friend, Harry Boland, and his passionate enemy, Cathal Brugha, both fell to Free State bullets. A government firing squad executed Erskine Childers for possessing a concealed weapon.

William Cosgrave and Kevin O'Higgins, successors to Griffith and Collins, determined that majority rule and liberal democracy should prevail over minority republican fanaticism, ended the Civil

War by shooting seventy-eight republican prisoners, including Childers and O'Connor. In less than a year, Free State authorities executed far more than the twenty-four rebels shot by the British government during the entire course of the Anglo-Irish War.

Free State severity plus the hostility of Irish public opinion and the opposition of the Catholic Church demoralized republicans. Emerging from the shadows, de Valera finally persuaded the anti-Treaty IRA to cease hostilities. In May 1923 commandants ordered their men to dump arms. Without officially surrendering, IRA members returned to civilian life without abandoning their animosity toward the Free State.

The Civil War left a legacy of hatred that continued to factionalize Irish politics. Instead of confronting pressing economic and social problems, from the 1920s through the 1940s politicians continued to debate the Treaty. Reflections on the past overshadowed the present and the future. Post–Civil War bitterness sometimes spilled over into violence. On July 10, 1927, assassins shot Kevin O'Higgins as he walked home from Sunday Mass.

Generally, the continuing Treaty debate existed within the narrow confines of political nationalism. In this context, Free Staters appeared as reasonable and practical people attempting to create a functioning nation-state while republicans seemed simpleminded fanatics oblivious to reality. But there were some Treaty foes who embraced republicanism as a protest against conservative post-1922 economic, political, and cultural policies. To them, the Free State symbolized an aborted revolution, a change of one establishment for another instead of a comprehensive transformation of society. From their perspective, the Catholic bishops and priests, large farmers, shopkeepers, and the former Protestant unionists who backed the Free State were counterrevolutionary preservers of the status quo and vested interests.

Republican writers such as Sean O'Faolain and Frank O'Connor, inheritors of Daniel O'Connell's liberal democratic political nationalism and the Literary Revival's inclusive cultural nationalism, found the ultra-Catholic, peasant-flavored, conservative Free State even more oppressive than British-dominated Ireland. They fought in the Anglo-Irish and civil wars to achieve a socially progressive, culturally diverse, and dynamic Ireland, and they were disappointed with the "pope's green island" results. Some enemies of the Free State were socialists, such as another distinguished writer, Peadar

O'Donnell. Although a small minority in Catholic Ireland, socialists were significant in the republican movement, sometimes exerting an influence far beyond their numbers.

Ideological distinctions between friends and enemies of the Treaty can distort reality. Personal loyalties, always an important part of Irish psychology, often determined commitments. Emotional attachments to Collins or de Valera or to IRA commandants could decide Free State or republican allegiances. Arthur Griffith was quite conservative on social, cultural, and economic issues, but that did not necessarily determine the Free State adherences of Catholic bishops, businessmen, large farmers, and wealthy Protestants, who were seeking law and order. However, the support that religion and property gave to the Free State did nudge it in a status-quo direction. Pro-Treaty Sinn Féin became the nucleus of conservative politics in post-Treaty Ireland.

In 1966, during the fiftieth anniversary celebration of Easter Week, politicians, historians, and folksingers paid tribute to the triumph of physical-force nationalism. An IRA demolition expert blew up Nelson's Pillar in O'Connell street, inspiring a rare example of President Eamon de Valera's sense of humor. Inventing a newspaper headline, he said: "Noted British Admiral Departs Dublin By Air." In the atmosphere of jubilation that surrounded the semicentennial, few doubted the contributions to Irish freedom of Pearse, Connolly, and their 1916 comrades or of the IRA during the Anglo-Irish War. The consensus held that revolutionary republicanism had emancipated Ireland from British colonialism, and established a nation-state that had survived as a successful example of liberal democracy.

By the early 1970s events in Northern Ireland initiated a historical revisionism challenging the pieties and tenets of physical-force republicanism. In the summer of 1972, *Studies*, a scholarly Jesuit quarterly, published the late Francis Shaw's "The Canon of Irish History—a Challenge," an essay that the journal's editors had thought inappropriate when the author submitted it in 1966. Father Shaw's piece dissected the revolutionary ideas of Theobald Wolfe Tone and Patrick Pearse, and their impact on Irish thought and action. He condemned Tone's adherence to French Revolutionary doctrine and his anti-Catholicism, and he accused him of hating Britain more than loving Ireland. Shaw was even more critical of Pearse, deploring his confusion of pagan Celtic mythology with

Christian theology and his equating patriotism with holiness. He said that Pearse's muddled thinking made Christianity an accessory to the moral evils of hatred and violence. Shaw rejected as myth the idea that 1916 redeemed Ireland from the decadence and West Britonism of constitutional nationalism.

Conor Cruise O'Brien is among the most significant and influential revisionists of Irish history. In a number of publications, principally *States of Ireland* (1972), he has denounced nationalism, especially the physical-force variety, as a great moral evil of modern times, particularly when associated with religious passions. O'Brien doubts that Easter Week or the Anglo-Irish War were necessary preludes to Irish independence. He is sure that England would have conceded Home Rule after World War I and, considering what has since happened in the empire and Commonwealth, the Irish could have expanded it to even greater degrees of sovereignty, including attaining republic status. O'Brien argues not only that 1916 and the Anglo-Irish War were a waste of lives, but that in glorifying blood sacrifice they have endangered the civility of Irish society. Ever since 1922, gunmen insisting that the majority have no right to be wrong have threatened the existence of Irish liberal democracy. O'Brien also unfavorably compares the exclusive Gaelic and Catholic post-1916 Irish nationalism with its inclusive Home Rule predecessor.

There is considerable merit in revisionist reassessments of revolutionary republicanism. In 1922, physical-force nationalism achieved a greater measure of sovereignty than O'Connell, Young Ireland, Butt, Parnell, or Redmond demanded, but it also abandoned most of Ulster. As we shall see, the Boundary Commission turned out to be a farce. And, as critics have remarked, the Irish nationalism that emerged from the alliance between Catholic and Gaelic Ireland and from the violence of revolution was narrow, provincial, and exclusive, discouraging economic modernization, social reform, intellectual creativity, and cooperation between north and south. Independent Ireland's static way of life encouraged ambitious and talented young people to continue the pattern of emigration.

Perhaps Conor Cruise O'Brien and other critics of revolutionary nationalism are right. The British might have kept faith and granted Home Rule, and it could have evolved into something much more, sparing Ireland the curses of fanaticism, intolerance, and violence. But after the 1912-14 Home Rule crisis it was difficult for Irish nationalism to have confidence in the integrity of Westminster politicians. In discussing what might have been, revisionists ignore the importance of legend and myth in the historical process. Easter Week and the Anglo-Irish War, like the American Revolution, provided examples of heroism and sacrifice that sustained a new nation through difficult times and adjustments. Because people did die and/or suffer for Irish independence, it became precious to succeeding generations.

The relevance of Ireland's struggle for freedom and the aftermath extends beyond the confines of a small island on the western fringe of Europe. The Anglo-Irish conflict was the twentieth century's first successful guerrilla war of liberation, an inspiration and model for revolutionary movements all over the globe. When it was over, Ireland faced the same problems of stability, civil war, and reconstruction that would later challenge other emerging nations in Asia, Africa, and the collapsing Soviet empire. Like them, Ireland confronted the challenge of independence with young leaders trained in the ideological rigidity of revolution rather than the compromise of politics. Men with years of legislative experience and political skill, the members of the Irish parliamentary party, were among the casualties of Easter Week and the Anglo-Irish conflict. Repudiated by their people, they were unable to contribute their considerable talents and common sense to the new nation they had served so well in the past. But despite the liabilities of limited political experience, the bitterness of civil war factionalism, and the narrowness of Gaelic and Catholic cultural nationalism, Ireland has survived as a relatively rare example of a successful post-revolutionary liberal democracy.

8

Unfinished Business
1922–1995

Collins and Griffith were right, de Valera and his friends were wrong: the Treaty was a "stepping stone" to complete political independence. Under William T. Cosgrave's Cummann na nGaedheal (Community of Irishmen) government, Ireland entered the League of Nations and articulated an independent foreign policy, appointed ambassadors to and established consulates in other countries, and issued passports. Led by Kevin O'Higgins and Desmond Fitzgerald, Irish delegates to Commonwealth conferences joined those from Canada and South Africa in demanding maximum dominion sovereignty. Due to their efforts, governors general became representatives of the Crown rather than the London government, the Westminster Parliament abandoned its claim to legislate for other members of the Commonwealth, and dominions no longer had to abide by British treaties with other nations.

Irish diplomats played an important role in formulating the 1931 Statute of Westminster, which defined the Commonwealth as a free association of sovereign and equal nations united in allegiance to the same monarch. This interpretation of dominion sovereignty came close to achieving de Valera's idea of external association.

Continuing to insist that the Free State was an impostor, and that the second Dáil elected in 1920 was the legitimate government, republicans refused to participate in Irish politics. In 1925 de Valera decided that this was a futile policy and created the Fianna Fáil (Soldiers of Destiny) party to achieve republican goals through constitutional methods. Because of the oath of allegiance, however, he refused to enter the Dáil. In 1927, after the assassination of Kevin O'Higgins, government legislation denying candidacy rights to those unwilling to subscribe to the oath forced Fianna Fáil reluctantly to take it and occupy their seats in Leinster House, the home of the Dáil. Five years later, in the midst of the world-wide depression, Fianna Fáil, campaigning on a platform including expanded social welfare, land for the rural proletariat, economic self-sufficiency, and refusal to pay annuities to Britain for land puchase, won a plurality in the Dáil and, with the support of the Labour party, formed a government.

From 1932 until 1948 Fianna Fáil held the reins of power in the Free State. Operating within the parameters of the Statute of Westminster, de Valera made Ireland a republic in fact if not in name. In 1933 he eliminated the oath of allegiance from the Irish constitution and diminished the role of the governor general. Two years later he did away with the right of appeal from Irish courts to the judicial committee of the British Privy Council. Taking advantage of the 1936 constitutional crisis in Britain, when Edward VIII abdicated and his brother became George VI, de Valera abolished the office of governor general and removed the Crown from the Irish constitution except for purposes of external association.

In 1937 de Valera offered the Irish people a new constitution. It changed the name of the Free State to Éire (Ireland), and replaced the discarded governor general with a president as symbolic head of state. The *taoiseach* (chief) or prime minister exercised real executive power. In a national referendum, 685,105 said yes to the new constitution while 526,945 said no, but 31 percent of eligible voters stayed home.

True to his campaign pledge, de Valera refused to pay land annuities to Britain. He collected them from Irish farmers in a reduced amount, and then applied the income to Irish needs. De Valera's refusal to continue payment on the annuities initiated a trade war with Britain, Ireland's almost exclusive outlet for exports. Britain placed tariffs on Irish agricultural products, and Ireland retaliated with duties on British industrial goods. The trade war hurt and antagonized large farmers, but de Valera believed it provided Ireland with an opportunity to develop its own small industries on the road to self-sufficiency.

Attempting to establish good relations with Ireland in an

increasingly troubled Europe, Britain's prime minister, Neville Chamberlain, invited de Valera to London for talks in 1938. The results were a considerable victory for the Irish leader. Chamberlain refused to discuss partition, but he made other significant concessions. De Valera agreed to pay Britain £10,000,000 as a settlement of the annuities claim. Britain lifted duties on Irish goods, Ireland responded accordingly, and the two countries signed a reciprocal trade pact. Chamberlain's most generous gesture was a surrender of the Treaty ports (Cobh, Berehaven, and Lough Swilly) to Éire, infuriating Winston Churchill as Britain faced serious threats from increasingly aggressive German Nazism and Italian fascism. And, as he predicted, for some time during World War II, until the British and Americans made use of facilities in Northern Ireland, the loss of the Treaty ports handicapped the Allies in their efforts to counteract the effect of German submarines in Atlantic shipping lanes.

The ultimate proof and test of Ireland's sovereignty was the decision, in the face of tremendous pressure from London and Washington, to stay neutral in World War II. Despite strong anti-communist emotions among her overwhelming Catholic majority, Ireland remained neutral throughout the Cold War, declining to join the North Atlantic Treaty Organization. Representatives of the coalition government that came into office in 1948 did tell the United States that it would consider NATO membership if Washington would pressure Britain to end partition. American strategists decided that since the Allies were able to win World War II despite Ireland's neutrality, they could survive another conflict without Irish participation. President Harry Truman informed the Dublin government that partition was an Anglo-Irish rather than an American problem.

The 1948-51 coalition government was a political alliance between the Fine Gael (United Ireland) party, a successor to Cummann na nGaedheal, Clann na Poblachta (Republican Family), a new breakaway Sinn Féin party with a social democrat agenda, Clann na Talmhan, the farmer's party, and independent James Dillon, the son of the former chair of the Irish party. Fine Gael's John Costello was *taoiseach*. To outflank Fianna Fáil and to please his Clann na Poblachta colleagues, Costello declared Ireland a republic in 1948 at a Commonwealth conference in Canada. (The Dáil's Republic of Ireland Bill was implemented on Easter Monday 1949.) De Valera had never taken that final step because he believed that by remaining in external association with Britain, Ireland would retain ties with the north that might someday result in a united Ireland. De Valera's fears were confirmed when Clement Attlee's Labour government responded to the Republic of Ireland Bill by pledging continuing British support for Northern Ireland's existence as long as it retained the allegiance of a majority of six-county citizens.

Northern Ireland was a peculiar concoction of a statelet. During the 1912-14 Home Rule crisis, and then again in 1920, British politicians decided that it was unfair to submit a 25 percent Protestant minority to the authority of a Dublin legislature. Instead, they included a 33 percent Catholic minority in Protestant-dominated Northern Ireland. Two of the six Northern Ireland counties, Fermanagh and Tyrone, had small Catholic majorities, and the South Down, South Armagh, and West Derry border areas were largely Catholic. Very early, Northern Ireland's prime minister, Sir James Craig, made it clear that he was leading a "Protestant nation for a Protestant people."

Most six-county Catholics, committed to the destiny and values of Irish nationalism, could not accept exclusion from the long-awaited Irish Zion or permanent inclusion in the United Kingdom. But in 1922, after local government councils in predominantly Catholic areas rejected the authority of the Northern Ireland Parliament and voted to join the Free State, Craig shut them down and, with the consent of Britain, eliminated the proportional representation feature of the 1920 Better Government of Ireland Act. Consequently, as a result of gerrymandering, extra votes for business properties, and a strict household suffrage, Catholic majorities had to suffer Protestant minority local government. Derry city was an obvious example of this injustice. There Catholics clearly outnumbered Protestants, but the city council had twelve Protestant to eight Catholic representatives.

Since local government distributed housing and jobs, Catholics had a shortage of both in Northern Ireland. They were denied private as well as public employment. Protestants owned most of the large businesses and industries and hired their own. Craig's successor as prime minister, Sir Basil Brooke, advised Protestants to drive Catholics out of Northern Ireland by not hiring them. In economic development programs, the Northern Ireland government ignored the territory west of the Bann river with its large Catholic numbers. There have been and are many poor Protestants in Northern Ireland, especially since the post-World War II decline in the linen and shipbuilding industries, but in many areas of the north Catholic unemployment has hovered around 40 percent. After three generations on the dole, many Northern Ireland Catholics are too psychologically disabled to work.

After Northern Ireland's Stormont Parliament fashioned a Protestant Ascendancy, Orange Order–influenced, Unionist-party state depriving Catholics of basic civil rights, economic opportunities, and adequate social services, the minority had good reason to believe that it was oppressed by an authoritarian regime. Stormont supplemented the Royal Ulster Constabulary with the exclusively Protestant B-Specials, which functioned as an Orange gestapo harassing and terrorizing Catholics. The 1922 Civil Authorities (Special Powers) Act made the work of the RUC and B-Specials easier by permitting authorities to arrest and detain suspected nationalist subversives for indefinite periods without trial.

There is some validity to the socialist view that large landowners and wealthy businessmen have promoted sectarian conflict and hatred in Northern Ireland in order to divide and control the working class. Six-county Protestant attitudes, however, represent more than capitalist manipulation. Protestants view themselves as separate and distinct from Catholics, and more British than Irish in cultural and national allegiances. Similar to the poor whites in the United States who despise poor blacks, working-class Ulster Protestants get a psychological lift from believing that they are superior to Catholics. Their xenophobia is expressed in racial rhetoric describing Catholics as treacherous, violent, improvident, filthy, and lazy scum who breed like rabbits. They believe that ignorant and superstitious "Fenians" are pawns of their priests, who are agents of Dublin and Rome.

In the north, anti-Catholicism has often moved beyond rhetoric to violence. During the 1920s and 1930s, Protestant mobs physically assaulted Catholics, burned their homes, and drove them out of shipyards and factories. On July 12, when Protestants celebrate the victory of William III over James II at the Boyne in 1690, or on August 11, when they commemorate successful resistance to the 1689 Siege of Derry, Catholics have not been safe on Northern Ireland streets, and sometimes not even in their homes.

Britain bears responsibility for the denial of civil rights to the Northern Ireland minority. During the discussion of the third Home Rule bill, British MPs insisted on and obtained guarantees safeguard-

ing Protestant interests in the proposed Irish state. When constructing Northern Ireland, why did Westminster ignore the interests of an
even larger Catholic minority? And why for over fifty years did British
governments tolerate discrimination and violence against Catholics
in a part of the United Kingdom? Throughout this period, Britain, a
self-proclaimed champion of liberal democracy, a foe of authoritarian
rule in other countries, gave tacit approval to the apartheid policies
of the Northern Ireland government, one that it sustained and
preserved with welfare-state subsidies.

Constant, often violent, Protestant persecution, poverty, and
second-class citizenship discouraged Catholics from participating in
the system. Most retreated into ghettos of the mind as well as of
place. Sectarian cultural separateness in Northern Ireland has been
even more pronounced than racial segregation in the pre-civil rights
American South. Northern Ireland has two distinct religious-cultural
communities, one essentially Irish, the other fanatically British.

Catholic conditions in the six counties produced fury as well
as passivity, and anti-British emotions far more intense than in the
rest of Ireland. Frustrated by poverty and oppression, disgusted with
the small Catholic, conservative nationalist party ("Green Tories) in
the Stormont Parliament—the voice of bishops, shopkeepers, professionals, and pub owners but not of the working class—some
nationalists joined the Irish Republican Army, illegal on both sides
of the border. The IRA engaged in acts of terrorism against symbols
of British authority: custom posts and RUC barracks. During World
War II, the IRA pursued subversive activities in Britain, but large
numbers of Catholics from both sides of the border fought bravely
and well in the British armed forces.

Although Protestant unionist prejudice, paranoia, and fears of
Irish nationalist irredentism, combined with British indifference to
injustices, were most responsible for discrimination and cultural
apartheid in Northern Ireland, politicians in the Free State, Éire, and
the Republic contributed their share. In their insistence that the
British presence was the only obstacle to a unified Ireland, they failed
to comprehend that the border was cultural as well as geographic.

During the Dáil Treaty debate, as previously discussed, parti-
tion was a minor issue compared to the oath of allegiance to the
Crown. No doubt participants from both sides trusted the Boundary
Commission to transfer so much of Northern Ireland to the Free
State that the former would cease to be a viable entity. But when the

Commission met in 1924, Justice R. Feetham of South Africa, its chair, and the British-chosen representative for Northern Ireland, J.R. Fisher, made it clear to Eoin MacNeill, the Free State member, that they would rule on the "economic and geographic" rather than the "wishes of the inhabitants" part of the Treaty's Article XII. After the Free State government learned that Feetham and Fisher were going to maintain Northern Ireland pretty much as it was—taking away a bit of South Armagh, adding some of East Donegal—it decided to negotiate with Britain to prevent the publication of the Commission report, which would have given it the force of law. In a tripartite agreement with Britain and Northern Ireland, Cosgrave's government accepted the existing frontier; in return Britain cancelled the Free State's and Northern Ireland's obligation to the British debt. The agreement also abolished the Council of Ireland, the intended bridge of eventual unity between north and south. In exchange, the Free State and Northern Ireland governments agreed to discuss and negotiate problems of mutual interest.

Free State leaders thought that they had salvaged something from the tripartite agreement, but Sinn Féin republicans accused them of sanctioning permanent partition. They said that the Free State sold out a united Ireland for a mess of British pottage. From 1925 on, partition was the principle item in the republican indictment of the Free State, and the target of IRA activities against Britain and Northern Ireland.

Although both Free Staters and Sinn Féiners continually denounced Britain as the sustaining force of partition, and expressed determination to erase the border, their efforts to create a Gaelic and Catholic Ireland reinforced the cultural and religious boundaries between north and south. Attempting to achieve Pearse's goal of an Ireland not only free but Gaelic as well, Cumman na nGaedheal, Fianna Fáil, and coalition governments insisted on compulsory Irish in the schools and competence in the language as a requirement for the secondary school leaving certificate (and thus access to universities) and for civil service employment. They also appropriated considerable sums of money to preserve Irish-speaking (Gaeltacht) districts. Despite these efforts, emigration to the English-speaking world and economic, social, and tourism ties with Britain, the United States, and Commonwealth countries continued to decrease the number of Irish speakers. Many of the well-educated middle class were Gaelic language enthusiasts, but English was the vernacular for most business and professional people, as well as for farmers and the city and town working class.

Support for a Gaelic Ireland was more nationalist piety than conviction, but the Catholic tradition was deeply engrained. Legislation of Catholic morality, particularly in regard to marriage and sex, and the influence of bishops and priests on the lives of the people and government decisions turned Ireland into a confessional state, contradicting the inclusive theory of Irish nationalism. De Valera, the most outspoken foe of partition, did the most to create an Ireland religiously and culturally offensive to Northern Ireland Protestants. His vision of Ireland as essentially rural, Catholic, and Gaelic not only froze the economy in a pre-modern mold, driving masses of young men and women out of the country, it confirmed Ulster loyalist opinion that a British rather than an Irish identity best served their interests.

Formulated by the distinguished Cork writer Daniel Corkery, a narrow, provincial cultural nationalism gave support to the Gaelic, Catholic Ireland efforts of politicians. Like the original thrust of the Gaelic League, it insisted that a true Irish literature had to be in the native language, and that Ireland should defend its spiritual supremacy from the secular materialism of the outside world. Corkery's one-time proteges, Sean O'Faolain and Frank O'Connor, led other writers in resisting the tide of Catholic clericalism and cultural isolationism. They defended the liberal, democratic, and inclusive beginnings of Irish nationalism, and pointed out that Irish culture blended the Anglo-Irish Protestant and Ulster Presbyterian with the Irish Catholic Gaelic tradition.

World War II, along with cultural, religious, and economic differences, played a part in maintaining a divided Ireland. The great crusade against fascism and Nazism was a defining twentieth-century event. Ireland's neutrality leaned toward the liberal democracies, and hundreds of thousands of its citizens served in the British armed forces or worked in British defense plants, but Northern Ireland was directly involved in the conflict, and served as host for American navy and army personnel patrolling the North Atlantic or preparing to invade France. Ireland's neutrality while Britain was in danger, and its postwar decision to remain outside NATO, contributed to another nongeographic aspect of a divided Ireland: unshared history.

During the late 1950s and into the 1960s, as Ireland experienced significant social, economic, and cultural changes, partition receded as a priority issue. Tourism, television, the printing press, and the cinema brought the outside world to Ireland, dissolving much of her provincial cultural and religious isolationism. De Valera moved to the presidency, and Sean Lemass replaced him as *taoiseach* and Fianna Fáil leader. Lemass encouraged foreign investment and the expansion of industry. Slowly but surely, Ireland became more urban than rural, gradually diminishing the influence of Catholicism and Gaelic nationalism. Citing its own experience of colonialism, Ireland entered the United Nations in 1956 as a champion of under-developed countries newly emancipated from imperialism and then joined the European Economic Community in 1973, changing its focus from the Third World to its partners in the Common Market. Cosmopolitanism and internationalism decreased hostility to and encouraged cooperation with Britain as a partner in a new Europe.

In the late 1960s Lemass and the Northern Ireland prime minister, Terence O'Neill, exchanged visits, and representatives of their two governments began to discuss problems of mutual con-cern—energy, foreign investment, and tourism. Just when observers predicted that tensions between north and south were disappearing and an epoch of harmony and peace was approaching, Northern Ireland burst into a passionate conflict of interests between the Protestant majority and the Catholic minority. The conflict began with peaceful civil rights demonstrations.

From the 1920s through the 1930s and 1940s, educational deficiencies, the product of poverty as well as of Protestant bigotry, victimized Catholics. This started to change in 1947 when the British Education Act opened secondary school and university doors to young people on the basis of talent rather than wealth. Bright young Catholics attended Queen's in Belfast, the New University of Ulster in Coleraine, Oxford, Cambridge, and other institutions of higher learning in Britain. But when they earned their degrees, they discov-ered that Northern Ireland unionists denied them the rewards of talent and training. Although bitter, they did not seek a solution in traditional nationalism. They decided that a united Ireland was a far off fantasy land, the catchword of politicians and the deluded IRA. They wanted first-class citizenship in the United Kingdom with all the benefits of its generous welfare state.

Inspired by the African-American struggle for equality, a mod-erate 1964 Catholic protest against discrimination in housing produced the Campaign for Social Justice. Four years later this movement evolved into the Northern Ireland Civil Rights Association, a coalition of middle-class Catholics, socialists, republicans, Protestant and Nonconformist liberals, and the People's Democracy, a radical student group from Queen's University, featuring the charismatic Bernadette Devlin. In 1968 anti-Catholic mobs violently responded to civil rights demonstrations. Frequently members of the RUC looked away while marchers suffered physical abuse; sometimes policemen participated in the beatings.

In the summer of 1969 unionist violence revived the IRA. It had been moribund since 1962, the time of its last terrorist campaign. After its resurrection, the IRA split into Official (Marxist) and Provisional (traditional republican terrorist) wings. Catholics retreated into barricaded ghettos in Belfast and Derry. To protect them from Protestant and Presbyterian violence and possible extermination, Britain sent troops to Northern Ireland in August 1969. At first, Catholics welcomed the soldiers as saviors, giving them tea and cookies, but when the army began to function as a police auxiliary of the Stormont regime, their attitude shifted and the IRA went to war against British troops.

On August 9, 1971, British soldiers assisted the constabulary in interning 342 people suspected of IRA connections. By mid-December authorities had apprehended over 1,500 suspects (943 were quickly released). The torture of some internees consolidated Catholic ghettos behind the IRA. When soldiers killed 13 Derry Catholic demonstrators on January 30, 1972, Catholic opinion exploded in anger. Reactions to "Bloody Sunday" in Britain, the United States, and the Irish Republic doomed the Stormont regime. In what was supposed to be a temporary measure, Britain suspended the Northern Ireland Parliament in March 1972, instituting direct rule from Westminster.

Following June 1973 elections, Britain established a Northern Ireland Assembly of eighty members, based on the principle of power sharing rather than majority rule. Official Unionists, led by Brian Faulkner, chair of the Assembly's Executive Committee, cooperated with Gerry Fitt (deputy chair) and John Hume of the Social Democratic and Labour party (SDLP), the successor of the Nationalist party, as the voice of majority Catholic opinion, and the unionist, pro–civil rights, non-sectarian Alliance party.

In December 1973 representatives of the Irish, British, and

Northern Ireland governments assembled for four days in Sunning-dale, England, and established a Council of Ireland to discuss problems affecting north and south. Shortly after this meeting, both the British and Irish governments published statements agreeing that an undivided Ireland was the best solution to the Ulster crisis, but that such an arrangement necessitated the consent of the Northern Ireland majority.

Opinion in Britain and the Irish Republic was optimistic that power sharing and Sunningdale would pacify the six counties and bring Ireland closer to unification. But the IRA insisted that only the end of partition would satisfy its demands, and unionist extremists, such as Reverend Ian Paisley of the Free Presbyterian Church, a fanatic no-popery bigot, and William Craig, leader of the Vanguard movement, a strong no-surrender pressure group in the Unionist party supported by anti-Catholic paramilitaries, rejected power sharing, demanded majority rule, and denounced the Council of Ireland as a stealthy approach to a unified Ireland. Meanwhile, the violence continued. The Provisional IRA's bullets killed British soldiers, and its bombs often took the lives of innocent women and children without sectarian or political discrimination. Loyalist paramilitaries killed Catholics. By the spring of 1974 over a thousand people had died from shootings, bombings, and fires; three years later the total number of fatalities approached fifteen hundred.

In May 1974 Craig's Protestant Workers' Council, allied with a variety of ultra-unionist groups and loyalist paramilitaries such as Vanguard and the Ulster Defense Association, began a general strike that intimidated the power-sharing government into rejecting participation in the Council of Ireland and finally into abolishing itself. Westminster resumed direct rule, frequently attempting to restore some form of Northern Ireland legislature, always to be thwarted by extreme unionist demands for majority rule, and the SDLP's refusal to abandon the principle of power sharing.

Intending to intimidate British public opinion—already opposed to involvement in Irish affairs—into pressuring its government to withdraw from Northern Ireland, the Provisional IRA decided to bring terrorism to Britain. Plans to assassinate prominent politicians failed, but in 1973 and 1974 IRA bombs caused extensive property damage and killed many innocent people. On Thursday, November 21, 1973, explosives planted in two Birmingham pubs slaughtered 21 and injured 162 people. In October and November 1974 the IRA killed 7 and wounded 92 in pub bombings in Guildford and Woolrich. The police arrested six Northern Ireland natives living in Birmingham for the atrocity in that city, and four, two from the six counties, for the Guildford and Woolrich murders. After torture-induced confessions, juries declared them guilty and judges sentenced them to life in prison. Later legal decisions reversed these verdicts, and released the prisoners.

Instead of increasing public opinion demands that Britain withdraw from Northern Ireland, IRA terrorism escalated anti-Irish sentiments and strengthened government resolve to remain in six-county Ulster until it achieved a satisfactory arrangement between majority and minority populations. Nevertheless, the IRA continued bombing British targets into the 1980s and 1990s, and the British reluctantly settled for an acceptable level of violence rather than law and order.

In 1972 the Official IRA agreed to a truce with the British military and, as the Workers' party, directed its energy to politics in both Irelands. In 1975 a militant Trotskyite faction broke with the Officials and formed the Irish Republican Socialist party. Its military expression, the Irish National Liberation Army (INLA), became the most promiscuously terrorist organization operating on the nationalist side of the Northern Ireland conflict. In addition to the indiscriminate slaughter of many innocents, it killed Aire Neave, MP, a prominent Conservative hard-liner on Northern Ireland.

Provisional Sinn Féin is the political wing of the Provisional IRA. Its leader, Gerry Adams, has argued that military efforts alone cannot drive the British out of Northern Ireland. He has insisted that political action is also necessary, and has projected an all-Ireland socialist republic as the ultimate goal of the armed, politically assisted struggle. Sinn Féin has contested elections in Northern Ireland and the Republic with little success in the south and a second-place showing to the SDLP among Catholics in the north.

For a long time, IRA, INLA, and unionist terrorists seemed indifferent to British, Irish, and world opinion that branded them murderers. Unionist paramilitaries have accused Britain of taking a soft line on the IRA, and of preparing to compromise the integrity of Northern Ireland. They have said that they are fighting fire with fire in order to preserve the existence of their community and its cultural values. Playing on the themes and traditions of Irish republicanism, IRA propagandists have argued that history demonstrates that Britain submits to Irish force rather than Irish reason. Heralding the justice of their cause in traditional republican rhetoric, they have replied to critics that even if most Irish nationalists disagree with their methods the majority has no right to be wrong. They also have reminded fault-finders that while most of the Irish rejected Pearse and Connolly during Easter Week 1916, their blood sacrifice redeemed and energized Irish nationalism for victory. And they have pointed out to people in the Republic that their freedom is a product of IRA terrorism during the Anglo-Irish War, and that Fianna Fáil was once a minority republican expression. IRA spokesmen have predicted that someday the Irish public will consider them, like the patriots of Easter Week and the Anglo-Irish War, as heroic freedom fighters. The Provisional IRA apologia disturbs old IRA veterans, who say "we did not kill our own people, especially women and children."

IRA members have represented a mixed bag of motives. Some come from families that for generations have played the patriot game. For many, the means—blood sacrifice—is more important than the end—one Ireland. Others in the organization are products of the poverty and hopelessness of Catholic ghettos. In other countries they might be members of street gangs. But in Northern Ireland patriotic slogans have sanctified thuggery and violence. Belonging to the IRA and fighting for the cause has given meaning to what were meaningless lives. The above explanations for the participation of Catholic nationalists in the IRA also apply to non-Catholics who have joined loyalist terrorist groups.

Nationalist and unionist patriotisms sanction extortion as well as murder. Terrorists often have more control over sectarian neighborhoods in Northern Ireland cities than do the RUC or British security forces, and they enforce codes of conduct. Suspected informers or moral delinquents are brutally punished, often by kneecapping. Many members of the IRA and the unionist Ulster Defense Association (which in 1971 synchronized the activities of a large number of loyalist paramilitary organizations) have found profit in intimidation and violence. They operate pubs, taxi services, and protection rackets. Because bombing has destroyed so many buildings in Belfast, the British government has poured money into reconstruction. The IRA and their unionist foes control hiring on building sites, often working in concert.

From the beginning of the civil rights movement through the early years of British army occupation, there was considerable sympathy and support in the Republic for Catholics in the North. The Fianna Fáil government protested their treatment to Britain, tried without success to get the United Nations to mediate the situation, and established camps for refugees fleeing anti-Catholic rage in the six counties. Irish spokesmen told the British that they could not idly stand by if Stormont and loyalist mobs continued to mistreat nationalists. The Fianna Fáil government also tolerated personnel from the Irish army training Northern Ireland Catholics in weaponry. Important members of the party encouraged Provisional IRA terrorism; some were indicted for arms smuggling into the north.

In 1970, two Fianna Fáil Cabinet ministers, Neil Blaney and Charles Haughey, were allegedly involved in a scheme to provide guns and ammunition to the IRA. Before they faced conspiracy charges in court, Jack Lynch, the *taoiseach*, dismissed them from the government for promoting a six-county policy in conflict with Fianna Fáil's. Haughey and Blaney were acquitted, but the arms smuggling scandal forced Lynch to realize the contagion of Northern Ireland violence. In 1972, after loyalist bombs exploded in Dublin, he rushed emergency anti-terrorist legislation through the Dáil, similar to that existing in the six counties.

More serious loyalist bombings in 1974 in Dublin and Monaghan, November 1975 explosions in various parts of Dublin, including the airport, the 1976 IRA assassination of the popular British ambassador to Ireland, Christopher Ewart-Biggs, the 1979 bomb that killed Lord Mountbatten and four of his boating party off the Sligo coast, and IRA bank robberies and kidnappings for ransom intensified apprehensions that northern madness had crossed the border. After the Ewart-Biggs murder, the Dáil and Senate passed resolutions declaring a state of emergency. Liam Cosgrave's Fine Gael-Labour Coalition government passed an Emergency Powers Bill increasing the authority of the state to apprehend and intern suspected terrorists. Since 1972 the Republic has incarcerated many of the IRA.

One of Ireland's leading intellectuals, Conor Cruise O'Brien, a Labour party TD (member of the Dáil) and a minister in the Coalition government, responded in his 1972 *States of Ireland* to the traditional nationalist position that Northern Ireland was an artificial state that the British created and preserved by their presence. He said that there were two nations in Ireland, and that Northern Ireland truly represented Ulster-Protestant culture and determination to remain British. While not prepared to go as far as O'Brien, other Irish politicians have realized that aggressive Gaelic nationalism and the Catholic confessional state prevent the possibility of a pluralistic united Ireland. They have also understood that the Republic's meager social benefits would not entice northern Protestants away from the generosity of the British welfare state.

In an effort to demonstrate the Republic's good intentions to Ulster unionists, a 1972 referendum removed Article 44 from the constitution, canceling the special status of the Catholic Church. The government also raised most welfare benefits up to the British level and removed Irish as a requirement for civil service employment. In 1973 the Irish Supreme Court ruled that existing prohibitions on contraceptives violated the constitution, forcing the Dáil to legalize birth-control devices. In 1983, however, by an almost two-to-one majority, an Irish referendum added an anti-abortion amendment to the constitution. There is not a strong abortion movement in Ireland, but the *taoiseach*, Garret Fitzgerald, opposed the amendment because it would preserve the international view that Ireland was a narrow-minded, Catholic confessional state, impeding progress toward a pluralistic, united Ireland. But Catholic pressures on both the Fianna Fáil and Fine Gael parties overcame Fitzgerald's opposition to a strongly-worded referendum amendment. Three years later, for social as well as religious reasons, a majority of voters in another referendum refused to lift the ban on divorce.

Easing some of the burdens of Gaelic chauvinism and Catholic clericalism extended the freedom of Irish citizens, but failed to impress loyalists in the north. They suspected that these reforms were hypocritical, and that popery still reigned south of the border. Protestants and Presbyterians continued to insist on their cultural uniqueness and their intention to remain British.

Money and guns for the IRA have come from the diaspora, especially the American branch. Before the Northern Ireland troubles began, upwardly mobile, well-educated, middle-class Irish-American suburbanites had shed much of their interest in or knowledge of Ireland. Like their fellow countrymen, they considered Britain, America's ally in two world wars and the cold war, a friendly nation. But when they turned on their television sets in the summer of 1969 and watched loyalist mobs, with the connivance of the RUC, brutalizing civil rights marchers in Northern Ireland, their genetic memories came into play. Many accepted the IRA as freedom fighters and generously gave money to its front organizations, most notably the Northern Ireland Aid Committee. NORAID claimed that it collected funds in the United States to distribute to families of interned nationalists in the six counties. But the Irish, British, and American governments have said that NORAID finances the IRA.

Eventually, barbarous IRA tactics disgusted and alienated law-and-order, middle-class Irish-Americans who share the antipathy to terrorism of the majority of people in the United States. They continue to endorse the Northern Ireland Catholic demand for civil rights, and they sympathize with the idea of a united Ireland, but they believe that these goals are best accomplished through negotiations, not violence. Encouraged by the Irish ambassador to the United States, Sean Donlon, such leading Irish-American politicians as former Speaker of the House of Representatives Thomas P. "Tip" O'Neill, Senators Daniel Patrick Moynihan and Edward Kennedy, and former New York Governor Hugh Carey asked Irish-Americans to encourage the political process in Northern Ireland rather than funding terrorism. A Friends of Ireland group in Congress, representing both parties, has continually worked for a negotiated settlement to sectarian and political tensions in the six counties.

A diminishing minority of Irish-Americans has continued to supply dollars to NORAID and other IRA support groups. For the most part, they represent immigrants of the 1950s, and sometimes their families, who left Ireland bitter because de Valera and other politicians could not provide them with jobs or a decent standard of living. When they arrived in the United States, they found it difficult to assimilate into middle-class, suburban Irish America. Their support for the IRA indicates not only anger with the hereditary enemy, Britain, and with an Ireland that let them down, but also a sense of alienation and a search for identity in the United States.

For a brief time, IRA and INLA hunger strikes in Belfast's Long Kesh (Maze) prison rekindled widespread Irish-American support for nationalist militancy in Northern Ireland. Early in the 1970s British authorities gave a special status to interned nationalists and unionists, permitting them to wear civilian clothes and to mingle with their comrades. From 1976 to 1979, on the orders of the government, prison officials phased out special treatment, touching off a series of protest tactics culminating in the 1981 hunger strike that resulted in the death of Bobby Sands and eight other IRA and INLA republicans in Long Kesh.

Northern Ireland's Protestants and Britain's Catholics and Protestants condemned hunger strikes as suicide, and the Irish-Catholic hierarchy and clergy pleaded with the strikers to halt their death journeys. Sinn Féin propagandists rejected the suicide charge. Using both Catholic and republican blood sacrifice symbolism, they argued that it was noble to give up one's life for a just cause, and that Sands and his colleagues were engaged in a redemptive process to free their people and create one Ireland. The influence of Father Denis Faul, a close friend of the internees, helped create parental pressure that ended the hunger strike.

At first the hunger strike brought significant dividends to the IRA. Each loss of life resulted in riots. Death watches and patriot funerals focused television cameras on Northern Ireland. American monetary contributions increased. In the midst of his ordeal, voters in Fermanagh and Tyrone elected Sands to the British Parliament. And Sinn Féin candidates drew considerable votes for another proposed Northern Ireland assembly and for local government offices.

As time passed, however, people outside Northern Ireland lost interest in the macabre events taking place in the Maze. American reactions became increasingly negative, dwindling the NORAID treasury. Like other Americans, the Irish in the United States are not great admirers of lost causes and martyrdom. They believe that it is more important to live than to die for one's country; blood sacrifice symbolizes an "un-American" loser mentality.

In 1980 and early 1981 there was a marked improvement in Anglo-Irish relations. Charles Haughey, the Irish *taoiseach*, had friendly discussions with Margaret Thatcher, the British prime minister. And his successor, Garret Fitzgerald, leader of a Fine Gael-Labour Coalition, had a summit conference with Thatcher. They agreed that representatives of their two countries would frequently meet to discuss common problems. The Anglo-Irish atmosphere darkened during the hunger strike when Irish Catholics in Northern Ireland, Ireland, and the United States directed considerable venom toward Thatcher for her inflexibility in regard to Maze prisoner demands. Relations between Britain and Ireland continued to deteriorate in 1982, when much of Irish public opinion was sympathetic to Argentina in the war over the Falklands, and when the *taoiseach*, Charles Haughey, back in power, gave only reluctant support to the EEC's economic sanctions against the Buenos Aires government.

A major breakthrough in the Northern Ireland situation occurred in May 1983 when, on the suggestion of John Hume, leader
of the SDLP, Fitzgerald, once more *taoiseach*, organized the New
Ireland Forum to arrive at a formula for solving the six-county
dilemma. After hearing evidence from a variety of sources (Sinn Féin
was not invited), the Forum suggested three possibilities: a federal
Ireland with considerable autonomy for each province; a single state
guaranteeing minority rights; or dual Irish and British administration
of Northern Ireland. Thatcher's immediate response to the Forum
report was "No, No, No!" but continuing negotiations led in 1985 to
the Hillsborough Conference in County Down, close to Belfast.

At Hillsborough, Fitzgerald and Thatcher established an In-
tergovernmental Conference through which Irish and British representatives could discuss matters of mutual interest and concern
regarding Northern Ireland. The Hillsborough Accord also gave the
Irish Republic an advisory role in the administration of the six
counties. During discussions, the British said that they would be
willing to relinquish their authority in Northern Ireland and recognize a united Ireland when a majority of the six-county population
consented to such an arrangement. Fitgerald also agreed that the
unification of Ireland depended on the wishes of the Northern
Ireland majority. President Jimmy Carter and his successor, Ronald
Reagan, both promised American financial aid if there was progress
toward peace in Northern Ireland. Seven months after Hillsborough,
the United States Congress passed a $50 billion aid bill for Northern
Ireland. It was intended as the beginning of a long-range effort to
revitalize the areas's beleaguered economy.

Both the British Parliament and the Dáil ratified the Hillsborough Accord. Although it did little to reduce six-county poverty and
unemployment, most Northern Ireland Catholics considered it a
major step in the right direction. Nationalist and unionist extremists
rejected the Fitzgerald-Thatcher agreement. Ian Paisley and his
cohorts vehemently insisted that Britain had sold out to Irish nationalism, compromising the integrity of Northern Ireland. Provisional
Sinn Féin and the IRA argued that instead of leading to an undivided
Ireland, Hillsborough perpetuated partition.

Despite Hillsborough, violence still troubled Northern Ireland. The IRA continued its war against the British army, other
security forces, and loyalist enemies, as well as its bombing strategy
at home and in Britain. In their opposition to the Anglo-Irish Accord,

unionist terrorist groups found themselves in conflict with the army and the constabulary as well as the IRA. The Ulster Freedom Fighters, the sociopathic loyalist equivalent to the INLA, from 1992 to 1994 killed more people than the IRA, murdering Catholics solely on the basis of their religion. There were also frequent tensions between Ireland and Britain. The latter protested Dublin's reluctance to extradite IRA members who fled south of the border to escape arrest; the former accused Westminster of insensitivity to Irish feeling. To buttress this charge, the Irish government pointed to Britain's decision not to punish members of the RUC responsible for killing six unarmed Catholics in 1982, the slaughter of weaponless IRA members in Gibraltar by the British army in 1988, the slowness in reexamining the evidence that jailed six innocent Catholics for the 1974 Birmingham pub bombings (they were eventually released), and the revelation in 1989 that members of the RUC turned over the identities of suspected IRA members to Protestant terrorists.

Although hatred and misery have continued to cloud life in Northern Ireland, the the condition of Catholics has certainly improved. Starting in 1969, British pressure and pragmatic necessity persuaded the Stormont government to curtail most aspects of Protestant Ascendancy. Change continued under Westminster supervision. Equity exists in public housing and the dispensation of social services, and the substitution of one-person-one-vote for dual and household franchises and the end of gerrymandering have transferred control of local government to Catholics in Derry and other places where they are a majority. British cultural and educational policies in Northern Ireland support Catholics in their Gaelic heritage interests, encourage Protestants, Nonconformists, and Catholics to comprehend and appreciate each other's traditions, and prod schools to teach Irish as well as British history. The presence of Catholic majorities in the student bodies at Queen's and the New University of Ulster is an indication of an increasingly important Catholic middle class with a stake in Northern Ireland. The works of poets such as Seamus Heaney and John Montague and playwright Brian Friel from the Northern Ireland Catholic community are evidence that Irish nationalism continues to inspire and foster the self-consciousness of literary genius.

While the overwhelming majority of educated Protestants remain unionists, many have converted to belief in civil rights and social justice for all Northern Irelanders. Dismal employment prospects trouble Catholics and non-Catholics alike in the six counties. British rule, however, has opened civil service opportunities to the former and is attempting to ensure fair employment practices in the private sector.

Since the founding of Northern Ireland, the Catholic proportion of the population has increased from approximately 33 to more than 40 percent, strengthening its local government potential. It is conceivable that by the middle of the twenty-first century, if not before, Catholics could outnumber Protestants and Nonconformists and vote the six counties into a united Ireland. But it appears that a large block of Catholics are not especially enthusiastic about such an outcome. For them, equal citizenship in the United Kingdom, with all of its advantages, benefits, and opportunities, is a more pressing concern than an undivided Ireland. Britain still has the attraction of a generous if reduced welfare state and has provided more funds for Catholic education in the north than the Dublin government has in the south.

John Hume, head of the Social Democratic and Labour Party, has been the most courageous, imaginative, pragmatically liberal, and intelligent leader involved in the search for a Northern Ireland solution. His goal is a united Ireland but he understands Protestant fears of incorporation into a majority Catholic state and their intense British identity, as well as the reservations some of his own people have about severing the United Kingdom connection. He has consistently tried to make other Irish nationalists, north and south, aware of Ulster loyalist emotions, including Gerry Adams, Martin McGuinness, and other Sinn Féin leaders. Hume is trying to educate his own people to realize that a united Ireland is a long process needing the consent of the non-Catholic majority in Northern Ireland. He also attempts to reassure British and Northern Ireland unionists that in the long-run one Ireland would serve the best interests of all concerned.

Hume's influence encouraged continuing negotiations between the British and Irish governments that led to another major Anglo-Irish agreement. Meeting in London on December 15, 1993, *Taoiseach* Albert Reynolds, head of a Fianna Fáil-Labour Coalition government, and Prime Minister John Major, leader of Britain's Conservative party, issued a joint statement concerning Northern Ireland. Major rejected the idea of any British selfish or economic interest there. He said that the future of both parts of Ireland was up to the Irish people, north and south, and if they eventually decided to become one nation, Britain would help speed the process. The prime minister emphasized, however, that Britain would continue to support the principle that the Northern Ireland majority must decide its nationality, British or Irish. Major promised full British coopera- tion with the Irish government in the effort to reconcile differences between Catholics and Protestants in the six counties while at the same time respecting their separate cultures.

Reynolds agreed with Major that the final status of the six counties depended on majority consent in the province, and he pledged that the Republic would not try to force a united Ireland. The *taoiseach* acknowledged that there were elements in the Irish constitution offensive to Protestant unionists, and that his govern- ment would carefully examine and do its best to remove them, particularly those relating to irredentist claims on the north. Reynolds said that Ireland in cooperation with Britain would try to end a long history of conflict in Ulster, always paying respect to Protestant unionist as well as Catholic nationalist traditions. The Irish and British leaders indicated their intention to negotiate with all constitutional parties in Northern Ireland, including Sinn Féin if it renounced violence.

The Downing Street Declaration received enthusiastic re- sponses in Britain and Ireland, but there was more dissension than unanimity in Northern Ireland. As expected, Paisley described the Major-Reynolds agreement as another British sellout to Irish nation- alism and popery. Speaking for Sinn Féin, Gerry Adams asked for clarifications before he would agree to join with other parties in discussing and mapping out the future of the six counties. On August 1, 1994, after a Sinn Féin convention in Letterkenny, County Don- egal, Adams announced that his party favored the peace process, but not the Downing Street Declaration. He said that Sinn Féin could not accept the proposition that Northern Ireland loyalists could have a veto over the future of Ireland. Adams said a referendum on national unity should involve all of the thirty-two county population.

Refusing to give up on the peace process, John Hume contin- ued to talk with Adams in an effort to involve him in negotiations with all parties in Northern Ireland and with representatives of the Irish and British governments. It appears that the Sinn Féin leader, like de Valera in the 1920s and Sean McBride, Clan na Poblachta head in the 1940s, came to realize that the persuasive powers of violence had reached a dead end. Funds from Irish America had dwindled to a trickle, and the IRA had been caught up in an international revulsion against terrorism. But it took some time for Adams to persuade republican hard-liners that it was time to give politics a chance. He did, however, succeed. On August 31, 1994, Adams announced an IRA ceasefire to begin at midnight. Irish Catholics throughout the world, along with other advocates of peace, celebrated what might be the end of twenty-five years of violence that has killed over thirty-one hundred and wounded over thirty thousand. On September 2, President Bill Clinton promised the Irish foreign minister and deputy *taoiseach*, Dick Spring that the United States would guarantee a peace dividend by contributing more to Irish economic development.

Despite the jubilation, the IRA ceasefire did not guarantee the end of six-county violence. *Taoiseach* Albert Reynolds, optimistic about prospects for resolving conflicts between nationalists and unionists in the north, urged an early start to negotiations with Sinn Féin and other interested parties. Prime Minister Major, dependent on Ulster Unionist MPs to sustain an increasingly unpopular Conservative government at Westminster, complained that the IRA had not explicitly promised a permanent cessation of violence. But it was clear that if the IRA kept its promise for three months, Sinn Féin would be included in talks about the future of Northern Ireland.

Loyalist extremists, Paisleyites and paramilitaries, interpreted the IRA ceasefire as the product of a conspiracy between nationalists and the Irish and British governments to maneuver Northern Ireland into an eventual union with the Republic. Loyalist extremists continued to assassinate Catholics and planted a bomb on a Belfast to Dublin train that exploded without any casualties. Despite provocations, the IRA maintained its ceasefire, and Prime Minister Major continued to assure Northern Ireland Protestants and Presbyterians that they would not be coerced into a united Ireland and that they would decide their own future. *Taoiseach* Albert Reynolds, John Hume, and Gerry Adams, in Ireland, Northern Ireland, and during an American tour, kept urging Major to begin negotiations with Sinn Féin, but the British leader kept insisting that the IRA must give pledges of a permanent ceasefire.

Finally, on October 13, loyalist paramilitaries announced a ceasefire, and ten days later Major said that negotiations on a Northern Ireland arrangement would soon begin. A temporary hitch in the peace and solution process developed in late November when a split in the Fianna Fáil-Labour Coalition government forced Reynolds to resign as *taoiseach* and Fianna Fáil leader. He had made the mistake of appointing the attorney general, Harry Whelehan, president of the high court, without consulting Spring and other Labour leaders. As attorney general, Whelehan had not responded to a seven-month British request to extradite a Catholic priest, Brendan Smyth, who had fled south of the border after being accused of pedophilia in Northern Ireland. Finally, the cleric returned to Northern Ireland, gave himself up, was convicted, and is now in prison. Spring reacted to Whelehan's appointment to the high court by resigning as *taniste* (deputy prime minister), and Labour left the coalition. After negotiations between Spring and other party leaders, on December 11 a new coalition government was agreed on. It involves Fine Gael, Labour, and the Democratic left (the former Official Sinn Féin Workers' party). Fine Gael's John Bruton is the *taoiseach*, and Spring resumes his position as *taniste*. Ideologically, the coalition is fragile and has only a five-seat majority in the Dáil.

In December 1994, representatives of the British government held exploratory conversations with Sinn Féin and unionist leaders. Negotiations between all parties involved in the Northern Ireland situation are expected to start in early 1995. But the joy and optimism that dialogue has replaced violence should not obscure the difficulty of arriving at a satisfatory conclusion. There are tremendous insecurities in the loyalist community. Although Gerry Adams said in an October 30, 1994, Ulster Television interview that he was prepared to compromise on a united Ireland, when Sinn Féin enters negotiations, it and the IRA will not have abandoned their ultimate objective, a single Irish nation, and a shorter-range goal, the withdrawal of British troops. The former will not be on the table and the latter probably will not happen until a political settlement guarantees peace and law and order. Britain cannot concede a united Ireland until it has the support of a Northern Ireland majority. At present, with few exceptions, non-Catholics in the six counties remain loyal to their British allegiance, and a portion of the Catholic minority is either indifferent or hostile to giving up United Kingdom citizenship benefits. And in the Irish Republic, with its own severe unemployment problems, there are reservations about assimilating the economically and socially troubled north. Furthermore, there are many in the Republic who are reluctant to surrender the cultural and religious homogeneity of their country. They worry about the disruptions that could come from trying to cope with the discontent and potential violence of a large non-Catholic minority.

Many experts doubt that, after centuries of cultural and physical conflict and unshared history and the bitterness and bloodshed of the past twenty-five years, Catholic nationalists and Protestant and Presbyterian unionists can reach a satisfactory accommodation. But if Sinn Féin can control the IRA and exhibit the patience to sit down and negotiate with moderate unionists, the SDLP, the Alliance party, and representatives of the Irish and British governments, and if fair-minded unionists can prevent temper tantrums from extremists in the loyalist camp during the talks and their aftermath, and if everyone at the bargaining table accepts the necessity of compromise, positive things can happen. Perhaps all sides can agree on a form of power sharing in a restored Northern Ireland parliament. A political settlement could lead to a gradual withdrawal of British troops, a larger advisory role for the Irish Republic in Northern Ireland affairs and the removal of irredentist clauses from its constitution, and an increase in foreign investment that could alleviate the economic aspect of sectarian tensions.

If these changes take place, Northern Ireland politics could evolve from parties based upon sectarian interests to those representing differing opinions on social and economic issues. And perhaps some time in the distant future, peaceful coexistence and a shared history will result in a pluralistic, united Ireland, providing the final answer to the Irish Question.

Conclusion

Contradicting George Santayana's admonishment that "Those who cannot remember the past are condemned to repeat it," the Irish obsession with their past has seemed to guarantee repetition. Many Irish share James Joyce's view that history "is a nightmare from which I am trying to escape." G.M. Young, the distinguished historian of Victorian Britain observed that what England "could never remember, Ireland could never forget." Of course it is much easier for victors than losers to have a memory loss. But a number of recent historians insist that what the Irish remember is myth calculated to preserve and incite bitterness and hatred rather than objective history. They would agree with José Ortega y Gasset's comment that "We have need of history in its entirety, not to fall back into it, but to see if we can escape from it."

Revisionist scholars argue that nationalism—substituting ideology for reality—has influenced the interpretation of Irish history, especially on the popular level. They claim that historians, professionals and amateurs, have concentrated too much on the British presence, neglecting indigenous, pre-Union aspects such as landlord-tenant tensions, overpopulation, a primitive agrarian economy, and religious and cultural conflicts between Irish Catholics, Anglo-Irish Protestants, and Ulster Presbyterians. Would an Irish Commons and Lords, dominated by the Anglo-Irish aristocracy and gentry, have been much more sensitive to the social and economic problems of

Irish-Catholic peasants than their Westminster counterparts? Perhaps yes, probably no.

All capable historians are revisionists in the sense of bringing new methods, research, and questions to the examination of old issues. But some historians of Ireland have accused many of their colleagues of overreacting to the revolutionary nationalism that terrorizes Northern Ireland and threatens political stability in the Republic. They say that this has led to the replacement of old myths with new ones that underestimate British responsibility for Irish misfortunes, and denigrate heroes, traditions, and values essential to the psychological health of the Irish nation.

Revisionists such as R.F. Foster are correct in their accusation that a number of historians have paid too much attention to British and not enough to local sources of Irish discontent, but in the period 1801-1922 Ireland was part of the United Kingdom—its fate was in Westminster's hands. The contemporary Ulster crisis is the product of Britain partitioning Ireland, and its indifference to injustices in Northern Ireland that have been the source of considerable pain and suffering for a large Catholic minority.

Of course the tensions between Ireland and Britain, and the antagonisms that divide religious groups in the former, commenced long before the 1920 Better Government of Ireland Act, which split the country in two. Britain engineered the 1800 Act of Union to insure her own security from a potential French invasion of an Ireland seething with Catholic, liberal Protestant, and Ulster Presbyterian unrest. British politicians worried that an Ireland dominated by a hostile Continental power would neutralize their country's most important defensive weapon, naval supremacy, exposing it to enemy attacks from both east and west. Although Britain insisted that the Union was a security necessity, it never fully integrated Ireland into the United Kingdom. Ireland retained separate administrations and institutions. More important, the 75 percent Catholic majority entered the Union as second-class citizens, denied their basic civil rights.

In addition to the religious issue, the disparity between Ireland, with one of the most underdeveloped agrarian economies in Europe, and Britain, the most industrially advanced country in the world, also complicated Anglo-Irish relations. With the exception of Sir Robert Peel's attempt to solve Ireland's religious, educational, and economic problems in the 1840s, and William Ewart Gladstone's efforts to deal with the total spectrum of Irish discontent, including the national question, in the 1860s, 1870s, and 1880s, few British politicians wanted to address the Irish situation until the Unionist plan to "kill Home Rule with kindness" in the 1890s. British politicians found it difficult to view Ireland from an Irish perspective. Those on the left, dogmatically insisting that what was good for Britain must also be right for Ireland, imposed an Irish policy instructed by laissez-faire precepts. Fearing that radical changes in Ireland would create precedents threatening privileged class interests in Britain, those on the right defended Protestant Ascendancy and the social, economic, and political status quo across the Irish Sea.

The anti-Catholic core of British nativism generated much of the insensitivity exhibited by British governments to the Irish Question. Encouraging and exploiting British, Anglo-Irish Protestant, and Ulster Presbyterian no-popery, Westminster politicians were antagonistic to a people they considered an alien and subversive threat to British cultural values and traditions. Affected by Social Darwinism in the late nineteenth century, British nativism's conviction that Irish Catholics were religiously and culturally inferior was expanded into the belief that they were also biologically defective. Religious and racial prejudices as well as economic doctrines explain half-hearted British responses to Ireland's great disaster, the Famine of the 1840s.

Throughout the nineteenth century, Conservative politicians manipulated anti-Catholicism to oppose reformist Liberal policies in Ireland and obstruct the progress of Irish nationalism. During the 1912-14 crisis over the third Home Rule bill, this strategy brought the United Kingdom to the brink of civil war. Not only did Conservative exploitation of religious and ethnic bigotry do much to destroy the Liberal party and frustrate Home Rule, it undermined faith in constitutional nationalism in Ireland, opening the door to revolutionary republicanism, escalating the Irish plea for limited self-government to a demand for complete separation from Britain.

British anti-Catholicism energized as well as thwarted Irish nationalism. In his agitation for Catholic Emancipation, Daniel O'Connell expanded a religious into a national identity. Although his success in providing Catholics with political rights and opportunities frightened Anglo-Irish Protestants and Ulster Presbyterians with the prospect of a Catholic peasant democracy, O'Connell did not intend to substitute a Catholic for a Protestant Ascendancy. Influenced by the ideas of such liberal democrats as Thomas Paine, William Godwin, and Jeremy Bentham, he injected their values into the blood-stream of Irish nationalism. Moving beyond O'Connell's Enlightenment political attitudes, Young Ireland romanticism defined and articulated an Irish cultural nationalism that insisted on the uniqueness and brilliance of the Gaelic tradition. Maintaining that their country could never be truly sovereign unless liberated from the cultural tentacles of British industrial materialism, Young Irelanders insisted on de-Anglicization. They worked for the preservation of the Irish language where it survived and for its restoration where it had perished as the proper vernacular of the people, the true expression of their folk soul.

Young Irelanders intended their cultural nationalism as an inclusive alternative to the sectarian and class loyalties that divided the Irish people. Instead, it proved to be as divisive, if not more so, than O'Connell's political nationalism. Anglo-Irish Protestants and Ulster Presbyterians associated the Gaelic with the Catholic tradition, reinforcing their loyalty to the Union and their identity as the British garrison in Ireland.

In the late nineteenth century, Anglo-Saxon racism, growing cynicism toward political nationalism after the fall of Charles Stewart Parnell and the split in the Irish party, and blocked opportunities in the British civil service for middle-class Irish Catholics sparked a revival of cultural nationalism in athletic, linguistic, and literary forms. But conflicts between Gaelic Leaguers, who demanded the subordination of literature to the national purpose, and Literary Revivalists, who insisted on artistic independence and integrity, and the alliance between Irish and Catholic Ireland converted cultural nationalism from an inclusive to an exclusive movement. Revolutionary republicans infiltrated and eventually captured Gaelic Irish-Ireland movements, using them to destroy constitutional efforts to obtain Home Rule, and as an inspirational theme for the blood sacrifice of Easter Week 1916 and the 1919-22 guerrilla war of liberation.

Anglo-Irish relations during the Union not only reveal the impact of British policy, politics, and nativism on Ireland, they also exhibit a significant Irish influence on Britain. O'Connell's Catholic Association and his agitation techniques provided models of organization and public opinion pressure for a variety of English reform movements. Parnell's Home Rule MPs were the first effectively organized, disciplined, and financed party in the House of Commons, an exemplar for Liberals and Conservatives.

Constitutional Irish nationalism offered more than a model for British imitation, it also installed and sustained British governments. Irish, like Scottish and Welsh voters, tended to be more liberal than the English. Therefore, the Celtic fringe often put Liberals in power against the wishes of English opinion. Without O'Connell's Repealers, Melbourne's Whigs would not have been in office for much of the 1830s. Parnell decided whether Liberals or Conservatives would rule Britain before making an alliance with the former in 1885. From 1910 to 1914 Herbert Asquith's Liberal government depended on the votes of John Redmond's Irish party.

Not only did Irish nationalism at times determine which party ruled the United Kingdom, it also played a significant role in defining the content of British politics, making the Conservatives more conservative and the Liberals more liberal. Wellington's and Peel's concession of Catholic Emancipation split their party into Tory and Conservative factions. During the 1830s, right-wing Whigs left the party over the issue of applying funds from the Church of Ireland to general purposes, eventually finding their way to the Conservative side of the House of Commons. Peel's efforts in the 1840s to destroy Irish nationalism by satisfying the needs of its ally, Irish Catholicism, enraged Tories, who satisfied their appetite for revenge by destroying his Conservative administration. Peelites, most notably William Ewart Gladstone, took a route that finally led to the Liberal benches. In the 1880s, anti-Home Rule Whigs and Joséph Chamberlain's Radical imperialists abandoned Gladstone, dubbed themselves Liberal Unionists, and finally joined with Conservatives under a Unionist party banner. Reactions to the Irish Question demarcated the boundaries between British liberalism and conservatism, distinguishing between the conflicting impulses for change and reform and for the preservation of the status quo.

Ireland's impact on Britain went beyond the issue of party politics. When Westminster politicians finally addressed the social and economic dimensions of the Irish Question, they created, sometimes unintentionally, precedents applying to Britain as well. Parliamentary legislation in regard to land tenure and purchase, public works projects, and economic development in Ireland did much to move British economic and social theory and practice away from an individualistic to a communal liberalism.

In general, pressures from Irish nationalism promoted the advance of liberal democracy throughout the United Kingdom. O'Connell's Catholic Emancipation agitation was the first successful political mass movement in the two islands. It was a major breakthrough in civil rights, preceding and inspiring Jewish emancipation and the abolition of slavery in the British empire. As previously mentioned, O'Connell's Catholic Association was a model for British reform movements, and he and his Repeal party played an important part in the passage of the 1832 Reform Bill and other Whig reform legislation. Peel's Irish policy began the dissolution of Protestant Ascendancy in Ireland, completed when his protege, Gladstone, disestablished the Church of Ireland in 1869. Election intimidation by landlords, nationalists, and priests in Ireland induced Parliament in 1872 to pass the Ballot Act, which enabled voters to make a private decision on candidates for office. At the beginning of the twentieth century the absolute veto power of the House of Lords and the denial of women's suffrage were the last two obstacles to British political and social democracy. The Irish and Labour parties, holding the balance of power, forced the Liberal government in 1911 to put an end to the former obstruction.

Irish-Catholic contributions to Britain extended beyond politics. Although many, but not all, voiced objections to the empire, they served in the armed and security forces that conquered and maintained it in numbers far above their proportion of the United Kingdom population. They were also a large majority of the Royal Irish Constabulary that preserved British rule and law and order in Ireland. A significant number of middle-class Catholics served Britain and the empire as civil servants. And the priests, nuns, and religious brothers who ministered to the Irish spiritual empire at home, in Britain, and the Irish diaspora, also were an advance guard and stabilizing force for British imperialism in Africa and Asia.

Influences have traveled east and west across the Irish Sea. Despite the objections of cultural nationalists, Ireland has been Anglicized in a number of ways. English became the vernacular for a large majority of the population, as well as for Irish novelists, short story writers, poets, and playwrights, considered some of the foremost in the world. English popular entertainments, manners of dress, values, and (unfortunately) culinary tastes successfully invaded Ireland. Irish puritanism owes almost as much to the influence of British Victorian prudery as it does to the teachings of the Roman Catholic

Church. Although there are unique features to Irish politics, much of it is based on the British parliamentary model. The Irish and British legal and educational systems are basically the same.

After the Anglo-Irish War and the creation of the Free State, the Irish continued to put their stamp on British affairs. As delegates to Commonwealth conferences, they were the most outspoken and effective champions of maximum dominion sovereignty. Desmond Fitzgerald and Kevin O'Higgins were largely responsible for passage of the 1931 Statute of Westminster, which defined the Commonwealth as a union of equals bound by common allegiance to the British monarch. Later, the Commonwealth expanded its definition of membership to include republics, a principle of external association that Eamon de Valera originally suggested to the British during the 1921 Treaty negotiations.

Although Ireland remained neutral in World War II and the subsequent Cold War and left the Commonwealth to become a republic in 1949, the Irish have continued their contribution to British life. More citizens of Éire than Northern Ireland fought for Britain in World War II, and many others worked in British defense industries. Since 1920 far more Irish emigrants have settled in Britain than in the United States. Most are members of the working class, but a good number are professionals or important in the arts. Studies of the Irish in Britain indicate a rather rapid assimilation. Since 1973, Britain and Ireland have been partners in the Common Market and European community.

Considering the centuries of conflict between British colonialism and Irish nationalism, Anglo-Irish relations since 1922 have been surprisingly cordial. But the existence of Northern Ireland has promoted discord.

In 1920, during the Anglo-Irish War, Britain partitioned Ireland to appease Ulster Protestants and Nonconformists, mostly Presbyterian, who fanatically opposed incorporation in a predominantly Catholic state. To persuade Irish nationalists to sign a treaty establishing the Free State, David Lloyd George, the British prime minister, promised them a Boundary Commission to settle the border between north and south, suggesting that a large Catholic portion of the former would be transferred to the latter, leading to the collapse of an economically unviable Northern Ireland and its merger with the rest of the country. This did not happen, and the six-county statelet continued its existence, much to the consternation of nation-alists in both Irelands.

Northern Ireland's two-thirds Protestant majority deprived its one-third Catholic minority of basic civil rights, economic opportu-nities, and social services, and terrorized them with the B-Special emergency security force and the Special Powers Act. Northern Ireland had a home rule parliament, but remained part of the United Kingdom under British sovereignty. Westminster politicians, how-ever, were not only indifferent to the political, social, and economic inequities and injustices that six-county Catholics suffered, they assured the survival of Northern Ireland through generous subsidies for social and educational services.

Leaders in the Free State and Republic focused on partition as a key issue in Anglo-Irish relations and domestic politics. But they failed to understand the inconsistency in their demand for a united Ireland and the Gaelic and Catholic state that they insisted on for their own people. Protestants and Nonconformists were guilty of creating an oppressive and discriminatory Northern Ireland, British politicians were responsible for permitting the violation of civil rights and the denial of social justice in the Irish portion of the United Kingdom, and politicians in the Free State, Éire, and the Republic, rejecting the earlier ideal of an inclusive Irish nationalism, reinforced the psychological, sectarian, and cultural boundary between north and south.

Inspired by the African-American civil rights movement, Northern Ireland Catholic responses to their minority position shifted in the 1960s from physical and mental ghettoization or physi-cal-force resistance to an agitation to achieve equal citizenship and opportunities in the United Kingdom. But Northern Ireland unionist opposition to Catholic equality quickly escalated to sectarian vio-lence and the intervention of British troops, who came to save Catholics from Protestant and Presbyterian anger and hatred, but remained to support the security policies of the Northern Ireland government. The result was a war between the revived Irish Repub-lican Army and the British army and other security forces, and between the IRA and numerous loyalist paramilitaries.

Over the twenty-five years of the latest Northern Ireland crisis, relations between Britain and Ireland have evolved from an-tagonism and suspicion to cooperation and finally to a common policy. In the late 1960s and early 1970s nationalists in the Republic were furious at Northern Ireland Protestant resistance to Catholic civil rights, the internment and sometimes torture of suspected IRA members and collaborators, and with British army atrocities, particularly the January 1972 Bloody Sunday slaughter of thirteen Catholic protest marchers in Derry. But when the violence of the north threatened to spread south, politicians and people in the Republic began to reassess their original reactions to the six-county situation. They condemned and outlawed IRA terrorism and attempted to make Ireland more culturally inclusive.

Meanwhile, British politicians finally began to take responsibility for Northern Ireland. They abolished the Stormont Parliament and ruled the six counties from Westminster. They then attempted to establish a power-sharing Northern Ireland Assembly that loyalist extremists managed to sabotage, forcing Britain to resume direct rule. Under British administration, most of the injustices that oppressed and enraged the Catholic minority have been eliminated. In fact, a significant portion of the expanding Catholic population has reservations about giving up the benefits of the United Kingdom for the questionable advantages of a united Ireland.

With Ireland taking a realistic look at the north and Britain finally accepting accountability for a province it created and subsidized, representatives of the two governments found it possible to find common ground. In a series of conferences that began in December 1973 at Sunningdale in England, British and Irish heads of government have agreed that a united Ireland is desirable if a majority of Northern Irelanders consents to such an arrangement. At the Hillsborough meeting in 1986, Britain conceded Ireland an advisory role in the administration of the six counties. In December 1993, Britain's prime minister, John Major, and Ireland's *taoiseach*, Albert Reynolds, repeated that the fate of Northern Ireland, Irish or British, rested on the decision of a majority of its people. Both leaders agreed to work for reconcilation between Catholic and Protestant communities in the north, and to negotiate with all parties in the province (including the IRA if it would agree to cease military operations). On August 31, 1994, Gerry Adams, the leader of Sinn Féin, the political wing of the IRA, announced a republican ceasefire. On October 13, loyalist paramilitaries also decided to stop fighting.

When negotiations begin, a united Ireland will not be the result. But a power-sharing government is a possibility. Peace and stability could lead to a British military withdrawal, economic investment, particularly from the the United States, and a reduction in the massive (almost 18 percent) unemployment that increases religious antagonisms in Northern Ireland. In time, politics there could focus on economic and social rather than sectarian issues. Someday, far down the road, a climate of cooperation in the north, the retreat of Catholic clericalism in the south, continuing good relations between Dublin and London, and an increasing European identity on both sides of the Irish Sea might lead to a united Ireland. Despite these possibilities and the optimism that existed in Ireland, Britain, and the United States following the announcement of the IRA ceasefire, experts who understand the complexities of the Northern Ireland situation know that maintaining peace will be difficult, and negotiating a satisfactory settlement even more so.

Historians such as Conor Cruise O'Brien, F.S.L. Lyons, and John A. Murphy have pointed out that there is more than one cultural nation in Ireland. Anglo-Irish Protestants, Ulster Presbyterians, and Irish Catholics have separate historical experiences and perspectives. Heroes and victories to one side are villains and defeats to the other. Both sides have a siege mentality. Catholic defensiveness reflects the reality of oppression, while the Protestant version is based more on fear of what might be than on what actually did occur. In the United States, tensions between North and South existed long after the Civil War, but after the descendents of Confederate and Union soldiers fought together in the Spanish-American conflict, World Wars I and II, Korea, and Vietnam, an American patriotism superceded sectional loyalties. Irish unionists and nationalists have fought together in the British army but for Britain and the empire, not for Ireland. To Irish nationalists, Easter Week 1916 was a brave and noble event, a prelude to the liberating Anglo-Irish War; to Ulster unionists it was a stab in the back to Britain fighting a war against Germany on the Western Front. And in World War II, a loyalty-defining event, when Britain faced defeat and perhaps extermination, the Irish Republic remained neutral, as it did when the Western democracies confronted the Soviet Union during the Cold War.

While events in Northern Ireland have brought Britain and the Irish Republic closer together, violence has increased sectarian bitterness and hatred in the six counties. It will be difficult if not impossible for victims of nationalist or unionist terrorism or the brutality of security forces to forget what has happened. Many well-educated middle-class Catholics, Protestants, and Nonconformists seem to have developed a tolerance for one another's religion, traditions, and culture, but among the working class fanatic sectarian and political loyalties have increased.

Vested interests also are at work to perpetuate a politically, religiously, and culturally divided Ireland. Many of nationalist and unionist paramilitaries have been playing their separate patriot games for a long time. In an economically depressed province with a long history of anger and distrust, revolutionary republicanism and British loyalism give meaning to meaningless lives. And there are paramilitary leaders on both sides who have an economic stake in civil conflict. They operate public houses, taxi services, and protection rackets and control jobs on business sites. Real peace and understanding would put them out of business.

For many reasons Britain would like to wash her hands of Northern Ireland. The cost of maintaining security and subsidizing social services and education in the six counties is a tremendous burden on British taxpayers, many of whom really do not understand what Northern Ireland is all about. Their religiously indifferent, recently multicultural society has passed beyond the anti-Catholic nativism of the nineteenth century that continues to define the loyalism of Northern Ireland unionists. Much to their credit, British politicians understand their country's responsibility for sectarian bitterness in the six counties and its role in partitioning Ireland. Therefore, they have resisted public opinion pressures to desert their Irish obligation, and have tried, in concert with the Republic, to reach some workable settlement in the Ulster province.

Although politicians in the Republic have rejected irredentism and have acknowledged the reality of Ulster Protestant and Presbyterian resistance to a united Ireland, they still stubbornly pursue it as an objective of Irish nationalism. Their persistence may not accurately represent the views of their constituents. A modernizing, increasingly cosmopolitan and sophisticated Irish Republic expresses a growing indifference to Northern Ireland and its multiplicity of problems. A united Ireland would only enlarge an already massive unemployment problem in the south, necessitate incurring the expense of implementing standard British educational, social, and medical services, and introduce a stubborn unionist faction into the life and politics of the Republic.

In *All I Survey*, G.K. Chesterton wrote: "The disadvantage of men not knowing the past is that they do not know the present.

History is a hill or high point of vantage from which alone men see the town in which they live or the age in which they are living." In Northern Ireland unionists and nationalists look at history from different heights and see segregated towns, and for many of them the past is indistinguishable from the present.

Recommended Reading

There are a number of general surveys of Irish history that cover the period interpreted in this book, including J.C. Beckett, *The Making of Modern Ireland, 1603-1923* (New York, 1966); Karl S. Bottigheimer, *Ireland and the Irish: A Short History* (New York, 1982); R.F. Foster, *Modern Ireland, 1600-1972* (New York, 1989); Thomas E. Hachey, Joseph M. Hernon, and Lawrence J. McCaffrey, *The Irish Experience* (Englewood Cliffs, N.J. 1989); K. Theodore Hoppen, *Ireland since 1800: Conflict and Conformity* (New York, 1989); F.S.L. Lyons, *Ireland since the Famine* (New York, 1971); Nicholas Mansergh, *The Irish Question, 1840-1920* (Toronto, 1964); Lawrence J. McCaffrey, *Ireland from Colony to Nation State* (Englewood Cliffs, N.J., 1979); T.W. Moody and F.X. Martin, eds., *The Course of Irish History* (Cork, 1978); and Robert Kee, *Ireland: A History* (London, 1980). Beckett and Bottigheimer are strong on the seventeenth and eighteenth centuries, sketchy on the nineteenth and twentieth. The Hachey, Hernon, and McCaffrey and the McCaffrey surveys are relatively brief studies of Irish history since the arrival of the Normans; their strength is in the early and recent modern periods. Mansergh was a pioneer in the analysis of Anglo-Irish relations and his work still deserves attention. Moody and Martin contains stimulating and expert essays. F.S.L. Lyons is reliable on detail and analysis and is well-written. It is the most thorough historical examination of Ireland from the Famine into the 1970s. Hoppen's succinct study is an excellent combination of strong writing, interesting information, and brilliant and challenging interpretation. For readers who know a good deal about Irish history, Foster's book is essential—it is considered the most important example of contemporary revisionism in Irish historiography. At times it does seem that Foster is excessive in absolving Britain of blame for Ireland's misfortunes, but on balance his judgments are mostly sound and thoughtful. In addition, Foster writes with masterful clarity and grace. His book is an enjoyable and informative contribution. Kee's well-written book is the base for his popular BBC/RTE series on Irish history. Alan J. Ward, *The Irish Constitutional Tradition: Responsible Government and Modern Ireland, 1782-1992* (Washington, D.C., 1994), examines Irish history from constitutional perspectives, stressing the importance of the British model and tradition in the governance of independent Ireland.

W.E. Vaughn, ed., *Ireland under the Union I: 1801-1870* (Oxford, 1989), vol. 5 of *The New History of Ireland* series, contains significant essays by a number of historians on a variety of subjects. D.G. Boyce, *The Irish Question and British Politics, 1868-1986* (London, 1988), is a short but comprehensive view of how British politicians perceived and acted on Irish issues—Boyce concludes that they have attempted to satisfy British rather than Irish opinion. In general, surveys of British history do not give adequate attention to the Irish dimension, but recently two historians have integrated English, Welsh, Scottish, and Irish history: Hugh Kearney, *The British Isles: A History of Four Nations* (New York, 1989), and Thomas William Heyck, *The Peoples of the British Isles: A New History from 1688 to 1870*, and *The Peoples of the British Isles: A New History from 1870 to the Present* (Belmont, Cal., 1992). Heyck is particularly good at blending the various ethnic strands of the British experience. An important addition to any Irish studies library is Ruth Dudley Edwards, *An Atlas of Irish History* (London, 1973).

In addition to historical surveys, there are other general studies of various aspects of the Irish experience that provide understanding of Anglo-Irish relations since the Union. Sean O'Faolain, *The Irish* (Harmondsworth, England, 1969), cleverly discusses and analyzes the multicultural contributions of Celts, Normans, and Anglo-Saxons, as well as poets, priests, writers, and politicians to the Irish character and personality. It is a pathbreaking effort in Irish intellectual history. Patrick O'Farrell, *Ireland's English Question* (New York, 1972), and *England and Ireland since 1800* (New York, 1975); and Oliver MacDonagh, *States of Mind: A Study of Anglo-Irish Conflict, 1780-1880* (Boston, 1983), are perceptive examinations of the differing values that have divided the British and Irish, people so close geographically and so far apart culturally. In *Ireland's English Question*, O'Farrell probably overestimates the Catholic element in Irish identity to the neglect of other aspects, but balance is restored in his *England and Ireland since 1800*. I have found the latter a successful reading assignment in both undergraduate and graduate Irish history courses. L.M. Cullen, *An Economic History of Ireland* (Baltimore, 1972), and Mary E. Daly, *Social and Economic History of Ireland since 1800* (Dublin, 1981), are the best surveys of important and, until rather recently, neglected aspects of Irish history.

Although it is not the only significant dimension of Irish nationalism,

Catholicism is and was the most important ingredient in developing Irish national self-consciousness, and the Catholic Church remains the most prestigious institution in modern Ireland. Emmet Larkin is the pioneer and premier historian of the Irish Catholic Church. His brilliant essay, "The Devotional Revolution in Ireland, 1850-1875," *American Historical Review* 77 (June 1972), 625-52, sparked a significant controversy in Irish historiography and inspired important research on nineteenth-century Irish Catholicism. This essay and three others from the *AHR* are combined in his *The Historical Dimensions of Irish Catholicism* (Washington, D.C., 1984). In his massive effort to present the total picture of nineteenth-century Irish Catholicism, Larkin has published *The Making of the Roman Catholic Church in Ireland, 1850-1860* (Chapel Hill, N.C., 1980); *The Consolidation of the Roman Catholic Church in Ireland, 1860-1870* (Chapel Hill, N.C., 1987); *The Roman Catholic Church and the Home Rule Movement in Ireland, 1870-1874* (Chapel Hill, N.C., 1990); *The Roman Catholic Church and the Creation of the Modern Irish State, 1878-1886* (Philadelphia, 1975); *The Roman Catholic Church and the Plan of Campaign, 1886-1888* (Cork, 1978); and *The Roman Catholic Church and the Fall of Parnell, 1888-1891* (Chapel Hill, N.C., 1979). Larkin also edited and translated *Alexis de Tocqueville's Journey in Ireland, July-August, 1835* (Washington, D.C., 1990).

In the "Devotional Revolution" essay, Larkin argues that pre-Famine Irish Catholicism featured an ignorant laity lax in religious practice; an inadequately educated, rebellious clergy; quarreling bishops; and a shortage of priests and chapels. He attributed reform to the elimination by the Famine of the surplus population, particularly agricultural laborers, reducing the chapel and priest shortages, and lessening the difficulty of priests in instructing the people on their religious faith and its obligations. But according to Larkin, it was the leadership of Paul Cardinal Cullen that Romanized the Church in Ireland and made the Irish the most devotionally religious Catholics in the Western world. Desmond Bowen, *Paul Cardinal Cullen and the Making of Modern Irish Catholicism* (Dublin, 1983) is a harsh judgment on Cullen as a main source of sectarian enmity in Ireland. Larkin's view of Cullen is more balanced.

Larkin's depiction of the pre-Famine Catholic Church is supported in S.J. Connolly, *Priests and People in Pre-Famine Ireland, 1780-1845* (New York, 1982). In another volume, *Religion and Society in Nineteenth-Century Ireland* (Dublin, 1985), Connolly credits the Famine for accelerating a Catholic reform that had already begun, and claims that the disaster was more important than Cullen's leadership. David W. Miller's "Irish Catholicism and the Great Famine," *Journal of Social History* 9 (September 1975), 81-98, is a perceptive analysis of the impact of the Famine on Irish Catholicism. In "The Great Hunger and Irish Catholicism," *Societas* 8 (Spring 1978), 137-56, Eugene Hynes argues that Irish-Catholic puritanism stemmed from the impact of the Famine more than from the Church's teachings on sex.

Determined to avoid another social disaster, the Irish married late if at all, with the Catholic moral code reinforcing economic necessity. Larkin's description of the condition of pre- and post-Famine Irish Catholicism is challenged in Patrick Corish's excellent overview, *The Irish Catholic Experience: A Historical Survey* (Wilmington, Del., 1985); James O'Shea's thorough local study, *Priests, Politics and Society in Post-Famine Ireland: A Study of County Tipperary, 1850-1891* (Atlantic Highlands, N.J., 1983); and K. Theodore Hoppen's thought-provoking, revisionist *Elections, Politics, and Society in Ireland, 1832-1885* (Oxford, 1984). These studies indicate that pre-Famine Catholicism differed in various parts of Ireland depending on economic and social conditions and the quantity and quality of priests. They and Larkin's introduction to *The Historical Dimensions of Irish Catholicism* have modified the interpretation of the Devotional Revolution into an evolution. But Larkin sticks to his guns in claiming important significance for the Famine and Cullen's leadership. For comprehensive, well-written, and intelligently interpreted examinations of the Irish Catholic church in the twentieth century and its relationships to politics and nationalism, see David W. Miller, *Church, State, and Nation in Ireland, 1898–1921* (Pittsburgh, 1973); and John Whyte, *Church and State in Modern Ireland* (New York, 1971).

Irish Protestantism is the topic for Donald Harmon Akenson, *The Church of Ireland: Ecclesiastical Reform and Revolution, 1800-1885* (New Haven, Conn., 1971); and Desmond Bowen, *The Protestant Crusade in Ireland, 1800-1870: A Study of Protestant Catholic Relations between the Act of Union and Disestablishment* (Montreal, 1978). As in his biography of Cullen, Bowen accuses the Cardinal of provoking religious antagonisms in Ireland while not placing sufficient blame on Protestant persecution for creating Catholic defensiveness.

Despite the new historiographic interest in other subjects, Irish nationalism still attracts scholarly analysis and significant popular interest. The most readable and highly informative survey of the subject is Robert Kee, *The Green Flag: The Turbulent History of the Irish National Movement* (New York, 1972). Excellent competition is D. George Boyce, *Nationalism in Ireland* (Baltimore, 1982).Owen Dudley Edwards has a long section on Ireland in his *Celtic Nationalism* (New York, 1968). Tom Garvin, *The Evolution of Irish Nationalist Politics* (Dublin, 1981), is a first-rate, highly intelligent, and imaginative discussion and interpretation of various aspects of Irish nationalism from the eighteenth century to the present. In his *Nationalist Revolutionaries in Ireland, 1858-1928* (Oxford, 1987), Garvin describes Irish nationalist leaders as mainly lower middle-class Catholics, many from Munster, who were anti-Protestant and anti-British. They were radical in technique but conservative in goals with little vision of the Ireland they were attempting to create. Thomas E. Hachey tells part of the story of Irish constitutional and physical force nationalism in *Britain and Irish Separatism:*

From the Fenians to the Free State, 1867-1922 (Skokie, Ill., 1977). In Thomas E. Hachey and Lawrence J. McCaffrey, eds., *Perspectives on Irish Nationalism* (Lexington, Ky., 1988), such scholars as the editors, R.V. Comerford, Mary Helen Thuente, Thomas Flanagan, James Donnelly, and Emmet Larkin discuss the language, folklore, literature, agrarian, and religious aspects of Irish nationalism. A most important contribution to a comprehension of Irish nationalism is Thomas N. Brown, "Nationalism and the Irish Peasant, 1800-1848," *Review of Politics* 15 (October 1953), 403-45, republished in the American Committee for Irish Studies Reprint Series, Emmet Larkin and Lawrence J. McCaffrey, eds., and in Lawrence J. McCaffrey, ed., *Irish American Nationalism and the American Contribution* (New York, 1976).

Because of the significance of Irish literature and its connections with Irish nationalism, cultural nationalism has been a major subject for scholarly investigation and interpretation. Thomas Flanagan's beautifully written and perceptive "Literature in English, 1801-1891" is one of the most valuable contributions to *Ireland under the Union, I: 1801-1870*, vol. 5 of *The New History of Ireland*. Malcolm Brown, *The Politics of Irish Literature from Thomas Davis to W. B. Yeats* (Seattle, 1972), is a useful survey of Irish literary nationalism from Young Ireland through the Literary Revival. In *The Harp Restrung: The United Irishmen and the Rise of Irish Literary Nationalism* (Syracuse, 1994), Mary Helen Thuente makes the point that there was a cultural as well as a political dimension to the nationalism of the Society of United Irishmen and that the United Irishmen anticipated Young Ireland and other subsequent expressions of cultural nationalism. Her essays on Thomas Moore and Young Ireland are also quite well done. Thomas Flanagan, *The Irish Novelists, 1800-1850* (New York, 1959), intelligently discusses the search for an Irish identity among such Irish writers as Maria Edgeworth, Lady Morgan, John Banim, Gerald Griffin, and William Carleton. Benjamin Kiely, *Poor Scholar: A Study of the Works and Days of William Carleton, 1794-1869* (London, 1947), remains the best study of Carleton. Charles Kickham, the Fenian leader, was far from a great writer, but his novels about Ireland inspired nationalist sentiments in Ireland and among the diaspora. R.V. Comerford, *Charles Kickham (1828-82): A Study in Irish Nationalism and Literature* (Dublin, 1979), is a quality portrait of the man and his work.

There are several valuable studies of the Literary Revival worth a readers attention: Richard Fallis, *The Irish Renaissance* (Syracuse, 1977); Ulick O'Connor, *All the Olympians: A Biographical Portrait of the Irish Literary Renaissance* (New York, 1987); and Herbert Howarth, *The Irish Writers: Literature and Nationalism, 1880-1940* (New York, 1959). John Wilson Foster has made significant contributions to Irish literary studies. His *Fictions of the Irish Literary Revival: A Challenging Art* (Syracuse, 1987) gives credit to the much-neglected prose dimension of the Revival. Two other major Foster contributions are *Forces and Themes in Ulster Fiction* (Totowa, N.J., 1974), and

Colonial Consequences (Dublin, 1991), a collection of essays. In the latter he pays attention to Irish modernism. G.J. Watson, *Irish Identity and the Literary Revial: Synge, Yeats, Joyce and O'Casey* (London, 1979), is another valuable volume. Richard J. Loftus, *Nationalism in Modern Anglo-Irish Poetry* (Madison, 1964), connects the work of W.B. Yeats, George W. Russell (A.E.), Patrick Pearse, Thomas MacDonagh, Joseph Mary Plunkett, Padraic Column, James Stephens, F.R. Higgins, and Austin Clarke to nationalism. John Hutchinson, *The Dynamics of Cultural Nationalism: The Gaelic Revival and the Creation of the Irish Nation State* (London, 1987), is a brilliant attempt to use the Irish experience as a paradigm of modern cultural nationalism, and to integrate historical analysis and sociological definitions. Hutchinson compares and contrasts the purposes of political and cultural nationalism, discusses the authors and propagandists of cultural nationalism, and explains the blocked mobility that converted a generation of bright young people into cultural nationalists.

Although literature is the most recognized contribution of Ireland and has been closely associated with Irish nationalism, Irish intellectual history has been a neglected subject. O'Faolain's *The Irish* was a pioneer effort and, more recently, F.S.L. Lyons, *Culture and Anarchy in Ireland, 1890-1939*, is an accomplished piece of work. The latter intelligently discusses the conflicts between Irish Catholics, Anglo-Irish Protestants, and Ulster Presbyterians that have resulted in a culturally divided Ireland. Terence Brown, *Ireland: A Social and Cultural History, 1922-79* (Ithaca, 1985), is intelligent, nicely written, and the only comprehensive analysis of Irish intellectual and social history since the Treaty. Daniel Corkery, *The Hidden Ireland* (Dublin, 1924, 1967) and *Synge and Anglo-Irish Literature* (Cork, 1935, 1955), articulate a post-Treaty cultural nationalism that rested on Catholicism, land, and the Gaelic tradition, and insisted that true Irish literature must be in the native language. In his "Proem" to *The King of the Beggars* (Dublin, 1938, 1980), Sean O'Faolain, a Corkery protege, brilliantly attacked the basic premises of *The Hidden Ireland*. In "Daniel Corkery," *Dublin Magazine* 11 (April-June 1936): 49-61; *The Irish;* and in his autobiography, *Vive Moi* (London, 1963), he criticizes Corkery's exclusive view of Irish nationalism while emphasizing the many influences on Irish culture. *Eire-Ireland* 8 (spring 1973), 35-51, published Lawrence J. McCaffrey, "Daniel Corkery and Irish Cultural Nationalism," and Emmet Larkin, "A Reconsideration: Daniel Corkery and His ideas of Cultural Nationalism," two essays on Daniel Corkery's literary accomplishments and the strengths and weaknessess of his Irish identity views.

Stimulated by the crisis in Northern Ireland, Irish intellectuals have been attempting to define an Irish identity separate from sectarian considerations. The *Crane Bag* was an important periodical that sought a multicultural, inclusive Ireland as did the *Field Day* pamphlets. For an example of the latter see Seamus Deane, Seamus Heaney, Richard Kearney, Declan Kiberd, and Tom Paulin, *Ireland's Field Day* (Notre Dame, 1986).

In the nineteenth century, land as well as religion motivated the forces of Irish nationalism. John Pomfret, *The Struggle for Land in Ireland* (Princeton, 1930), was a pioneer study in the agrarian dimension of the Irish Question and still offers a useful analysis. James S. Donnelly Jr. has contributed two valuable volumes to the historiography of the land issue. His *The Land and People of Nineteenth Century Cork* (London, 1975) is a prize-winning classic. In it Donnelly states that Cork is a representative county with which to analyze the Irish agrarian economy in all of its complexity. Donnelly's *Landlord and Tenant in Nineteenth Century Ireland* (Dublin, 1973) was designed for the use of secondary school students, but it is effective on all levels and deserves republication. Another worthy study of landlord and tenant relations is W.E. Vaughn, *Landlords and Tenants in Ireland, 1848-1904* (Dublin, 1984). R.D. Crotty's highly regarded *Irish Agricultural Production: Its Volume and Structure* (Cork, 1966) concerns the economics of Irish farming. Barbara Lewis Solow, *The Land Question and the Irish Economy, 1870-1903* (Cambridge, Mass., 1971), is an important contribution to an understanding of the economic reality as distinct from the propaganda of agrarian agitation. Her evidence makes clear that in terms of prices and tenant security the post-Famine agrarian situation improved economically and socially, and that land reform, including peasant proprietorship, did not increase production. The results of Solow's efforts suggest that land was more of a social and national than an economic issue. Paul Bew, *Land and the National Question in Ireland, 1858-82* (Dublin, 1978), is a good analysis of the relationship between agrarian and nationalist agitations. Maureen Wall, "The Whiteboys," and Joseph Lee, "The Ribbonmen," in T. Desmond Williams, ed., *Secret Societies in Ireland* (Dublin, 1973), discuss two of the leading agrarian protest movements of the pre-Famine period. Perhaps the best published material on secret agrarian societies and their intimidation tactics is contained in the essays by David Dickson, Paul E.W. Roberts, and James S. Donnelly Jr. in Samuel Clark and James S. Donnelly Jr., eds., *Irish Peasants and Political Unrest, 1780-1914* (Madison, 1983). This work also contains informative essays on a variety of topics dealing with the agrarian situation. Clark has also authored *Social Origins of the Irish Land War* (Princeton, 1979), one of the most significant examinations of that subject. In it, the author reveals how important the shopkeepers in the towns were to Land League leadership. Another important contribution to the history of agrarian agitation and its contribution to Irish nationalism is Laurence M. Geary, *The Plan of Campaign, 1886-1891* (Cork, 1987). Irish agrarian agitation and British responses are the subjects of E.D. Steele, *Irish Land and British Politics: Tenant Right and Nationality, 1865-1870* (Cambridge, 1974); and Charles Townshend's fascinating *Political Violence in Ireland: Government and Resis-*

tance since 1848 (New York, 1983). Irish peasant life involved more than agitation, politics, and nationalism. Using the parish of Killashandra in County Cavan, Kevin O'Neill's *Family and Farm in Pre-Famine Ireland* (Madison, 1984) points to British economic policy as the main factor in the collapse of rural Irish social structures and eventually of the Famine. His book is the product of extensive research and thoughtful analysis. Daniel J. Casey and Robert E. Rhodes, eds., *Views of the Irish Peasantry, 1800-1916* (Hamden, Conn., 1977), contains a number of informative essays on the lives and problems of Irish rural folk. Conrad Arensberg was a trailblazer in anthropological studies of Irish peasants. His *The Irish Countryman* (Gloucester, 1937) remains a classic, as does his *Family and Community in Ireland* (Cambridge, Mass., 1968), co-authored with Solon T. Kimball. But the most important and artistic folklore approaches to Irish rural life are Henry Glassie, *Irish Folk History* (Philadelphia, 1982), and *Passing the Time in Ballymenone: Culture and History of an Ulster Community* (Philadelphia, 1982).

Emigration affected Ireland more than any other European country, and the diasporic Irish had considerable influence on the course of Irish nationalism and Anglo-Irish relations. David Fitzpatrick, *Irish Emigration, 1801-1921* (Dundalk, Ireland, 1984), focuses on the social and economic factors that encouraged or forced young people to leave Ireland. Fitzpatrick's essay, "Irish Emigration in the Later Nineteenth Century," *Irish Historical Studies* 22 (September, 1980), 126-43, has informative and useful information concerning the class and gender backgrounds of people emigrating to the United States, Canada, Australia, and New Zealand, where they settled, and what they did in their new homelands. In his prize-winning *Emigrants and Exiles: Ireland and the Exodus to North America* (New York, 1985) Kerby A. Miller discusses the reasons that persuaded Irish Catholics and Ulster Presbyterians to leave Ireland, and describes their American experiences. Leaning on emigrant letters, Miller argues that Irish Catholics were too culturally and psychologically disabled to cope with Protestant and urban America and as a result felt alienated and saw themselves as exiles. He interprets Irish-American nationalism as an expression of loneliness and discontent. Donald H. Akenson, *The Irish Diaspora: A Primer* (Toronto, 1994), offers evidence that relatively easy Irish social mobility in the United States and various parts of the British empire disproves Miller's thesis that Irish Catholics were culturally and psychologically unready for life outside of Ireland. The problem with Akenson's book is that he tries too hard to minimize differences between Irish Catholics, Anglo-Irish Protestants, and Ulster Presbyterians, arguing that geography is more important than culture and religion in determining national identity. He also stretches the comparisons between various branches of the diaspora, neglecting the considerable situational differences. The Canadian or Australian experiences of the Irish reveal very little about problems and developments in the United States. Arnold Schrier's *Ireland and the American Emigration, 1850-1900* (Minneapolis, 1956) is another study making use of immigrant letters.

In my "From a Land Across the Sea" in *Textures of Irish America* (Syracuse, 1992), I take issue with both Miller's thesis on alienation and Akenson's opinion that American Irish ethnic identity was not essentially Catholic and urban. Terry Coleman, *Going to America* (New York, 1971), and Philip Taylor's *The Distant Magnet* (New York, 1971) discuss the emigration process. Coleman features the departure from Liverpool, the harsh Atlantic crossing, and the sometimes painful American reception. Taylor reviews the entire scope of European emigration, the journey to and the entry into the United States. Robert E. Kennedy, *The Irish: Emigration, Marriage, and Fertility* (London, 1973), is a social science masterpiece. One of the unique aspects of Irish emigration is the large number of single women involved. In *Ourselves Alone: Female Emigration from Ireland, 1825-1920* (Lexington, Ky., 1989), Janet Ann Nolan intelligently and interestingly argues that the Great Famine so altered Irish marriage patterns that women had more reasons to leave Ireland than men. Nolan's position finds support in an exceptionally well-written article, "'She Never Then After that Forgot Him': Irishwomen and Emigration to the United States in Irish Folklore," by Grace Neville, *Mid-America* 74 (October 1992), 271-90. Thomas N. Brown, the leading investigator of the subject, in his "Origins and Character of Irish-American Nationalism," *Review of Politics* 18 (July 1956), 327-58, reprinted in *Irish Nationalism and the American Contribution* (New York, 1976), indicates that Irish-American nationalism originated in "loneliness, poverty and prejudice." In his *Irish-American Nationalism* (Philadelphia, 1966), Brown, while describing the element of alienation involved in their support for freedom efforts in Ireland, provides strong evidence that by the late nineteenth century economically mobile Irish-Americans, deeply in love with the United States and searching for respectability, decided that an independent Ireland could provide it.

In *Fenians and Anglo-American Relations during Reconstruction* (Ithaca, N.Y., 1969), Brian Jenkins relates how the United States government encouraged Fenianism to intimidate Britain into settling claims concerning the British-built Confederate blockade runner *Alabama* and recognizing the naturalization of former British citizens. Michael Funchion, *Chicago's Irish Nationalists, 1881-1890* (New York, 1976), focuses on conflict in the Clan na Gael when Chicago's A.M. Sullivan was its dominant personality. Joseph Patrick O'Grady, *Irish-Americans and Anglo-Irish Relations, 1880-1888* (New York, 1976); Francis M. Carroll, *American Opinion and the Irish Question, 1910-1923* (New York, 1978); Joseph Edward Cuddy, *Irish America and National Isolationism, 1914-1920* (New York, 1976); Alan J. Ward, *Ireland and Anglo-American Relations, 1880-1921* (London, 1969); Sean Cronin, *Washing-*

ton's Irish Policy, 1916-1989: Independence, Partition, Neutrality (Dublin, 1986); and Jack Holland, *The American Connection: U. S. Guns, Money, and Influence in Northern Ireland* (New York, 1987), all discuss the significance of Irish America on Irish nationalism and Anglo-Irish and Anglo-American relations. There are a number of general studies of Irish America that have valuable information: those that highlight its contributions to Irish nationalism include Donald Akenson, *The United States and Ireland* (Cambridge, Mass., 1973); John B. Duff, *The Irish in America* (Belmont, Cal., 1971); Dennis Clark, *Hibernia America: The Irish and Regional Cultures* (New York, 1986); Marjorie Fallows, *Irish-Americans: Identity and Assimilation* (Englewood Cliffs, N.J., 1977); Andrew M. Greeley, *The Irish-Americans: The Rise to Money and Power* (New York, 1981); William D. Griffin, *A Portrait of the Irish in America* (New York, 1981), and *The Book of Irish-Americans* (New York, 1990); Lawrence J. McCaffrey, *The Irish Diaspora in America* (Bloomington, Ind., 1976; Washington, D.C., 1984), and *Textures of Irish America;* William V. Shannon, *The American Irish* (New York, 1974); and Carl Wittke, *The Irish in America* (New York, 1970). Wittke is rich in detail, Shannon offers informative and perceptive essays on important Irish-American individuals, politics, literature, sports, entertainment, and religion. Greeley offers a sociological perspective, insisting that Irish America evolved into a prosperous, respectable, and progressive force in the United States. Fallows also blends historical and sociological approaches into an informative, lively analysis. Duff is a short study but useful in ethnic courses. Griffin's *Portrait of the Irish* is a pictorial look at Irish America. In my two books I emphasize the impact of the Irish experience on Irish America and conclude that they gave as much as they took from the United States; I agree with Greeley and others that Irish America deserves to be seen as a success story. With great skill, Clark compares and contrasts the Irish experience in various parts of the United States, describing regional impacts on the Irish personality. Patrick Blessing's "The Irish" in the *Harvard Encyclopedia of American Ethnic Groups* (Cambridge, Mass., 1980), Stephen Thernstrom, ed., is an exceptionally informative and intelligent analysis of its subject. David Noel Doyle and Owen Dudley Edwards, eds., *America and Ireland* (Westport, Conn., 1980), and P.J. Drudy, *The Irish in America* (New York, 1985), both contain some first-rate essays, but the Drudy book is more consistent in quality.

Other branches of the diaspora have lacked the attention given to the American, but important work has been done. Patrick O'Farrell, *The Irish in Australia* (Notre Dame, Ind., 1989), deservedly is a highly regarded book; so is L.H. Lees, *Exiles of Erin: Irish Migrants in Victorian London* (Manchester, England, 1979). Other studies of the Irish in Britain worth consulting are John Archer Jackson, *The Irish in Britain* (Cleveland, 1963); Kevin O'Connor, *The Irish in Britain* (London, 1972); and John Hickey, *Urban Catholics* (London, 1967). Robert O'Driscoll and Lorna Reynolds, *The Irish in Canada*, 2 vols. (Toronto, 1988), has a number of excellent articles. As previously mentioned, Donald H. Akenson's *The Irish Diaspora: A Primer* attempts with uneven success to compare and contrast the various branches of the diaspora.

The 1798 rebellion was an important prelude to the Act of Union. Thomas Pakenham, *The Year of Liberty: The Great Rebellion of 1798* (London, 1966), offers a scholarly description of the rising. Thomas Flanagan, *The Year of the French* (New York, 1979), is a gem of a historical novel. It discusses the ideologies, interests, and issues involved in the events of 1798, provides excellent character studies of the various class, religious, and political components of Irish society, and describes the events in Mayo during the rising. Marianne Elliott has produced two masterful books on the Society of United Irishmen: *Partners in Revolution: The United Irishmen and France* (New Haven, Conn., 1982), and *Wolfe Tone: Prophet of Irish Independence* (New Haven, Conn., 1989). In the first book, Elliott not only discusses the ideology and personnel of the United Irishmen, she describes their French contacts and their role in international revolutionary activities. In her biography of Tone, Elliott rescues him from nationalist iconolatry, showing how his anti-British republicanism slowly evolved from a reformist beginning. Elliott's Tone is not an original thinker but a first-rate propagandist. Though flawed in character, he deserves honor and respect, and his idea of a non-sectarian nationalism is still a noble objective. Tom Dunne, *Theobald Wolfe Tone: Colonial Outsider* (Cork, 1982), questions Tone's nationalist and radical integrity. Dunne's Tone ends up as an Irish patriot after he is unable to find an important place within the British imperial system. In her gracefully written, thoroughly researched, and thoughtful *The United Irishmen: Popular Politics in Ulster and Dublin, 1791-1798* (Oxford, 1994), Nancy Curtin portrays the United Irishmen as elitist reformers *who* educated the people on active citizenship and good government. Their Society evolved into a mass revolutionary movement. She also indicates that United Irishmen were troubled by insubordination, sectarianism, and disagreements over objectives. Curtain blames timid leadership rather than faltering support for the failures of 1798. In *A Deeper Silence: The Hidden Origins of the United Irishmen* (London, 1994), A.T.Q. Stewart emphasizes the Ulster Presbyterian contribution to the radicalism of the United Irishmen. He also points out that Freemasonry was a significant factor in the Society. Stewart claims that a radical inspiration for the United Irishmen was the republicanism of Oliver Cromwell.

G.C. Bolton, *The Passing of the Act of Union* (Oxford, 1966), ably argues that nationalists have exaggerated the charge that corruption carried the Act of Union through the Irish Parliament. He points out that the use of patronage to win votes was an accepted practice in eighteenth-century Britain and Ireland. Bolton says that selfish and idealistic motives influenced those for and against the British connection. For a study of the British administration of Ireland in the early nineteenth century see Brian Jenkins, *Era of Emancipation: The British Government of Ireland, 1812-1830* (Montreal, 1988). Sir Robert Peel was the most important British administrator in Ireland during the immediate post-Union period. His career there is described in Norman Gash, *Mr. Secretary Peel* (Cambridge, Mass., 1961). One of Peel's most influential decisions was the establishment of a police force in Ireland, an act discussed in Galen Broeker, *Rural Disorder and Police Reform in Ireland, 1812-1836* (Toronto, 1970).

Gearóid Ó Tuathaigh, *Ireland before the Famine, 1798-1848* (The Gill History of Ireland 9; Dublin, 1972), is a perceptive survey of pre-Famine Ireland under the Union with a strong emphasis on the Gaelic tradition. Donal McCartney, *The Dawning of Democracy: Ireland, 1800-1870* (Helicon History, of Ireland; Dublin, 1987), is also a valuable introduction to nineteenth-century Irish history. Kenneth Connell, *The Population of Ireland, 1750-1845* (London, 1950), is a clever, pioneer social analysis of pre-Famine Ireland, pointing to the potato as an important factor in overpopulation. Except for one essay, Connell's *Irish Peasant Society* (Oxford, 1968) is concerned with post-Famine Ireland. Thomas W. Freeman, *Pre-Famine Ireland: A Study in Historical Geography* (Manchester, 1957); and E. Estyn Evans, *Irish Heritage* (Dundalk, Ireland, 1949), and *The Personality of Ireland: Habitat, Heritage, and History* (Cambridge, England, 1973), are interesting views of Irish rural culture, as is Kevin Danaher, *In Ireland Long Ago* (Dublin, 1976), and the previously mentioned Conrad Arensberg, *The Irish Countrymen.*

Penal Laws that oppressed Catholics are the subject of Robert E. Burns, "The Irish Penal Code and Some of Its Historians," *Review of Politics* 21 (January 1959), 276-99; and Maureen Wall, *The Penal Laws, 1691-1760* (Irish History Series, No. 1; Dundalk, Ireland, 1961). Burns interprets the Penal Laws as an effort to convert Catholics through punitive measures; Wall describes them as physical and psychological terrorism. She explains how their restrictions on landed propery purchase led to a relatively large Catholic middle class in "The Rise of a Catholic Middle Class in Eighteenth Century Ireland," *Irish Historical Studies* 11 (September 1958), 91-115.

One of the most significant contributions to recent Irish historiography is Maurice R. O'Connell, ed., *The Correspondence of Daniel O'Connell,* 8 vols. (New York, 1973-1980). This work made possible Oliver Mac-Donagh's excellent two-volume biography, *The Hereditary Bondsman: Daniel O'Connell, 1775-1829* (New York, 1987), and *The Emancipist: Daniel O'Connell, 1830-1847* (New York, 1989). Although MacDonagh's is by far the best scholarly biography of O'Connell, Sean O'Faolain's *King of the Beggars* has an unmatched appeal. It is full of insights that only the creative and imaginative novelist can bring to the complicated and charismatic O'Connell. O'Connell's resurrection in Irish historiography has been aided by two interesting books of essays: Kevin Nowlan and Maurice O'Connell, eds., *Daniel O'Con-*

nell: Portrait of a Radical (Belfast, 1984); and Donal McCartney, ed., *The World of Daniel O'Connell* (Cork, 1980). James A. Reynolds, *The Catholic Emancipation Crisis in Ireland, 1823-1829* (New Haven, Conn., 1954), was an important analysis of the Catholic agitation crisis with rather harsh judgments on the personality of O'Connell. It has been superceded in value and information by Fergus O'Ferrall, *Catholic Emancipation: Daniel O'Connell and the Birth of Irish Democracy, 1820-1830* (Dublin, 1985). According to O'Ferrall, O'Connell, along with Andrew Jackson, created modern political democracy in action. Gash's *Mr. Secretary Peel*, and G.I.T. Machin, *The Catholic Question in British Politics, 1820-1830* (London, 1964), present British political perspectives on the Catholic Emancipation issue. British-instituted education in Ireland is the subject of D.H. Akenson, *The Irish Education Experiment: The National System of Education in the Nineteenth Century* (Toronto, 1970).

O'Connell's nationalist activities in the 1830s and 1840s and his relations with the Whigs are the subjects of Angus MacIntyre, *The Liberator: Daniel O'Connell and the Irish Party, 1830-1847* (London, 1965). There are a number of informative and interesting studies concerning O'Connell's Repeal movement and British reactions; most important are Kevin Nowlan, *The Politics of Repeal* (Toronto, 1965), Lawrence J. McCaffrey, *Daniel O'Connell and the Repeal Year* (Lexington, Ky., 1966); John F. Broderick, S.J., *The Holy See and the Irish Movement for Repeal of the Union with England, 1829-1847* (Rome, 1951); Donal A. Kerr, *Peel, Priest, and Politics* (Oxford, 1982); George Kitson-Clark, *Peel and the Conservative Party, 1822-1841* (Hamden, Conn., 1964); and Norman Gash, *Politics in the Age of Peel* (London, 1953). British anti-Catholicism frustrated Peel's Irish policy, a subject carefully described and analyzed by Gilbert A. Cahill in "Irish Catholicism and English Toryism," *Review of Politics* 19 (January 1957), 62-76, and "The Protestant Association and the Anti-Maynooth agitation of 1845," *Catholic Historical Review* 43 (October 1957), 273-308. E.R. Norman, ed., *Anti-Catholicism in Victorian England* (London, 1968), also treats British no-popery.

Charles Gavan Duffy, *Young Ireland: A Fragment of Irish History, 1840-45* (London, 1896), is a readable but highly partisan examination. For a more objective approach see R. Davis, *The Young Ireland Movement* (Dublin, 1987). For discussions of events leading up to and during the 1848 rebellion see Denis Gwynn, *O'Connell, Davis, and the Colleges Bill* (Cork, 1948), and *Young Ireland and 1848* (Cork, 1949); and Thomas P. O'Neill, "The Economic and Political Ideas of James Fintan Lalor," *Irish Ecclesiastical Record* 74 (November 1950), 398-409. Brendan O'Cathaoir, *John Blake Dillon, Young Irelander* (Dublin, 1990), rescues an important intellectual influence on Young Ireland and one of the leading figures in 1860s constitutional nationalism from undeserved neglect. Blanche M. Touhill, *William Smith O'Brien and His Irish Revolutionary Companions in Penal Exile* (Columbia, Mo., 1981), pays tribute to another important Young Irelander who merits attention. The best analyses of Young Ireland's cultural nationalism are Malcolm Brown, *The Politics of Irish Literature From Thomas Davis to W. B. Yeats*, Part II; and Mary Helen Thuente, "Young Ireland Poetry," *The Harp Unstrung: The United Irishmen and the Rise of Irish Literary Nationalism*.

R.D. Dudley Edwards and T. Desmond Williams, eds., *The Great Famine: Studies in Irish History, 1845-1852* (Dublin, 1956), was the first significant scholarly investigation of the Famine containing essays on a number of subjects connected to this important event. Cecil Woodham-Smith's *The Great Hunger, Ireland, 1845-49* (New York, 1962) leaned on the work of scholars to present an excellent, well-written, popular examination of the Famine. Woodham-Smith is quite harsh on the insensitivity and prejudice of British politicians in regard to their Irish subjects. Recently there have been a number of Famine studies. From an economic historian's perspective, Joel Mokyr, in *Why Ireland Starved: A Quantitative and Analytic History of the Irish Economy, 1800-1850* (London, 1983), rejects the idea that the Famine was the result of too many people for available resources. He insists that a more productive agricultural and capital investment in industry could have saved Ireland. Mokyr also blames British attitudes and policies for starvation in Ireland. Mary E. Daly, *The Famine in Ireland* (Dundalk, Ireland, 1986), is revisionist in its calm analysis and explanation of British policy in Ireland. My own preferences in Famine studies are Cormac Ó Gráda, *The Great Irish Famine* (Atlanic Highlands, N.J., 1988); the eight chapters on "The Great Hunger, 1845-1851" by James S. Donnelly Jr. in *Ireland under the Union, I (1801-1870)*, vol 5 of *The New History of Ireland* and Christine Kinealy, *This Great Calamity: The Irish Famine, 1845-52* (Dublin, 1994). In less than two hundred clearly presented pages Ó Gráda synthesizes the best available research, including his own, on the subject and interprets it in an exciting and interesting manner. Donnelly also applies superb writing and synthesis skills to his discussion of the great disaster in Irish history. His effort deserves to be published separately to reach the wider reading audience it deserves. Both Ó Gráda and Donnelly absolve British officials of genocidal motives, but neither hesitates to blame them for causing considerable Irish misery. Kinealy effectively argues that British laissez-faire ideology and anti-Irish racism translated a serious but manageable food shortage into a massive calamity. Robert James Scally, *The End of Hidden Ireland: Rebellion, Famine, and Emigration* (Oxford, 1995) illuminates social and economic conditions in Famine Ireland by focusing on a community in Roscommon. It is a thoroughly researched, perceptive, and exceptionally well-written condemnation of British policy in Ireland and responses to the Great Hunger.

In *The Modernization of Irish Society, 1848-1918* (The Gill History of Ireland 10; Dublin, 1973), Joseph Lee challenges the historical consensus on many issues. In a sprightly and provocative manner, Lee rejects the notion that British legislation in regard to Ireland was an experiment in modernization, arguing that it perpetuated the status quo rather than change. Lee credits Parnell and the Irish party and Cullen's religious reforms with modernization tendencies. R.V. Comerford's four chapters on the 1850-70 period in *Ireland under the Union, I (1801-1870)*, is another stimulating interpretation of political, economic, social, and cultural trends and events. But Comerford does see modernization, Anglicization, and adjustments to the United Kingdom in Irish life. He does not find evidence that a complete break with Britain was inevitable.

John Whyte, *The Independent Irish Party, 1850-59* (London, 1958), is a clear and comprehensive treatment of the 1850s tenant-right movement and the independent Irish party. It clears away the partisan distortions of Charles Gavan Duffy, *The League of the North and South* (London, 1886). There are a number of competent Fenian studies, including Maurice Harmon, ed., *Fenians and Fenianism* (Seattle, 1970); and T.W. Moody, ed., *The Fenian Movement* (Cork, 1968). But the best look at the Irish Republican Brotherhood is R.V. Comerford, *The Fenians in Context: Irish Politics and Society* (Atlantic Highlands, N.J., 1985). Comerford interprets the Fenians in Ireland as bright, lower middle-class young men, often journalists, blocked by the O'Connellite and Young Ireland establishments. Revolutionary republicanism gave them an audience and status. Comerford also stresses the importance of Fenianism as a recreational and social outlet in a repressive rural environment. This aspect of Fenianism is adeptly explored in Brian Griffin, "Social Aspects of Fenianism in Connacht and Leinster, 1858-1870," *Eire-Ireland* 12 (Spring 1986), 16-38. There are two historical novels that provide perceptive insights into nineteenth century Irish history. Thomas Flanagan, *The Tenants of Time* (New York, 1988), covers the period from the Fenians to the fall of Parnell. Sean O'Faolain, *A Nest of Simple Folk* (London, 1989), takes the reader from pre-Fenian times to Easter Week 1916. Valuable information on the National Association can be found in E.R. Norman, *The Catholic Church and Ireland in the Age of Rebellion, 1859-1873* (Ithaca, N.Y., 1965).

The beginnings of Home Rule and Issac Butt's leadership are the subjects of Lawrence J. McCaffrey, *Irish Federalism in the 1870s: A Study in Conservative Nationalism* (Philadelphia, 1962); and David Thornley, *Isaac Butt and Home Rule* (London, 1964). Terence De Vere White, *The Road of Excess* (Dublin, 1946), is a sympathetic and informative biography of Butt. The best analysis of the origin and contents of the New Departure is in Thomas N. Brown, *Irish American Nationalism*. Some of the above-mentioned books on the agrarian dimension of Irish nationalism refer to the Land League and its war on landlordism. T.W. Moody, *Davitt and Irish Revolution, 1848-1882* (New York, 1982), is an outstanding biography of the founder of the Land League. Among a number of books on the life of

Parnell, I strongly recommend two: F.S.L. Lyons, *Charles Stewart Parnell* (New York, 1977); and Robert Kee, *The Laurel and the Ivy: The Story of Charles Stewart Parnell* (New York, 1994). Lyons's *The Fall of Parnell* (Toronto, 1960) details the events that led to Committee Room 15 and the split in the Irish Party. Frank Callanan, *The Parnell Split, 1890-91* (Syracuse, 1992), argues that the debate between Parnell and his enemies involved more than the struggle over Irish party leadership and the role of the Catholic Church in the dispute. According to Callanan, Parnell offered the Irish an inclusive, secular, liberal, and democratic nationalism while Tim Healy and his allies presented an exclusive, Catholic, and conservative Home Rule Ireland. Conor Cruise O'Brien, *Parnell and His Party, 1880-1890* (Oxford, 1960), is still the leading study of Parnell's leadership and the character of the Irish party in the 1880s. During the struggle for Home Rule, Irish nationalists began to take control over local government in Ireland. This process is the topic of William Féingold, *Revolt of the Tenantry: The Transfer of Local Government in Ireland* (Boston, 1984). *In The English Face of Irish Nationalism: Parnellite Involvement in British Politics, 1880-1886* (Dublin, 1977), Alan O'Day points out that many members of the Irish party had lived in Britain and accepted the values of British radicalism. In Parliament they became involved in British as well as Irish issues. For years J.L. Hammond, *Gladstone and the Irish Nation* (Hamden, Conn., 1962), was a standard and is still useful, but it has been challenged by James Loughlin, *Gladstone, Home Rule, and the Ulster Question, 1892-93* (Atlantic Highlands, N.J., 1987). Loughlin accuses Gladstone of considerable ignorance concerning Ireland. He claims that the Liberal leader believed Home Rule was a conservative solution to the Irish Question, one that would restore the reputations and leadership of landlords. Thomas William Heyck, *The Dimensions of British Radicalism: The Case of Ireland, 1874-1895* (Urbana, Ill., 1974), tests the radical integrity of British radicals on the Irish Question and finds it wanting.

L.P. Curtis Jr., *Coercion and Conciliation in Ireland, 1880-1892: A Study in Conservative Unionism* (Princeton, N.J., 1963), focuses on the Conservative (Unionist) party's Irish policies. Under Arthur Balfour's guidance, the party blended coercion and concilation into an effort to impose law and order on Ireland while at the same time "killing Home Rule with kindness." In *Ireland and the Death of Kindness: The Experience of Constructive Unionism, 1890-1905* (Cork, 1987), Andrew Gailey says that there was much more to Unionist Irish policy than the destruction of Home Rule nationalism. He claims that Conservative leaders wanted to pacify Ireland so that they could concentrate on British and imperial affairs, appease Liberal Unionists in the coalition, and keep class-and sectarian-divided Ulster unionists in the party. For the best examination of the Irish phase of Arthur J. Balfour's career, see Catherine Shannon's thoroughly researched and clearly written *Arthur J. Balfour and Ireland, 1874-1922* (Washington, D.C., 1988). Patrick Buckland,

Irish Unionism, i: The Anglo-Irish and the New Ireland, 1885-1922 (Dublin, 1972), and *Irish Unionism, ii: Ulster Unionism and the Origins of Northern Ireland, 1886-1922* (Dublin, 1973), combine to make a comprehensive examination of their subject. In *Ulster Politics: The Formative Years, 1868-1886* (Belfast, 1989), Brian M. Walker discusses the shift in Ulster politics from a conflict between Liberals and Conservatives to Unionists versus nationalists, setting the stage for the 1912-14 Home Rule crisis and the present conflict in Northern Ireland. Alvin Jackson, *The Ulster Party: Irish Unionists in the House of Commons, 1884-1911* (Oxford, 1989), tells of the impact of Ulster unionism on British Conservatives and how after 1905 Protestants in the north begin to lose confidence in Parliament to preserve the United Kingdom.

For a study of the Irish parliamentary party from the fall of Parnell to the eve of the 1912-14 Home Rule crisis see F.S.L. Lyons, *The Irish Parliamentary Party, 1890-1910* (London, 1951). Paul Bew, *Conflict and Conciliation in Ireland, 1890-1910: Parnellites and Agrarian Radicals* (Oxford, 1987), demonstrates that the land question continued to be an important factor in Irish nationalism and Anglo-Irish relations after the land war of the late 1870s and early 1880s.

In the late nineteenth century there was a revival of cultural nationalism that was both a supplement to and an alternative to Home Rule political nationalism. In my previous listing of books on cultural nationalism I mentioned a number of works pertinent to this subject. Janet Gareth Dunleavy and Gareth W. Dunleavy, *Douglas Hyde: A Maker of Modern Ireland* (Berkeley, Cal., 1991), is an important study of the co-founder of the Gaelic League. F.X. Martin and F.J. Byrne, eds., *The Scholar Revolutionary: Eoin MacNeil, 1867-1945 and the Making of the New Ireland* (New York, 1973), discusses the life of the other founding father of the Gaelic League and the head of the Irish Volunteers. Racist Anglo-Saxon contempt for the Irish had much to do with the revival of Irish cultural nationalism. Anglo-Saxon racial attitudes are the subject of L.P. Curtis Jr., *Anglo-Saxon and Celts: A Study in Anti-Irish Prejudice in Victorian England* (Bridgeport, Conn., 1968), and *Apes and Angels: The Irishman in Victorian Caricature* (Washington, 1971); and Richard Ned Lebow, *White Britain and Black Ireland: The Influence of Sterotypes on Colonial Policy* (Philadelphia, 1976). R.F. Foster's revisionist *Paddy & Mr Punch: Connections in Irish and English History* (New York, 1993) is a book of essays that rejects exclusive views of Irish identity, pointing out the contributions of various traditions to Ireland, appealing for Irish multiculturalism, and arguing that Curtis exaggerates British anti-Irishness.

Sinn Féin nationalism also questioned Home Rule. Richard Davis, *Arthur Griffith and Non-violent Sinn Féin* (Dublin, 1974), is a study of Sinn Féin's originator. The peasant orientation of Home Rule nationalism was challenged by labor militancy. Joseph V. O'Brien, *Dear Dirty Dublin: A City in Distress, 1899-1916* (Berkeley, Cal., 1982), describes the social and economic conditions that created working-class unrest. Emmet Larkin, *James Larkin, Irish Labour Leader, 1876-1947* (London, 1989), is not only an excellent study of the founder of the Irish Transport and General Workers Union, it also provides interesting material on Irish urban social and economic problems. Dunsmore J. Clarkson, *Labour and Nationalism in Ireland* (New York, 1925), remains a classic study. Beresford P. Ellis, *A History of the Irish Working Class* (New York, 1973), and Arthur Mitchel, *Labour in Irish Politics, 1890-1930* (Shannon, 1974), are valuable contributions to the bibliography of the Irish working class.

In the highly readable *The Strange Death of Liberal England* (New York, 1961), George Dangerfield attributes the collapse of British Liberalism to three problems that it could not cope with: the radicalism of labor, the feminist movement, and the resistance of Ulster Unionists to Home Rule. Of the three, Dangerfield claims the last was most important. A.T.Q. Stewart, *The Ulster Crisis* (London, 1967), is sympathetic to the Ulster Unionist cause. The Curragh incident, which increased Liberal fears that the army could not be depended on in a conflict with Ulster unionists, is the subject of Ian W.F. Beckett, *The Army and the Curragh Incident, 1914* (London, 1986); Sir James Ferguson, *The Curragh Incident* (London, 1964); and A.P. Ryan, *Mutiny at the Curragh* (New York, 1956). A new biography of John Redmond, a truly tragic figure in Irish history, is badly needed, but Denis Gwynn, *The Life of John Redmond* (London, 1932), is a more than competent portrait. In his perceptive *Ideology and the Irish Question: Ulster Unionism and Irish Nationalism, 1912-1916* (Oxford, 1994), Paul Bew gives a favorable estimate of John Redmond's impact on Irish nationalism. Biographies of importance in understanding the 1912 Home Rule crisis are Roy Jenkins, *Asquith* (London, 1965); Joseph V. O'Brien, *William O'Brien and the Course of Irish Politics, 1881-1918* (Berkeley, Cal., 1976); and Leon Ó Broin, *The Chief Secretary: Augustine Birrell in Ireland* (London, 1969).

Two books of value that cover key issues in the early twentieth century are Cliona Murphy, *The Woman's Suffrage Movement and Irish Society in the Early Twentieth Century* (Philadelphia, 1989); and Thomas J. Morrisey, S.J., *Toward a National University: William Delaney, S. J., 1835-1924* (Atlantic Highlands, N.J., 1985). Murphy criticizes some Irish party leaders for their hostility to the women's suffrage movement. The most comprehensive examination of the place of women in late nineteenth and early twentieth century Ireland is Joanna Bourke, *Husbandry to Housewifery: Women, Economic Change, and Housework in Ireland, 1890-1914* (Oxford, 1993).

The most satisfying concise study of Easter Week 1916 is Alan J. Ward, *The Easter Rising: Revolution and Irish Nationalism* (Arlington Heights, Ill., 1980). Ward discusses the prelude to and aftermath of the rising as well as the event itself. William Irwin Thompson, *The Imagination of an Insurrection: Dublin, Easter, 1916* (New York, 1967), treats the impact of the poetic imagination on Irish revolutionary nationalism. Other worthwhile examinations of Easter Week are Thomas Coffey, *Agony at Easter* (Baltimore, 1969); Roger McHugh, ed., *Dublin, 1916* (London, 1966); and Kevin B. Nowlan, ed., *The Making of 1916* (Dublin, 1969). Ruth Dudley Edwards *Patrick Pearse: The Triumph of Failure* (London, 1977), is an exceptionally good and impartial study of Easter Week's most prominent hero. Edwards also has contributed another biography of a 1916 martyr, *James Connolly* (Dublin, 1981). Another interpretation of the labor dimension of the rising is John Boyle, "Irish Labour and the Rising," *Eire-Ireland* 2 (Autumn 1967), 122-31.

For the political background of the Anglo-Irish War see Michael Laffan, "The Unification of Sinn Féin" *Irish Historical Studies* 27 ((March 1971), 353-79; Brian Farrell, *The Founding of Dáil Eireann: Parliament and Nation Building* (Dublin, 1971); and David Fitzpatrick, *Politics and Irish Life, 1913-1921: Provincial Experience of War and Revolution* (Dublin, 1977). Fitzpatrick traces the political triumph of Sinn Féin over the Irish party on the local level and how the former absorbed the organizational apparatus of the latter. The Anglo-Irish conflict and the following Civil War have been treated in a number of studies, including Edgar Holt, *Protest in Arms: The Irish Troubles, 1916-1923* (London, 1960); Charles Townshend, *Political Violence in Ireland: Government and Resistance since 1848*, and *The British Campaign in Ireland, 1919-1922: The Development of Political and Military Policies* (Oxford, 1975); and T.D. Williams, ed., *The Irish Struggle, 1916-1926* (London, 1966). The Townshend material is particularly good. Tom Garvin, *The Evolution of Irish Nationalist Politics* and *Nationalist Revolutionaries in Ireland, 1858-1928*, certainly help in an understanding of the dynamics of the Anglo-Irish and Civil Wars. D.G. Boyce, *Englishmen and Irish Troubles: British Public Opinion and the Making of Irish Policy, 1918-1922* (Cambridge, Mass., 1972), explains how Sinn Féin won the propaganda phase of the Anglo-Irish War, building British and world opinion against Lloyd George's government. Charles Loch Mowat, *Britain Between the Wars, 1918-1940* (Chicago, 1969), is one of the few British history texts that appreciates the full significance of the Irish Question. Two books that deal specifically with the Civil War are Eoin Neeson, *The Civil War in Ireland* (Cork, 1966); and Carlton Younger, *Ireland's Civil War* (London, 1968). Tim Pat Coogan, *Michael Collins* (London, 1991), is an informative and flattering picture of the most dashing and romantic figure of the Anglo-Irish and Irish Civil War. Frank O'Connor, *The Big Fellow: A Life of Michael Collins* (London, 1961), is insightful and readable. R. Taylor, *Michael Collins* (London, 1958), is useful. Earl of Longford and T.P. O'Neill, *Eamon de Valera* (London, 1970), tells the reader a great deal about de Valera in a sympathetic way. Tim Pat Coogan, *De Valera: Long Fellow, Long Shadow* (London, 1973), is a highly unflattering look at the dominant personality in twentieth-century Irish life, seldom giving him the benefit of the doubt on any issue. J.P. O'Carroll and John A.

Murphy, eds., *De Valera and His Times* (Cork, 1983), contains a number of valuable and enlightening essays. In *De Valera and the Ulster Question, 1917-1973*, (Oxford, 1982), John Bowman says that de Valera's concept of a Gaelic, Catholic Ireland worked against Irish unity, but that he was more flexible toward the north than most historians believe. De Valera was prepared to give considerable autonomy to the six counties in a united Ireland, and toward the end of his life he did begin to realize and appreciate the unique historical and cultural heritages of Anglo-Irish Protestants and Ulster Presbyterians. A most important biography dealing with the Anglo-Irish and Irish Civil Wars and the start of Irish independence is Maryann Gialanella Valiulis, *Portrait of a Revolutionary: General Richard Mulcahy and the Founding of the Irish Free State* (Lexington, Ky., 1992). Thomas Flanagan, *The End of the Hunt* (New York, 1994), presents the ideological and personality complexities of the Anglo-Irish and Irish Civil Wars in an exceptionally fine historical novel. Joseph M. Curran, *The Birth of the Irish Free State, 1921-1923* (University, Alabama, 1980), is a well-written, thoroughly researched, and masterful discussion of the Anglo-Irish negotiations that resulted in the Free State and the resulting Irish Civil War. In *The Greening of Dublin Castle: The Transformation of Bureaucratic and Judicial Personnel in Ireland, 1892-1922* (Washington, D.C., 1991), Lawrence W. McBride describes and discusses the increasing number of Irish Catholic civil servants in the British administration of Ireland. They proved to be an important factor in the stability of post-revolutionary Ireland.

John A. Murphy, *Ireland in the Twentieth Century* (Gill History of Ireland 11; Dublin, 1975); and Ronan Fanning, *Independent Ireland* (Helicon History of Ireland; Dublin, 1983), are informative, nicely written, relatively brief surveys of Ireland in the twentieth century. J.J. Lee, *Ireland, 1912-1985* (New York, 1989), is a comprehensive look at Ireland from the beginning of the Home Rule crisis to recent times. Lee is quite critical of de Valera, blaming him and other politicians for freezing Ireland in the myths of rural romanticism and not facing up to economic realities, solving problems by emigration rather than change, and failing to understand the nuances of the Ulster problem. He credits Sean Lemass for bringing Ireland into the twentieth century. Lemass's impact is the subject of Paul Bew and Henry Patterson, *Sean Lemass and the Making of Modern Ireland, 1945-1966* (Dublin, 1982). Ronan Fanning, *The Irish Department of Finance, 1922-1958* (Dublin, 1978), is an exceptionally good example of administrative history and reveals much about the problems of the Free State before Lemass's period of power. Terence Brown, *Ireland: A Social and Cultural History, 1922-79*, and F.S.L. Lyons, *Culture and Anarchy in Ireland, 1890-1939*, cover Irish intellectual life in the twentieth century. In *The Restless Dominion: The Irish Free State and the British Commonwealth of Nations, 1921-1931* (Dublin, 1969), D.W. Harkness explains how Irish representatives at Commonwealth conferences expanded dominion sovereignty and played a key role in designing the Statute of Westminster. Anglo-Irish relations are the topic for Paul Canning, *British Policy toward Ireland, 1921-1941* (Oxford, 1985); Deirdre McMahon, *Republicans and Imperialists: Anglo-Irish Relations in the 1930s* (New Haven, Conn., 1984), and "A Transient Apparition: British Policy towards the de Valera Government, 1932-1935," *Irish Historical Studies* 22 (1981); and D.W. Harkness, "Mr. de Valera's Dominion: Ireland's Relations with Britain and the Commonwealth, 1932-1938," *Journal of Commonwealth Political Studies* 8 (November 1970), 206-28. In *Almost a Rebellion: The Irish Army Mutiny of 1924* (Cork, 1985), Maryann Gialanella Valiulis discusses how civilian authority over the army at a critical time exemplified the liberal-democratic success of independent Ireland. World War II tested Ireland's sovereignty and aggravated her relations with Britain. These issues are discussed in Joseph T. Carroll, *Ireland in the War Years, 1939-1945* (Dublin, 1976); and Kevin B. Nowlan and T. Desmond Williams, eds., *Ireland in the War Years and After, 1939-1951* (Dublin, 1969). In *Nationalism and Socialism in Twentieth-Century Ireland* (New York, 1977), E. Rumpf and A.C. Hepburn analyze why Irish nationalism and unionism, closely tied to sectarian loyalties, have triumphed over socialism in attracting popular allegiances.

The contemporary crisis in Northern Ireland has generated a multitude of books. Patrick Buckland, *A History of Northern Ireland* (Dublin, 1981), is a useful volume. Peter Collins, ed., *Nationalism and Unionism: Conflict in Ireland, 1885-1921* (Belfast, 1994), includes many valuable essays on events and issues that resulted in partition. Eamonn Phoenix, *Northern Nationalism: Nationalist Politics, Partition, and the Catholic Minority in Northern Ireland, 1890-1940* (Belfast, 1994), discusses the anguish of the Catholic community in six-county Ulster, isolated from their brethren in the south, persecuted by their Protestant neighbors. For readers interested in the background and ingredients of the conflict in the six counties, John Darby, *Conflict in Northern Ireland: The Development of a Polarized Community* (New York, 1976), is the best place to start. Darby also edited *Northern Ireland: The Background to the Conflict* (Syracuse, 1983), which has ten essays uneven in quality and not well integrated, but the editor's "The Historical background" is first-rate, as are Paddy Hillyard, "Law and Order"; Dominic Murray, "Schools and Conflict"; and Bill Rolston, "Reformism and Sectarianism: The State of the Union after Civil Rights." J. Bowyer Bell, *The Irish Troubles* (Dublin, 1993), demonstrates thorough research and objectivity and contains an encyclopedic amount of material on all aspects of the Ulster crisis. Bell is particularly good on terrorism, Irish-American involvement, the impact of the hunger strike, and the crisis-management policies of the British government. One of the early and most interesting scholarly books on Northern Ireland is Rosemary Harris, *Prejudice and Tolerance in Ulster: A Study of Neighbors and Strangers in a Border Community* (Manchester, 1972). Harris describes the social and economic relationships between Catholics and Protestants, the things that unite and divide them. In *The Uncivil Wars: Ireland Today* (Boston, 1983), and *Biting at the Grave: The Irish Hunger Strikes and the Politics of Despair* (Boston, 1990), Padraig O'Malley offers perceptive and penetrating studies of the Northern Ireland conflict that have the quality of great literature. *Biting at the Grave* shows how Pearse's "blood sacrifice" theories, which melded Catholic redemptive theology and revolutionary republicanism, persist in Northern Ireland and how they influenced the hunger strike mentality. O'Malley makes it clear that to some nationalists the permanence of the cause is more important than victory. Andrew J. Wilson's forthcoming volume *Irish America and the Ulster Conflict, 1967-1987* (Washington, D.C., and Belfast, 1995), is the most comprehensive examination of the role of the American Irish in the Northern Ireland crisis.

A number of interesting studies have discussed the cultural and social dimensions of partition. M.W. Heslinga, *The Irish Border as a Cultural Divide: A Contribution to the Study of Regionalism in the British Isles* (Assen, Netherlands, 1962), pioneered this approach. F.S.L. Lyons, *Culture and Anarchy in Ireland, 1890–1939*, insists on the divisiveness of an Irish cultural pluralism that involved Irish Catholics, Anglo-Irish Protestants, and Ulster Presbyterians. Confronting nationalist myths that blame British ambitions for a divided Ireland, Conor Cruise O'Brien, in *States of Ireland* (New York, 1973), convincingly argues that the Protestant majority culture of Northern Ireland is quite distinct from the Irish-Catholic culture of the Republic, and that the border is cultural as well as geographic. My "Irish Nationalism and Irish Catholicism: A Study in Cultural Identity," *Church History* 42, 4 (December 1973), 524-34, emphasizes the inseparability of Irish nationalist and Catholic identities and the connection between Anglo-Irish Protestant and Presbyterian sectarianism in Northern Ireland and British loyalty. Modifying Conor Cruise O'Brien's two-nations theory, David W. Miller, in *Queen's Rebels: Ulster Loyalism in Historical Perspective* (New York, 1978), brilliantly discusses and analyzes the origins of Ulster Protestant (mainly Presbyterian) loyalism, describing it as a pre-modern Scottish "public banding," from the covenanting tradition rather than a cultural nationalism. A.T.Q. Stewart, *The Narrow Ground: Aspects of Ulster, 1609-1969* (London, 1977), is another valuable look at the character and ethos of Ulster Unionism. Geoffrey Bell, *The Protestants of Ulster* (London, 1976), is also recommended. For excellent studies of Northern Ireland Catholicism see Oliver P. Rafferty, *Catholicism in Ulster, 1603-1983* (Columbia, S.C., 1994); and Mary Harris, *The Catholic Church and the Foundation of the Northern Irish State* (Cork, 1993). Both volumes discuss a conservative Catholicism making pragmatic adjustments to a "Protestant state for a Protestant people." Rafferty suggests that these adjustments weakened the Church's response to the Catholic community's post-1968 anger and frustration.

If Ulster unionism does represent a separate cultural nation or community that justifies partition, what about the rights of the large Catholic minority in the six counties? Liam Kennedy, *Two Ulsters: A Case for Repartition* (Belfast, 1986), and Joseph M. Curran, "Ulster Repartition: A Possible Answer," *America* 134 (January 31, 1976), 66-68, advocate a repartition (Curran also favors repatriation) of Northern Ireland, placing most Catholics in the Republic. In *Partition and the Limits of Irish Nationalism* (Dublin, 1987), Clare O'Halloran maintains that despite all the grumbling from south of the border, partition made it easier for nationalists to create the kind of Catholic state they desired.

The IRA is the subject of Tim Pat Coogan, *The IRA* (London, 1970); J. Bowyer Bell, *The Secret Army: A History of the IRA, 1916-1970* (London, 1972); and Patrick Bishop and Eamon Mallie, *The Provisional IRA* (London 1987). As their titles suggest, Coogan and Bell offer examinations of the IRA from its beginnings while Bishop and Mallie focus on more recent times. The Irish National Liberation Army is the most vicious and sadistic of the nationalist paramilitary organizations. Jack Holland and Henry McDonald tell its story in *INLA: Deadly Divisions* (Torc, 1994). In "Making a Killing: The High Cost of Peace in Northern Ireland," *Harper's Magazine* 288 (February 1994), 45-54, Scott Anderson exposes paramilitary racketeering and the cooperation between nationalist and loyalist groups in controlling Belfast building-site employment.

Some revealing books on the responses of Northern Irelanders, nationalists and loyalists, are found in three perceptive, exceptionally well-written books by Chicago, London, and Irish visitors to the six counties: John Conroy, *Belfast Diary: War as a Way of Life* (Boston, 1987); Sally Belfrage, *Living with War: A Belfast Year* (New York, 1987); and Dervla Murphy's *A Place Apart* (London, 1978).

The development of Irish historiography since I wrote my first version of *The Irish Question* has advanced in both quality and quantity. No doubt in this "Recommended Reading" section I have forgotten or overlooked works that deserve the attention of readers. For those I have missed I apologize to both authors and readers. Although I do not agree with the theses of some of the books I have mentioned, I am indebted to all for my understanding of Irish history since 1800.

Index